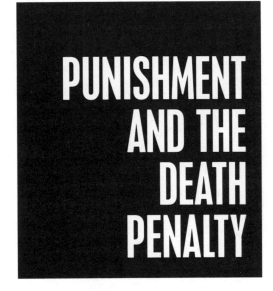

PUNISHMENT AND THE DEATH PENALTY

Contemporary Issues

Series Editors: Robert M. Baird
Stuart E. Rosenbaum

Other titles in this series:

EDITED BY ROBERT M. BAIRD
AND STUART E. ROSENBAUM

PUNISHMENT AND THE DEATH PENALTY

THE CURRENT DEBATE

Prometheus Books

59 John Glenn Drive
Amherst, New York 14228-2197

Published 1995 by Prometheus Books

99 98   5 4 3

Library of Congress Cataloging-in-Publication Data

Punishment and the death penalty : the current debate / edited by Robert M. Baird and Stuart E. Rosenbaum.
     p.   cm. — (Contemporary issues series)
    Includes bibliographical references (p.   ).
    ISBN 0-87975-946-1 (pbk.)
    1. Capital punishment—United States. 2. Punishment—United States.
I. Baird, Robert M., 1937-   . II. Rosenbaum, Stuart E. III. Series.
HV8694.P86   1995
364.6'6'0973—dc20   94-47521
                                                CIP

Printed in Canada on acid-free paper.

Contents

6   Contents

Introduction

The sentencing of the 18-year-old American Michael Fay to a caning in Singapore and Supreme Court Justice Harry Blackmun's unequivocal public renunciation of capital punishment have intensified current debate over punishment in general and capital punishment in particular—the two topics of this collection of essays.

Michael Fay, a high school student visiting Singapore, was convicted of minor vandalism and sentenced to a brief imprisonment, a small fine, and a caning. The caning part of his sentence has occasioned an international controversy. Some think caning is a cruel punishment, inappropriate for use in civilized societies; others regard caning as inappropriately harsh for so minor an offense as Fay's vandalism (spray painting two automobiles). Still others think it's about time somebody did something to keep teenagers in line, and if caning will do the trick then so be it.

On the eve of his retirement, 85-year-old Justice Harry Blackmun, after nearly a quarter century on the Court, has reversed his position on capital punishment. Declaring that "from this day forward" he would "no longer tinker with the machinery of death," Blackmun argued (in a dissenting opinion which appears in this collection) that capital punishment as practiced in the United States is unconstitutional because it is applied in a discriminatory manner. He has taken this position at a time when capital punishment has been revived in this country, and is proceeding at a rate of thirty to forty executions annually.

The practice of punishment is standard in all societies. The ways in which punishment is inflicted vary with history and culture. The Michael Fay case brings to our attention cultural differences in enforcing punishment. In late twentieth-century America, the infliction of punishment does not allow deliberate physical pain or torture. In Singapore, by contrast, it routinely does include bodily pain for those convicted of a crime, the extent of the torture varying with the magnitude of the crime. Andrew Glass, in an editorial

7

column about the Michael Fay case, remarks that America's Founding Fathers saw public whippings as effective and efficient punishments, and, further, that contemporary Saudi Arabia sentences petty thieves to the pain and disfigurement of having a hand chopped off. ("A second mugging, and it is the head that is lost."[1]) Particular cultural traditions obviously have a marked effect on the kind of punishment regarded as appropriate for a particular offense; this point is most obvious in the cross-cultural controversy over Michael Fay's caning.

The Fay controversy and the Blackmun declaration raise deep questions about how to get "the punishment to fit the crime," and about what sort of guidance might be available, apart from particular historical and cultural traditions of punishment, to achieve this. This is a difficult issue.

A more basic issue concerns why we think punishment is appropriate at all. In some ways this question is more difficult to answer because the practice of punishment is so "close" to us, so taken for granted in our societies, that we rarely think to question its legitimacy. Nevertheless, we must ask, what justifies the institution of punishment? What purposes do we have in inflicting injury or deprivation on those we punish? An extreme version of this question arises in connection with our practice of capital punishment: what justifies our institutionalized killing of those guilty of murder or other offenses? Why do, or should, we seek the death of some criminals? This question is much more pressing as a result of the crime bill now sought by the Clinton administration, which mandates the death penalty for a much wider range of offenses than ever before.

How might we define institutionalized punishment, the justification of which is being debated here? Widespread philosophical agreement holds that legal punishment involves five characteristics.[2] First, punishment must involve unpleasant consequences for the one being punished, for example, a fine, imprisonment, or death. Second, the punishment must follow from the violation of a law (a rule of conduct prescribed by a properly constituted governing authority and enforced by sanctions). Third, the one punished must have been found guilty of violating the law. Fourth, the suffering must be administered by someone other than the guilty party, and fifth, the one administering the punishment must be a properly designated authority.

Is it justifiable for an authorized representative of society to inflict suffering on those found guilty of violating the law? Questions about the justification for this customary social practice are addressed by the essays in Part One of this volume. In addressing the question of justification, several of the essays distinguish between justifying the institution of punishment and justifying the punishment of a particular individual. Do the same arguments justify both? Or may it be that one kind of argument is needed to justify the institution of punishment and a different kind needed to justify the punishment of a particular individual?

Two ostensibly opposing positions, retributivism and utilitarianism, are traditional efforts to justify punishment. The retributivists maintain that punishment is simply what one deserves for having broken the law. Their view is captured by the ancient Latin phrase *lex talionis,* "an eye for an eye." For retributivists, punishment is inherently justified in the act of lawbreaking. Children who steal candy from younger siblings or employees who embezzle from employers deserve, by the very nature of their acts, to be punished. The explication of this position is complex, but one plausible account is offered by Walter Berns in "The Morality of Anger" (chapter 13).

One problem with the retributivist view is that it appears to justify punishment even when that punishment has highly unfortunate consequences. A woman may be conscience-stricken about the plight of her family, which has been without food for three days. As a result she decides to steal from a wealthy neighbor. The retributivist view may justify imprisoning the woman for theft even though the punishment leaves her family without support or possibility of relief.

Utilitarians seek to avoid such difficulties of retributivism. Some utilitarians argue that penalties should be imposed only when doing so likely results in more desirable consequences than not doing so. More than simple lawbreaking is required to justify punishment. Why should the guilty be punished? Why is it permissible to inflict pain on one who has caused another suffering? The utilitarian answer is that punishment has socially desirable consequences. In the case of the conscience-stricken woman who steals to feed her family, a utilitarian might find punishment unjustified because of undesirable consequences for her family, which may be more severely disadvantaged by the woman's imprisonment than the wealthy neighbor was disadvantaged by the theft. For such a utilitarian, these consequences might mean that the punishment is unjustified; for retributivists, such consequences are not relevant to justifying the punishment. Although most utilitarians agree that inflicting pain or suffering on an individual is usually wrong, many would also agree that it is permissible when the desirable consequences more than offset the evil of imposing suffering.

Utilitarians usually emphasize two desirable consequences of punishment. The first is its deterrent effect: Punishment is socially valuable because it deters criminals from repeating their crimes and may also keep others from engaging in similar acts. The example of one criminal suffering imprisonment for his deed may make others reluctant to commit similar crimes. A second socially desirable consequence of punishment is reform of criminals. Since criminals behave in a destructive and antisocial way, they must be reformed so that they no longer have antisocial desires. When children are punished for inappropriate treatment of younger siblings, they may no longer be inclined to behave in such ways. Similarly, punishment criminals may change their inclinations toward criminal behavior.

Critics of utilitarianism argue that awkward results follow from seeking to justify punishment in terms of its desirable consequences. They suggest that if utilitarians are to remain consistent in their view, then they must maintain that sometimes innocent persons should be punished and sometimes guilty persons should not. If punishing the guilty yields worse results than not doing so, then it is not justified. On the other hand, if punishing the innocent yields better results than any alternative, then such punishment is justified. In an extreme case, law enforcement authorities may feel a need simply to arrest and punish any plausible suspect, even though they have no evidence that he or she is guilty. Some serious, perhaps gruesome, crime might, if unsolved, undermine public confidence in authority and perhaps even encourage potential criminals. Thus, the sacrifice of an innocent to avoid these evil consequences may sometimes appear justified on utilitarian grounds.

Utilitarians may reply to this criticism by distinguishing between justifying the institution of punishment and justifying a particular act enjoined by it. Only the social institution of punishment is justified by utilitarian considerations. Individual cases of criminal behavior are handled by the policies, procedures, and practices that constitute the institution, and justifications for the disposition of individual cases are supplied only within the context of that institution. Utilitarian considerations do not legitimately reach individual cases when questions of justification are involved. Hence, the institution of punishment, justified by utilitarian considerations, does not permit the sacrifice of innocent persons.

This distinction may also reconcile the apparent conflict between retributivist and utilitarian views. As suggested above, utilitarians may argue that utilitarian considerations are relevant only to justifying punishment as a social institution. Consistent with this utilitarian strategy, one may still argue that individuals should be punished only for retributive reasons, only if they deserve punishment as specified within the policies of the institution. While one might legitimately appeal to retribution in justifying the punishment of an individual, it does not follow that the same kind of appeal can legitimately be used to justify the institution of punishment itself.

In the essay that opens Part One of the volume, J. D. Mabbott appears to contest this effort to reconcile retributivist and utilitarian views. Mabbott sees retribution not only as justifying the punishment of individuals, but also as justifying the institution of punishment.

John Rawls's well-known essay "Two Concepts of Rules" refines the controversy by developing in detail the distinction between justifying a practice—a system of rules governing behavior—and justifying a particular act falling under the practice. Rawls agrees that utilitarian arguments are appropriate for justifying the institution of punishment, and that retributive arguments are needed to justify applying the institution in a particular case.

Karl Menninger, the noted psychiatrist, simply denies that punishment can be justified as a social institution. Arguing that punishment of criminals has failed to achieve desirable goals, Menninger maintains that punishment should be replaced by programs of therapeutic rehabilitation.

Richard Wasserstrom emphasizes the deterrent function of punishment. He challenges Menninger and others who propose to replace it with therapy. Their approach, he argues, focuses only on preventing repeated criminal acts, ignoring entirely the goal of preventing the offense in the first place. Since prevention is a major goal of punishment and the threat of punishment, Wasserstrom argues that Menninger's view fails.

Herbert Morris sides with Wasserstrom against Menninger, arguing that humans have a right to be punished. In his view, this right is involved in being a person who freely chooses, and to be treated as a free person is one of the most fundamental of all rights. Just as persons have the right to be praised when they do something noble, so have they the right to be punished when they do something wrong.

In the concluding essay of Part One, Richard Dagger comes to the defense of the Fair Play Principle as a means of justifying punishment. Dagger sees society as a system of cooperation which enables individuals to flourish, one in which rules make clear how cooperation is required. Since all benefit from this social arrangement, fair play demands that all jointly cooperate by obeying the rules. Violators take unfair advantage of those who obey, and their disobedience threatens the very existence of society. Hence, punishment is essential to the maintenance of a mutually advantageous social order. The Principle of Fair Play also justifies punishing particular individuals as a means of restoring balance between benefits and burdens. The heart of Daggers's essay is a defense of the fair-play justification of punishment against six specific objections, which charge that the principle fails to justify punishment, and also fails in a variety of ways to capture other features of punishment.

Part Two of this volume focuses on the issue of capital punishment. Several factors in recent years have intensified public debate on this issue. In 1972, the United States Supreme Court, in response to evidence that the death penalty was being administered across the country in a biased and prejudicial manner, declared in *Furman* v. *Georgia* that state laws as then written constituted cruel and unusual punishment, and were, therefore, in violation of the Eighth Amendment to the Constitution. This decision, in conjunction with the rewriting of state laws to conform with the requirements of *Furman* v. *Georgia,* and further Supreme Court decisions related to capital punishment, as well as a significant increase in the number of criminals executed, has greatly intensified the capital punishment debate.

In their book *Capital Punishment and the American Agenda,* Franklin Zimring and Gordon Hawkins open with the lines: "The pattern is so simple it is stunning. Every Western industrial nation has stopped executing criminals, except the United States."[3] Thoughtful people have to be concerned about this difference between the behavior of America and that of other nations. Is U.S. policy right and other policies wrong? Or, do significantly different circumstances justify these differences in policy? If so, what are those circumstances? Part Two of our book, a significant revision of the first edition,[4] is in an effort to stay abreast of these developments.

The vital issues surrounding the more specific question of capital punishment are, in part, a mirror image of issues concerning the question of punishment in general. This debate again pits retributivists against utilitarians, the former tending to support capital punishment and the latter frequently, though not always, opposing it. Additional issues are involved, however, and the essays added to this volume address many of these.

M. L. Radelet, H. A. Bedau, and C. E. Putnam lead off Part Two with an attempt to draw the reader into the capital punishment debate by raising the specter of killing the innocent. This essay is one of two selections taken from an important recent publication by these three researchers which serves both to demonstrate how often the innocent are convicted and to underline the horror of a wrongful conviction in a capital case.

The second and third essays are historical in nature, providing a broad context in which the current debate is better understood. The Information Plus essay (chapter 8) provides a general history of capital punishment in the United States from the settlement of the colonies to the more recent decisions of the Supreme Court. J. Gordon Melton examines the role of religious groups and religious attitudes in the history of capital punishment. He also discusses various biblical perspectives on capital punishment.

Ernest van den Haag has been a prominent defender of capital punishment, offering well thought-out arguments in its defense. Two of his essays are included in this volume: The first of these defends capital punishment against the charges of discriminatory application and miscarriages of justice, and sets forth his primary case for capital punishment, one that appeals to both retributive and utilitarian arguments.

Lloyd Steffen's "Casting the First Stone" argues against capital punishment on specifically Christian grounds. He appeals to the testimony of Jesus in support of the claim that those who engage in capital punishment arrogate to themselves "a power that was not theirs to assume . . . the power to destroy the life of a person who was a gift from God."

As van den Haag is the academician usually associated with defending capital punishment, Hugo Bedau is the academician usually associated with opposing it. Over the years he has written extensively against capital punishment. The second essay by Bedau included here, from his recent work published in collaboration with Radelet and Putnam, reflects "thirty years of intermittent research" aimed at documenting the "miscarriages of justice in capital cases in the United States." The possibility of taking the life of an innocent, always a danger in capital cases, is advanced as sufficient reason for eliminating the death penalty.

The selection by Walter Berns, "The Morality of Anger," expresses a retributivist perspective in defense of capital punishment. Berns finds justification for capital punishment in the legitimacy and necessity of communal anger.

Jeffrey Reiman also acknowledges the legitimacy of the retributivist case; however, he asserts that this rationale for the death penalty can be satisfied by the lesser penalty of life imprisonment. Since the legitimate demand for retribution can be satisfied by a nonlethal penalty, Reiman believes that a very important utilitarian consideration emerges. Since our institutions not only reflect but also mold our attitudes and character, we should use these institutions to help shape a more civilized general social character. In Reiman's opinion, refusing to sanction the death penalty would contribute to the civilizing mission of our social institutions.

Stephen Nathanson objects to the death penalty on the ground that, intentionally or not, it is in fact applied in discriminatory ways. Blacks who murder whites are far more likely to have the death penalty imposed on them than are whites who murder blacks. Since the death penalty is inevitably applied in discriminatory ways, says Nathanson, it is unjust to apply it at all.

The second of our selections from Ernest van den Haag is a further defense of capital punishment that involves specific rejoinders to the arguments of Reiman and Nathanson. (They in fact single out his defense of retributivism for critical treatment.)

Several of the authors in this volume maintain the widely held view that a majority of the electorate in the United States supports capital punishment. William Bowers challenges this belief, which he says has had a significant impact on the thinking of the Supreme Court. Evidence is available, argues Bowers, that most people prefer life imprisonment without the possibility of parole to capital punishment.

In a brief essay, Christie Davies defends capital punishment in a highly restricted class of cases. Davies, too, is concerned about the possibility of a totally innocent person being wrongly convicted of a capital offense, but Davies supports the execution of an individual who commits murder after already having been convicted of a long string of violent offenses such as "armed robbery, forcible rape, or inflicting grievous bodily harm."

The recently published views of Supreme Court Justices Harry Blackmun and Antonin Scalia conclude our study. Blackmun used the occasion of the Court's denying a writ of certiorari* to express his conviction that fair procedural and substantive rules governing the death penalty are not currently operative and that the death penalty is, therefore, unconstitutional under the Eighth Amendment's "cruel and unusual punishment" clause. Indeed, Blackmun argues that the Court has in recent capital punishment decisions developed two lines of jurisprudence that are logically incompatible. "From this day forward," he says, "I no longer shall tinker with the machinery of death." In his response, Scalia accuses Blackmun of appealing to his own moral and personal perceptions rather than, as he should, to the "text and tradition of the Constitution." Since the Fifth Amendment provides that "no person shall be held to answer for a capital crime . . . without due process of law," clearly, argues Scalia, capital punishment itself cannot be judged a "cruel and unusual punishment" proscribed by the Eighth Amendment."

The controversy surrounding the issue of capital punishment is especially important in the present social and political climate of America. After a long hiatus, executions are again becoming common. Controversy over the death penalty attracts and nourishes extremists; therefore, familiarity with the issues and the rationale behind competing positions is imperative. The selections offered here will prove helpful in gaining that familiarity.

NOTES

1. Andrew J. Glass, "Outcry for Punishment," *Waco Tribune Herald,* April 11, 1994.
2. See. H. L. A. Hart, *Punishment and Responsibility* (New York: Oxford University Press, 1968), pp. 4–5.
3. Franklin E. Zimring and Gordon Hawkins, *Capital Punishment and the America Agenda* (Cambridge, England: Cambridge University Press, 1986), p. 3.
4. *The Philosophy of Punishment,* edited by Robert M. Baird and Stuart E. Rosenbaum (Amherst, N.Y.: Prometheus Books, 1988).

---

*In February 1994, the Supreme Court denied the petition for a writ of certiorari in a capital murder case involving Bruce Callins. To deny a writ of certiorari in such a situation is to uphold the lower court's decision.

Part One

The Justification
for Punishment

1

Punishment

J. D. Mabbott

I propose in this paper to defend a retributive theory of punishment and to reject absolutely all utilitarian considerations from its justification. I feel sure that this enterprise must arouse deep suspicion and hostility both among philosophers (who must have felt that the retributive view is the only moral theory except perhaps psychological hedonism which has been definitely destroyed by criticism) and among practical men (who have welcomed its steady decline in our penal practice).

The question I am asking is this. Under what circumstances is the punishment of some particular person justified and why? The theories of reform and deterrence which are usually considered to be the only alternatives to retribution involve well-known difficulties. These are considered fully and fairly in Dr. Ewing's book, *The Morality of Punishment,* and I need not spend long over them. The central difficulty is that both would on occasion justify the punishment of an innocent man, the deterrent theory if he were believed to have been guilty by those likely to commit the crime in future, and the reformatory theory if he were a bad man though not a criminal. To this may be added the point against the deterrent theory that it is the threat of punishment and not punishment itself which deters, and that when deterrence seems to depend on actual punishment, to implement the threat, it really depends on publication and may be achieved if men believe that punishment has occurred even if in fact it has not. As Bentham saw, for a utilitarian apparent justice is everything, real justice is irrelevant.

Dr. Ewing and other moralists would be inclined to compromise with

From J. D. Mabbott, "Punishment," *Mind* 48 (April 1939). Reprinted by permission of Oxford University Press.

retribution in the face of the above difficulties. They would admit that one fact and one fact only can justify the punishment of this man, and that is a *past* fact, that he has committed a crime. To this extent reform and deterrence theories, which look only to the consequences, are wrong. But they would add that retribution can determine only *that* a man should be punished. It cannot determine how or how much, and here reform and deterrence may come in. Even Bradley,* the fiercest retributionist of modern times, says "Having once the right to punish we may modify the punishment according to the useful and the pleasant, but these are external to the matter; they cannot give us a right to punish and nothing can do that but criminal desert." Dr. Ewing would maintain that the whole estimate of the amount and nature of a punishment may be effected by considerations of reform and deterrence. It seems to me that this is a surrender which the upholders of retribution dare not make. As I said above, it is publicity and not punishment which deters, and the publicity though often spoken of as "part of a man's punishment" is no more part of it than his arrest or his detention prior to trial, though both these may be also unpleasant and bring him into disrepute. A judge sentences a man to three years' imprisonment not to three years *plus* three columns in the press. Similarly with reform. The vision of the prison chaplain is not part of a man's punishment nor is the visit of Miss Fields or Mickey Mouse.

The truth is that while punishing a man and punishing him justly, it is possible to deter others, and also to attempt to reform him, and if these additional goods are achieved the total state of affairs is better than it would be with the just punishment alone. But reform and deterrence are not modifications of the punishment, still less reasons for it. A parallel may be found in the case of tact and truth. If you have to tell a friend an unpleasant truth you may do all you can to put him at his ease and spare his feelings as much as possible, while still making sure that he understands your meaning. In such a case no one would say that your offer of a cigarette beforehand or your apology afterwards are modifications of the truth, still less reasons for telling it. You do not tell the truth in order to spare his feelings, but having to tell the truth you also spare his feelings. So Bradley was right when he said that reform and deterrence were "external to the matter," but therefore wrong when he said that they may "modify the punishment." Reporters are admitted to our trials so that punishments may become public and help to deter others. But the punishment would be no less just were reporters excluded and deterrence not achieved. Prison authorities may make it possible that a convict may become physically or morally better. They cannot ensure either result; and the punishment would still be just if the criminal took no advantage of their arrangements and

---

*F. H. Bradley, 1846–1924. English Idealist philosopher. (Edd.)

their efforts failed. Some moralists see this and exclude these "extra" arrangements for deterrence and reform. They say that it must be the punishment *itself* which reforms and deters. But it is just my point that the punishment *itself* seldom reforms the criminal and never deters others. It is only "extra" arrangements which have any chance of achieving either result. As this is the central point of my paper, at the cost of labored repetition I would ask the upholders of reform and deterrence two questions. Suppose it could be shown that a particular criminal had not been improved by a punishment and also that no other would-be criminal had been deterred by it, would that prove that the punishment was unjust? Suppose it were discovered that a particular criminal had lived a much better life after his release and that many would-be criminals believing him to have been guilty were influenced by his fate, but yet that the "criminal" was punished for something he had never done, would these excellent results prove the punishment just?

It will be observed that I have throughout treated punishment as a purely legal matter. A "criminal" means a man who has broken a law, not a bad man; an "innocent" man is a man who has not broken the law in connection with which he is being punished, though he may be a bad man and have broken other laws. Here I dissent from most upholders of the retributive theory—from Hegel, from Bradley, and from Dr. Ross. They maintain that the essential connection is one between punishment and moral or social wrongdoing.

My fundamental difficulty with their theory is the question of *status*. It takes two to make a punishment, and for a moral or social wrong I can find no punisher. We may be tempted to say when we hear of some brutal action "that ought to be punished"; but I cannot see how there can be duties which are nobody's duties. If I see a man ill-treating a horse in a country where cruelty to animals is not a legal offense, and I say to him "I shall now punish you," he will reply, rightly, "What has it to do with you? Who made you a judge and a ruler over me?" I may have a duty to try to stop him and one way of stopping him may be to hit him, but another way may be to buy the horse. Neither the blow nor the price is a punishment. For a moral offense, God alone has the *status* necessary to punish the offender; and the theologians are becoming more and more doubtful whether even God has a duty to punish wrongdoing.

Dr. Ross would hold that not all wrongdoing is punishable, but only invasion of the rights of others; and in such a case it might be thought that the injured party has a right to punish. His right, however, is rather a right to reparation, and should not be confused with punishment proper.

This connection, on which I insist, between punishment and crime, not between punishment and moral or social wrong, alone accounts for some of our beliefs about punishment, and also meets many objections to the retributive theory as stated in its ordinary form. The first point on which it helps us is with regard to retrospective legislation. Our objection to this practice is unaccountable on reform and deterrence theories. For a man who commits a wrong before the date on which a law against it is passed, is as much in need of reform as a man who commits it afterwards; nor is deterrence likely to suffer because of additional punishments for the same offense. But the orthodox retributive theory is equally at a loss here, for if punishment is given for moral wrongdoing or for invasion of the rights of others, that immorality or invasion existed as certainly before the passing of the law as after it.

My theory also explains, where it seems to me all others do not, the case of punishment imposed by an authority who believes the law in question is a bad law. I was myself for some time disciplinary officer of a college whose rules included a rule compelling attendance at chapel. Many of those who broke this rule broke it on principle. I punished them. I certainly did not want to reform them; I respected their characters and their views. I certainly did not want to drive others into chapel through fear of penalties. Nor did I think there had been a wrong done which merited retribution. I wished I could have believed that I would have done the same myself. My position was clear. They had broken a rule; they knew it and I knew it. Nothing more was necessary to make punishment proper.

I know that the usual answer to this is that the judge enforces a bad law because otherwise law in general would suffer and good laws would be broken. The effect of punishing good men for breaking bad laws is that fewer bad men break good laws.

[*Excursus on Indirect Utilitarianism.* The above argument is a particular instance of a general utilitarian solution of all similar problems. When I am in funds and consider whether I should pay my debts or give the same amount to charity, I must choose the former because repayment not only benefits my creditor (for the benefit to him might be less than the good done through charity) but also upholds the general credit system. I tell the truth when a lie might do more good to the parties directly concerned, because I thus increase general trust and confidence. I keep a promise when it might do more immediate good to break it, because indirectly I bring it about that promises will be more readily made in future and this will outweigh the immediate loss involved. Dr. Ross has pointed out that the effect on the credit system of my refusal to pay a debt is greatly exaggerated. But I have a more serious objection of principle. It is that in all these cases the indirect effects do not result from my wrong action—my lie or defalcation or bad faith—but from the publication of these actions. If in any instance the breaking of the rule were to remain unknown then I could consider only the direct or immediate consequences. Thus in my "compulsory chapel" case I could have considered which of my culprits were law-abiding men generally and unlikely to break any other college rule. Then I could have sent for each of these separately and said, "I shall let you off if you will tell no one I have done so." By these means the general keeping of rules would not have suffered. Would this course have been correct? It must be remembered that the proceedings need not deceive everybody. So long as they deceive would-be law-breakers the good is achieved.

As this point is of crucial importance and as it has an interest beyond the immediate issue, and gives a clue to what I regard as the true general nature of law and punishment, I may be excused for expanding and illustrating it by an example or two from other fields. Dr. Ross says that two men dying on a desert island would have duties to keep promises to each other even though their breaking them would not affect the future general confidence in promises at all. Here is certainly the same point. But as I find that desert-island morality always rouses suspicion among ordinary men I should like to quote two instances from my own experience which also illustrate the problem.

(i) A man alone with his father at his death promises him a private and quiet funeral. He finds later that both directly and indirectly the keeping of this promise will cause pain and misunderstanding. He can see no particular positive good that the quiet funeral will achieve. No one yet knows that he has made the promise nor need anyone ever know. Should he therefore act as though it had never been made?

(ii) A college has a fund given to it for the encouragement of a subject which is now expiring. Other expanding subjects are in great need of endowment. Should the authorities divert the money? Those who oppose the diversion have previously stood on the past, the promise. But one day one of them discovers the "real reason" for this slavery to a dead donor. He says, "We must consider not only the value of this money for these purposes, since on all direct consequences it should be diverted at once. We must remember the effect of this diversion on the general system of benefactions. We know that benefactors like to endow special objects, and this act of ours would discourage such benefactors in future and leave learning worse off." Here again is the indirect utilitarian reason for choosing the alternative which direct utilitarianism would reject. But the immediate answer to this from the most ingenious member of the opposition was crushing and final. He said, "Divert the money but keep it dark." This is obviously correct. It is not the act of diversion which would diminish the stream of benefactions but the news of it reaching the ears of benefactors. Provided that no possible benefactor got to hear of it no indirect loss would result. But the justification of our action would depend entirely on the success of the measures for "keeping it dark." I remember how I felt and how others felt that whatever answer was right this result was certainly wrong. But it follows that indirect utilitarianism is wrong in all such cases. For its argument can always be met by "Keep it dark."]

The view, then, that a judge upholds a bad law in order that law in general should not suffer is indefensible. He upholds it simply because he has no right to dispense from punishment.

The connection of punishment with lawbreaking and not with wrongdoing also escapes moral objections to the retributive theory as held by Kant and Hegel or by Bradley and Ross. It is asked how we can measure moral wrong or balance it with pain, and how pain can wipe out moral wrong. Retributivists have been pushed into holding that pain *ipso facto* represses the worse self and frees the better, when this is contrary to the vast majority of observed cases. But if punishment is not intended to measure or balance or negate moral wrong then all this is beside the mark. There is the further difficulty of reconciling punishment with repentance and with forgiveness. Repentance is the reaction morally appropriate to moral wrong and punishment added to remorse is an unnecessary evil. But if punishment is associated with lawbreaking and not with moral evil, the punisher is not entitled to consider whether the criminal is penitent any more than he may consider whether the law is good. So, too, with forgiveness. Forgiveness is not appropriate to lawbreaking. (It is noteworthy that when, in divorce cases, the law has to recognize forgiveness it calls it "condonation," which is symptomatic of the difference of attitude.) Nor is forgiveness appropriate to moral evil. It is appropriate to personal injury. No one has any right to forgive me except the person I have injured. No judge or jury can do so. But the person I have injured has no right to punish me. Therefore there is no clash between punishment and forgiveness since these two duties do not fall on the same person nor in connection with the same characteristic of my act. (It is the weakness of vendetta that it tends to confuse this clear line, though even there it is only by personifying the family that the injured party and the avenger are identified. Similarly we must guard against the plausible fallacy of personifying society and regarding the criminal as "injuring society," for then once more the old dilemma about forgiveness would be insoluble.) A clergyman friend of mine catching a burglar red-handed was puzzled about his duty. In the end he ensured the man's punishment by information and evidence, and at the same time showed his own forgiveness by visiting the man in prison and employing him when he came out. I believe any "good Christian" would accept this as representing his duty. But obviously if the punishment is thought of as imposed *by* the victim or *for* the injury or immorality then the contradiction with forgiveness is hopeless.

So far as the question of the actual punishment of any individual is concerned this paper could stop here. No punishment is morally retributive or reformative or deterrent. Any criminal punished for any one of these reasons is certainly unjustly punished. The only justification for punishing any man is that he has broken a law.

In a book which has already left its mark on prison administration I have found a criminal himself confirming these views. *Walls Have Mouths,* by W. F. R. Macartney, is prefaced, and provided with appendices to each chapter, by Compton Mackenzie. It is interesting to notice how the novelist maintains that the proper object of penal servitude should be reformation,[1] whereas the prisoner himself accepts the view I have set out above. Macartney says, "To punish a man is to treat him as an equal. To be punished *for an offense against rules* is a sane man's right."[2] It is striking also that he never uses "injustice" to describe the brutality or provocation which he experienced. He makes it clear that there were only two types of prisoner who were *unjustly* imprisoned, those who were insane and not responsible for the acts for which they were punished[3] and those who were innocent and had broken no law.[4] It is irrelevant, as he rightly observes, that some of these innocent men were, like Steinie Morrison, dangerous and violent characters, who on utilitarian grounds might well have been restrained. That made their punishment no whit less unjust. . . .[5]

It will be objected that my original question "Why ought X to be punished?" is an illegitimate isolation of the issue. I have treated the whole set of circumstances as determined. X is a citizen of a state. About his citizenship, whether willing or unwilling, I have asked no questions. About the government, whether it is good or bad, I do not inquire. X has broken a law. Concerning the law, whether it is well-devised or not, I have not asked. Yet all these questions are surely relevant before it can be decided whether a particular punishment is just. It is the essence of my position that none of these questions is relevant. Punishment is a corollary of law-breaking by a member of the society whose law is broken. This is a static and an abstract view but I see no escape from it. Considerations of utility come in on two quite different issues. Should there be laws, and what laws should there be? As a legislator I may ask what general types of action would benefit the community and, among these, which can be "standardized" without loss, or should be standardized to achieve their full value. This, however, is not the primary question since particular laws may be altered or repealed. The choice which is the essential *prius* of punishment is the choice that there should be laws. This choice is not Hobson's. Other methods may be considered. A government might attempt to standardize certain modes of action by means of advice. It might proclaim its view and say "Citizens are requested" to follow this or that procedure. Or again it might decide to deal with each case as it arose in the manner most effective for the common welfare. Anarchists have wavered between these two alternatives and a third—that of doing nothing to enforce a standard of behavior but merely giving arbitrational decisions between conflicting parties, decisions binding only by consent.

I think it can be seen without detailed examination of particular laws that the method of lawmaking has its own advantages. Its orders are explicit and general. It makes behavior reliable and predictable. Its threat of punishment may be so effective as to make punishment unnecessary. It promises to the good citizen a certain security in his life. When I have talked to businessmen about some inequity in the law of liability they have usually said, "Better a bad law than no law, for then we know where we are."

Someone may say I am drawing an impossible line. I deny that punishment is utilitarian; yet now I say that punishment is a corollary of law and we decide whether to have laws and which laws to have on utilitarian grounds. And surely it is only this corollary which distinguishes any law from good advice or exhortation. This is a misunderstanding. Punishment is a corollary not of law but of lawbreaking. Legislators do not *choose* to punish. They hope no punishment will be needed. Their laws would succeed even if no punishment occurred. The criminal makes the essential choice; he "brings it on himself." Other men obey the law because they see its order is reasonable, because of inertia, because of fear. In this whole area, and it may be the major part of the state, law achieves its ends without punishment. Clearly, then, punishment is not a corollary of law.

We may return for a moment to the question of amount and nature of punishment. It may be thought that this also is automatic. The law will include its own penalties and the judge will have no option. This, however, is again an initial choice of principle. If the laws do include their own penalties then the judge has no option. But the legislature might adopt a system which left complete or partial freedom to the judge, as we do except in the case of murder. Once again, what are the merits (regardless of particular laws, still more of particular cases) of fixed penalties and variable penalties? At first sight it would seem that all the advantages are with the variable penalties; for men who have broken the same law differ widely in degree of wickedness and responsibility. When, however, we remember that punishment is not an attempt to balance moral guilt this advantage is diminished. But there are still degrees of responsibility; I do not mean degrees of freedom of will but, for instance, degrees of complicity in a crime. The danger of allowing complete freedom to the judicature in fixing penalties is not merely that it lays too heavy a tax on human nature but that it would lead to the judge expressing in his penalty the degree of his own moral aversion to the crime. Or he might tend on deterrent grounds to punish more heavily a crime which was spreading and for which temptation and opportunity were frequent. Or again on deterrent grounds he might "make examples" by punishing ten times as heavily those criminals who are detected in cases in which nine out of ten evade detection. Yet we should revolt from all such punishments if they involved punishing theft more heavily than blackmail or negligence more heavily than premeditated assault. The death penalty for sheep-stealing might have been defended on such deterrent grounds. But we should dislike equating sheep-stealing with murder. Fixed penalties enable us to draw these distinctions between crimes. It is not that we can say how much imprisonment is right for a sheep-stealer. But we can grade crimes in a rough scale and penalties in a rough scale, and keep our heaviest penalties for what are socially the most serious wrongs regardless of whether these penalties will reform the criminal or whether they are exactly what deterrence would require. The compromise of laying down maximum penalties and allowing judges freedom below these limits allows for the arguments on both sides.

To return to the main issue, the position I am defending is that it is essential to a legal system that the infliction of a particular punishment should *not* be determined by the good *that particular punishment* will do either to the criminal or to "society." In exactly the same way it is essential to a credit system that the repayment of a particular debt should not be determined by the good that particular payment will do. One may consider the merits of a legal system or of a credit system, but the acceptance of either involves the surrender of utilitarian considerations in particular cases as they arise. This is in effect admitted by Ewing in one place where he says, "It is the penal system as a whole which deters and not the punishment of any individual offender."[6]

To show that the choice between a legal system and its alternatives is one we do and must make, I may quote an early work of Lenin in which he was defending the Marxist tenet that the state is bound to "wither away" with the establishment of a classless society. He considers the possible objection that some wrongs by man against man are not economic and therefore that the abolition of classes would not *ipso facto* eliminate crime. But he sticks to the thesis that these surviving crimes should not be dealt with by law and judicature. "We are not Utopians and do not in the least deny the possibility and inevitability of excesses by *individual persons,* and equally the need to suppress such excesses. But for this no special machine, no special instrument of repression is needed. This will be done by the armed nation itself as simply and as readily as any crowd of civilized people even in modern society parts a pair of combatants or does not allow a woman to be outraged."[7] This alternative to law and punishment has obvious demerits. Any injury not committed in the presence of the crowd, any wrong which required skill to detect or pertinacity to bring home, would go untouched. The lynching mob, which is Lenin's instrument of justice, is liable to error and easily deflected from its purpose or driven to extremes. It must be a mob, for there is to be no "machine." I do not say that no alternative machine to ours could be devised but it does seem certain that the absence of all "machines" would be intolerable. An alternative machine might be based on the view that "society" is responsible for all criminality, and a curative and protective system developed. This is the system of Butler's *Erewhon* and something like it seems to be growing up in Russia except for cases of "sedition."

We choose, then, or we acquiesce in and adopt the choice of others of, a legal system as one of our instruments for the establishment of the conditions of a good life. This choice is logically prior to and independent of the actual punishment of any particular persons or the passing of any particular laws. The legislators choose particular laws within the framework of this predetermined system. Once again a small society may illustrate the reality of these choices and the distinction between them. A Headmaster launching a new school must explicitly make both decisions. First, shall he have any rules at all? Second, what rules shall he have? The first decision is a genuine one and one of great importance. Would it not be better to have an "honor" system, by which public opinion in each house or form dealt with any offense? (This is the Lenin method.) Or would complete freedom be better? Or should he issue appeals and advice? Or should he personally deal with each malefactor individually, as the case arises, in the way most likely to improve his conduct? I can well imagine an idealistic headmaster attempting to run a school with one of these methods or with a combination of several of them and therefore without punishment. I can even imagine that with a small school of, say, twenty pupils all open to direct personal psychological pressure from authority and from each other, these methods involving no "rules" would work. The pupils would of course grow up without two very useful habits, the habit of having some regular habits and the habit of obeying rules. But I suspect that most headmasters, especially those of large schools, would either decide at once, or quickly be driven, to realize that some rules were necessary. This decision would be "utilitarian" in the sense that it would be determined by consideration of consequences. The question "what rules?" would then arise and again the issue is utilitarian. What action must be regularized for the school to work efficiently? The hours of arrival and departure, for instance, in a day school. But the one choice which is now no longer open to the headmaster is whether he shall punish those who break the rules. For if he were to try to avoid this he would in fact simply be returning to the discarded method of appeals and good advice. Yet the headmaster does not decide to punish. The pupils make the decision there. He decides actually to have rules and to threaten, but only hypothetically, to punish. The one essential condition which makes actual punishment just is a condition he *cannot* fulfill—namely that a rule should be broken.

I shall add a final word of consolation to the practical reformer. Nothing that I have said is meant to counter any movement for "penal reform" but only to insist that none of these reforms have anything to do with punishment. The only type of reformer who can claim to be reforming the system of punishment is a follower of Lenin or or Samuel Butler who is genuinely attacking the *system* and who believes there should be no laws and no punishments. But our great British reformers have been concerned not with punishment but with its accessories. When a man is sentenced to imprisonment he is not sentenced also to partial starvation, to physical brutality, to pneumonia from damp cells and so on. And any movement which makes his food sufficient to sustain health, which counters the permanent tendency to brutality on the part of his warders, which gives him a dry or even a light and well-aired cell, is pure gain and does not touch the theory of punishment. Reformatory influences and prisoners' aid arrangements are also entirely unaffected by what I have said. I believe myself that it would be best if all such arrangements were made optional for the prisoner, so as to leave him in these cases a freedom of choice which would make it clear that they are not part of his punishment. If it is said that every such reform lessens a man's punishment, I think that is simply muddled thinking which, if it were clear, would be mere brutality. For instance, a prisoners' aid society is said to lighten his punishment, because otherwise he would suffer not merely imprisonment but also unemployment on release. But he was sentenced to imprisonment, not imprisonment *plus* unemployment. If I promise to help a friend and through special circumstances I find that keeping my promise will involve upsetting my day's work, I do not say that I really promised to help him and to ruin my day's work. And if another friend carries on my work for me I do not regard him as carrying out part of my promise, nor as stopping me from carrying it out myself. He merely removes an indirect and regrettable consequence of my keeping my promise. So with punishment. The Prisoners' Aid Society does not alter a man's punishment nor diminish it, but merely removes an indirect and regrettable consequence of it. And anyone who thinks that a criminal cannot make this distinction and will regard all the inconvenience that comes to him as punishment, need only talk to a prisoner or two to find how sharply they resent these wanton additions to a punishment which by itself they will accept as just. Macartney's chapter on "Food" in the book quoted above is a good illustration of this point, as are also his comments on Clayton's administration. "To keep a man in prison for many years at considerable expense and then to free him charged to the eyes with uncontrollable venom and hatred generated by the treatment he has received in gaol, does not appear to be sensible." Clayton "endeavored to send a man out of prison in a reasonable state of mind. 'Well, I've done my time. They were not too bad to me. Prison is prison and not a bed of roses. Still they didn't rub it in. . . .' "[8] This "reasonable state of mind" is one in which a prisoner on release feels he has been punished but not *additionally* insulted or ill-treated. I feel convinced that penal reformers would meet with even more support if they were clear that they were *not* attempting to alter the system of punishment but to give its victims "fair play." We have no more right to starve a convict than to starve an animal. We have no more right to keep a convict in a Dartmoor cell "down which the water trickles night and day"[9] than we have to keep a child in such a place. If our reformers really want to alter the system of punishment, let them come out clearly with their alternative and preach, for instance, that no human being is responsible for any wrongdoing, that all the blame is on society, that curative or protective measures should be adopted, forcibly if necessary, as they are with infection or insanity. Short of this let them admit that the essence of prison is deprivation of liberty for the breaking of law, and that deprivation of food or of health or of books is unjust. And if our sentimentalists cry "coddling of prisoners," let us ask them also to come out clearly into the open and incorporate whatever starvation and disease and brutality they think necessary *into the sentences they propose.*[10] If it is said that some prisoners will prefer such reformed prisons, with adequate food and aired cells, to the outer world, we may retort that their numbers are probably not greater than those of the masochists who like to be flogged. Yet we do not hear the same "coddling" critics suggest abolition of the lash on the grounds that some criminals may like it. Even if the abolition from our prisons of all maltreatment other than that imposed by law results in a few down-and-outs breaking a window (as O. Henry's hero did) to get a night's lodging, the country will lose less than she does by her present method of sending out her discharged convicts "charged with venom and hatred" because of the additional and uncovenanted "rubbing it in" which they have received.

I hope I have established both the theoretical importance and the practical value of distinguishing between penal reform as we know and approve it— that reform which alters the accompaniments of punishment without touching its essence—and those attacks on punishment itself which are made not only by reformers who regard criminals as irresponsible and in need of treatment, but also by every judge who announces that he is punishing a man to deter others or to protect society, and by every juryman who is moved to his decision by the moral baseness of the accused rather than by his legal guilt.

NOTES

1. W. F. R. Macartney, *Walls Have Mouths* (London: V. Gollancz, 1936), p. 97.

2. Ibid., p. 165. My italics.

3. Ibid., pp. 165–66.

4. Ibid., p. 298.

5. Ibid., p. 301.

6. *The Morality of Punishment* (London: K. Paul, Trubner & Co., Ltd., 1929), p. 66.

7. *The State and Revolution* (Eng. trans.) (New York: International Publishers, 1943), p. 93. Original italics.

8. Macartney, *Walls Have Mouths,* p. 152.

9. Ibid., p. 258.

10. "One of the minor curiosities of jail life was that they quickly provided you with a hundred worries which left you no time or energy for worrying about your sentence, long or short. . . . Rather as if you were thrown into a fire with spikes in it, and the spikes hurt you so badly that you forget about the fire. But then your punishment would *be* the spikes not the fire. Why did they pretend it was only the fire, when they knew very well about the spikes?" (From *Lifer,* by Jim Phelan [Deltona, Fla.: Panther, 1966], p. 40.)

2

Two Concepts of Rules

John Rawls

In this paper I want to show the importance of the distinction between justifying a practice[1] and justifying a particular action falling under it, and I want to explain the logical basis of this distinction and how it is possible to miss its significance. While the distinction has frequently been made,[2] and is now becoming commonplace, there remains the task of explaining the tendency either to overlook it altogether, or to fail to appreciate its importance.

To show the importance of the distinction I am going to defend utilitarianism against those objections which have traditionally been made against it in connection with punishment. . . . I hope to show that if one uses the distinction in question then one can state utilitarianism in a way which makes it a much better explication of our considered moral judgments than these traditional objections would seem to admit.[3] Thus the importance of the distinction is shown by the way it strengthens the utilitarian view regardless of whether that view is completely defensible or not.

To explain how the significance of the distinction may be overlooked, I am going to discuss two conceptions of rules. One of these conceptions conceals the importance of distinguishing between the justification of a rule or practice and the justification of a particular action falling under it. The other conception makes it clear why this distinction must be made and what is its logical basis.

The subject of punishment, in the sense of attaching legal penalties to the violation of legal rules, has always been a troubling moral question.

From *The Philosophical Review* (1955): 3–13. Reprinted by permission of the publisher and the author.

The trouble about it has not been that people disagree as to whether or not punishment is justifiable. Most people have held that, freed from certain abuses, it is an acceptable institution. Only a few have rejected punishment entirely, which is rather surprising when one considers all that can be said against it. The difficulty is with the justification of punishment: various arguments for it have been given by moral philosophers, but so far none of them has won any sort of general acceptance; no justification is without those who detest it. I hope to show that the use of the aforementioned distinction enables one to state the utilitarian view in a way which allows for the sound points of its critics.

For our purposes we may say that there are two justifications of punishment. What we may call the retributive view is that punishment is justified on the grounds that wrongdoing merits punishment. It is morally fitting that a person who does wrong should suffer in proportion to his wrongdoing. That a criminal should be punished follows from his guilt, and the severity of the appropriate punishment depends on the depravity of his act. The state of affairs where a wrongdoer suffers punishment is morally better than the state of affairs where he does not; and it is better irrespective of any of the consequences of punishing him.

What we may call the utilitarian view holds that on the principle that bygones are bygones and that only future consequences are material to present decisions, punishment is justifiable only by reference to the probable consequences of maintaining it as one of the devices of the social order. Wrongs committed in the past are, as such, not relevant considerations for deciding what to do. If punishment can be shown to promote effectively the interest of society it is justifiable, otherwise it is not.

I have stated these two competing views very roughly to make one feel the conflict between them: one feels the force of *both* arguments and one wonders how they can be reconciled. From my introductory remarks it is obvious that the resolution which I am going to propose is that in this case one must distinguish between justifying a practice as a system of rules to be applied and enforced, and justifying a particular action which falls under these rules; utilitarian arguments are appropriate with regard to questions about practices, while retributive arguments fit the application of particular rules to particular cases.

We might try to get clear about this distinction by imagining how a father might answer the question of his son. Suppose the son asks, "Why was *J* put in jail yesterday?" The father answers, "Because he robbed the bank at *B*. He was duly tried and found guilty. That's why he was put in jail yesterday." But suppose the son had asked a different question, namely, "Why do people put other people in jail?" Then the father might answer, "To protect good people from bad people" or "To stop people from doing things that would make it uneasy for all of us; for otherwise we wouldn't be able to go to bed at night and sleep in peace." There are two very different questions here. One question emphasizes the proper name: it asks why *J* was punished rather than someone else, or it asks what he was punished for. The other question asks why we have the institution of punishment: why do people punish one another rather than, say, always forgiving one another?

Thus the father says in effect that a particular man is punished, rather than some other man, because he is guilty, and he is guilty because he broke the law (past tense). In his case the law looks back, the judge looks back, the jury looks back, and a penalty is visited upon him for something he did. That a man is to be punished, and what his punishment is to be, is settled by its being shown that he broke the law and that the law assigns that penalty for the violation of it.

On the other hand we have the institution of punishment itself, and recommend and accept various changes in it, because it is thought by the (ideal) legislator and by those to whom the law applies that, as a part of a system of law impartially applied from case to case arising under it, it will have the consequence, in the long run, of furthering the interests of society.

One can say, then, that the judge and the legislator stand in different positions and look in different directions: one to the past, the other to the future. The justification of what the judge does, *qua* judge, sounds like the retributive view; the justification of what the (ideal) legislator does, *qua* legislator, sounds like the utilitarian view. Thus both views have a point (this is as it should be since intelligent and sensitive persons have been on both sides of the argument); and one's initial confusion disappears once one sees that these views apply to persons holding different offices with different duties, and situated differently with respect to the system of rules that make up the criminal law.[5]

One might say, however, that the utilitarian view is more fundamental since it applies to a more fundamental office, for the judge carries out the legislator's will so far as he can determine it. Once the legislator decides to have laws and to assign penalties for their violation (as things are there must be both the law and the penalty), an institution is set up which involves a retributive conception of particular cases. It is part of the concept of the criminal law as a system of rules that the application and enforcement of these rules in particular cases should be justifiable by arguments of a retributive character. The decision whether or not to use law rather than some other mechanism of social control, and the decision as to what laws to have and what penalties to assign, may be settled by utilitarian arguments; but if one decides to have laws then one has decided on something whose working in particular cases is retributive in form.[6]

The answer, then, to the confusion engendered by the two views of punishment is quite simple: one distinguishes two offices, that of the judge and that of the legislator, and one distinguishes their different stations with respect to the system of rules which make up the law; and then one notes that the different sorts of considerations which would usually be offered as reasons for what is done under the cover of these offices can be paired off with the competing justifications of punishment. One reconciles the two views by the time-honored device of making them apply to different situations.

But can it really be this simple? Well, this answer allows for the apparent intent of each side. Does a person who advocates the retributive view necessarily advocate, as an *institution,* legal machinery whose essential purpose is to set up and preserve a correspondence between moral turpitude and suffering? Surely not.[7] What retributionists have rightly insisted upon is that no man can be punished unless he is guilty, that is, unless he has broken the law. Their fundamental criticism of the utilitarian account is that, as they interpret it, it sanctions an innocent person's being punished (if one may call it that) for the benefit of society.

On the other hand, utilitarians agree that punishment is to be inflicted only for the violation of law. They regard this much as understood from the concept of punishment itself.[8] The point of the utilitarian account concerns the institution as a system of rules: utilitarianism seeks to limit its use by declaring it justifiable only if it can be shown to foster effectively the good of society. Historically it is a protest against the indiscriminate and ineffective use of the criminal law.[9] It seeks to dissuade us from assigning to penal institutions the improper, if not sacrilegious, task of matching suffering with moral turpitude. Like others, utilitarians want penal institutions designed so that, as far as humanly possible, only those who break the law run afoul of it. They hold that no official should have discretionary power to inflict penalties whenever he thinks it for the benefit of society; for on utilitarian grounds an institution granting such power could not be justified.[10]

The suggested way of reconciling the retributive and the utilitarian justifications of punishment seems to account for what both sides have wanted to say. There are, however, two further questions which arise, and I shall devote the remainder of this section to them.

First, will not a difference of opinion as to the proper criterion of just law make the proposed reconciliation unacceptable to retributionists? Will they not question whether, if the utilitarian principle is used as the criterion, it follows that those who have broken the law are guilty in a way which satisfies their demand that those punished deserve to be punished? To answer this difficulty, suppose that the rules of the criminal law are justified on utilitarian grounds (it is only for laws that meet his criterion that the utilitarian can be held responsible). Then it follows that the actions which the criminal law specifies as offenses are such that, if they were tolerated, terror and alarm would spread in society. Consequently, retributionists can only deny that those who are punished deserve to be punished if they deny that such actions are wrong. This they will not want to do.

The second question is whether utilitarianism doesn't justify too much. One pictures it as an engine of justification which, if consistently adopted, could be used to justify cruel and arbitrary institutions. Retributionists may be supposed to concede that utilitarians *intend* to reform the law and to make it more humane; that utilitarians do not *wish* to justify any such thing as punishment of the innocent; and that utilitarians may appeal to the fact that punishment presupposes guilt in the sense that by punishment one understands an institution attaching penalties to the infraction of legal rules, and therefore that it is logically absurd to suppose that utilitarians in justifying *punishment* might also have justified punishment (if we may call it that) of the innocent. The real question, however, is whether the utilitarian, in justifying punishment, hasn't used arguments which commit him to accepting the infliction of suffering on innocent persons if it is for the good of society (whether or not one calls this punishment). More generally, isn't the utilitarian committed in principle to accepting many practices which he, as a morally sensitive person, wouldn't want to accept? Retributionists are inclined to hold that there is no way to stop the utilitarian principle from justifying too much except by adding to it a principle which distributes certain rights to individuials. Then the amended criterion is not the greatest benefit of society *simpliciter,* but the greatest benefit of society subject to the constraint that no one's rights may be violated. Now while I think that the classical utilitarians proposed a criterion of this more complicated sort, I do not want to argue that point here.[11] What I want to show is that there is *another* way of preventing the utilitarian principle from justifying too much, or at least of making it much less likely to do so: namely, by stating utilitarianism in a way which accounts for the distinction between the justification of an institution and the justification of a particular action falling under it.

I begin by defining the institution of punishment as follows: a person is said to suffer punishment whenever he is legally deprived of some of the normal rights of a citizen on the ground that he has violated a rule of law, the violation having been established by trial according to the due process of law, provided that the deprivation is carried out by the recognized legal authorities of the state, that the rule of law clearly specifies both the offense and the attached penalty, that the courts construe statutes strictly, and that the statute was on the books prior to the time of the offense.[12] This definition specifies what I shall understand by punishment. The question is whether utilitarian arguments may be found to justify institutions widely different from this and such as one would find cruel and arbitrary.

This question is best answered, I think, by taking up a particular accusation. Consider the following from [Edgar F.] Carritt:

> . . . the utilitarian must hold that we are justified in inflicting pain always and only to prevent worse pain or bring about greater happiness. This, then, is all we need to consider in so-called punishment, which must be purely preventive. But if some kind of very cruel crime becomes common, and none of the criminals can be caught, it might be highly expedient, as an example, to hang an innocent man, if a charge against him could be so framed that he were universally thought guilty; indeed this would only fail to be an ideal instance of utilitarian 'punishment' because the victim himself would not have been so likely as a real felon to commit such a crime in the future; in all other respects it would be perfectly deterrent and therefore felicific.[13]

Carritt is trying to show that there are occasions when a utilitarian argument would justify taking an action which would be generally condemned; and thus that utilitarianism justifies too much. But the failure of Carritt's argument lies in the fact that he makes no distinction between the justification of the general system of rules which constitutes penal institutions and the justification of particular applications of these rules to particular cases by the various officials whose job it is to administer them. This becomes perfectly clear when one asks who the "we" are of whom Carritt speaks. Who is this who has a sort of absolute authority on particular occasions to decide that an innocent man shall be "punished" if everyone can be convinced that he is guilty? Is this person the legislator, or the judge, or the body of private citizens, or what? It is utterly crucial to know who is to decide such matters, and by what authority, for all of this must be written into the rules of the institution. Until one knows these things one doesn't know what the institution is whose justification is being challenged; and as the utilitarian principle applies to the institution one doesn't know whether it is justifiable on utilitarian grounds or not.

Once this is understood it is clear what the countermove to Carritt's argument is. One must describe more carefully what the *institution* is which his example suggests, and then ask oneself whether or not it is likely that having this institution would be for the benefit of society in the long run. One must not content oneself with the vague thought that, when it's a question of *this* case, it would be a good thing if *somebody* did something even if an innocent person were to suffer.

Try to imagine, then, an institution (which we may call "telishment") which is such that the officials set up by it have authority to arrange a trial for the condemnation of an innocent man whenever they are of the opinion that doing so would be in the best interests of society. The discretion of officials is limited, however, by the rule that they may not condemn an innocent man to undergo such an ordeal unless there is, at the time, a wave of offenses similar to that with which they charge him and telish him for. We may imagine that the officials having the discretionary authority are the judges of the higher courts in consultation with the chief of police, the minister of justice, and a committee of the legislature.

Once one realizes that one is involved in setting up an *institution,* one sees that the hazards are very great. For example, what check is there on the officials? How is one to tell whether or not their actions are authorized? How is one to limit the risks involved in allowing such systematic deception? How is one to avoid giving anything short of complete discretion to the authorities to telish anyone they like? In addition to these considerations, it is obvious that people will come to have a very different attitude towards their penal system when telishment is adjoined to it. They will be uncertain as to whether a convicted man has been punished or telished. They will wonder whether or not they should feel sorry for him. They will wonder whether the same fate won't at any time fall on them. If one pictures how such an institution would actually work, and the enormous risks involved in it, it seems clear that it would serve no useful purpose. A utilitarian justification for this institution is most unlikely.

It happens in general that as one drops off the defining features of punishment one ends up with an institution whose utilitarian justification is highly doubtful. One reason for this is that punishment works like a kind of price system: by altering the prices one has to pay for the performance of actions it supplies a motive for avoiding some actions and doing others. The defining features are essential if punishment is to work in this way; so that an institution which lacks these features, e.g., an institution which is set up to "punish" the innocent, is likely to have about as much point as a price system (if one may call it that) where the prices of things change at random from day to day and one learns the price of something after one has agreed to buy it.[14]

If one is careful to apply the utilitarian principle to the institution which is to authorize particular actions, then there is *less* danger of its justifying too much. Carritt's example gains plausibility by its indefiniteness and by its concentration on the particular case. His argument will only hold if it can be shown that there are utilitarian arguments which justify an institution whose publicly ascertainable offices and powers are such as to permit officials to exercise that kind of discretion in particular cases. But the requirement of having to build the arbitrary features of the particular decision into the institutional practice makes the justification much less likely to go through.

NOTES

1. I use the word "practice" throughout as a sort of technical term meaning any form of activity specified by a system of rules which defines offices, roles, moves,

penalties, defenses, and so on, and which gives the activity its structure. As examples one may think of games and rituals, trials and parliaments.

2. The distinction is central to Hume's discussion of justice in *A Treatise of Human Nature,* bk. III, pt. II, esp. secs. 2–4. It is clearly stated by John Austin in the second lecture of *Lectures on Jurisprudence* (4th ed.; London, 1873), I, 116ff. (1st ed., 1832). Also it may be argued that J. S. Mill took it for granted in *Utilitarianism;* on this point cf. J. O. Urmson, "The Interpretation of the Moral Philosophy of J. S. Mill," *Philosophical Quarterly* 3 (1953). In addition to the arguments given by Urmson there are several clear statements of the distinction in *A System of Logic* (8th ed.; London, 1872), bk. VI, ch. xii, pars. 2, 3, 7. The distinction is fundamental to J. D. Mabbott's important paper, "Punishment," *Mind,* n.s., 48 (April 1939). More recently the distinction has been stated with particular emphasis by S. E. Toulmin in *The Place of Reason in Ethics* (Cambridge, 1950), see esp. ch. xi, where it plays a major part in his account of moral reasoning. Toulmin doesn't explain the basis of the distinction, nor how one might overlook its importance, as I try to in this paper, and in my review of his book (*Philosophical Review* 60 [October, 1951]), as some of my criticisms show, I failed to understand the force of it. See also H. D. Aiken, "The Levels of Moral Discourse," *Ethics* 62 (1952); A. M. Quinton, "Punishment," *Analysis* 14 (June 1954); and P. H. Nowell-Smith, *Ethics* (London, 1954), pp. 236–39, 271–73.

3. On the concept of explication see the author's paper *Philosophical Review* 60 (April 1951).

4. While this paper was being revised, Quinton's appeared; footnote 2 supra. There are several respects in which my remarks are similar to his. Yet as I consider some further questions and rely on somewhat different arguments, I have retained the discussion of punishment and promises together as two test cases for utilitarianism.

5. Note the fact that different sorts of arguments are suited to different offices. One way of taking the differences between ethical theories is to regard them as accounts of the reasons expected in different offices.

6. In this connection see Mabbott, "Punishment," pp. 163–64.

7. On this point see Sir David Ross, *The Right and the Good* (Oxford, 1930), pp. 57–60.

8. See Hobbes's definition of punishment in *Leviathan,* ch. xxviii; and Bentham's definition in *The Principle of Morals and Legislation,* ch. xii, par. 36, ch. xv, par. 28, and in *The Rationale of Punishment* (London, 1830), bk. I, ch. i. They could agree with Bradley that: "Punishment is punishment only when it is deserved. We pay the penalty, because we owe it, and for no other reason; and if punishment is inflicted for any other reason whatever than because it is merited by wrong, it is a gross immorality, a crying injustice, an abominable crime, and not what it pretends to be." *Ethical Studies* (2d ed., Oxford, 1927), pp. 26–27. Certainly by definition it isn't what it pretends to be. The innocent can only be punished by mistake; deliberate "punishment" of the innocent necessarily involves fraud.

9. Cf. Leon Radzinowicz, *A History of English Criminal Law: The Movement for Reform 1750–1833* (London, 1948), esp. ch. xi on Bentham.

10. Bentham discusses how corresponding to a punitory provision of a criminal law there is another provision which stands to it as an antagonist and which needs a name as much as the punitory. He calls it, as one might expect, the *anaetiosostic,* and of it he says: "The punishment of guilt is the object of the former one: the preservation of innocence that of the latter." In the same connection he asserts that it is never thought fit to give the judge the option of deciding whether a thief (that is, a person whom he believes to be a thief, for the judge's belief is what the question

must always turn upon) should hang or not, and so the law writes the provision: "The judge shall not cause a thief to be hanged unless he have been duly convicted and sentenced in course of law" (*The Limits of Jurisprudence Defined,* ed. C. W. Everett [New York, 1945], pp. 238–39).

11. By the classical utilitarians I understand Hobbes, Hume, Bentham, J. S. Mill, and Sidgwick.

12. All these features of punishment are mentioned by Hobbes; cf. *Leviathan,* ch. xxviii.

13. *Ethical and Political Thinking* (Oxford, 1947), p. 65.

14. The analogy with the price system suggests an answer to the question how utilitarian considerations ensure that punishment is proportional to the offense. It is interesting to note that Sir David Ross, after making the distinction between justifying a penal law and justifying a particular application of it, and after stating that utilitarian considerations have a large place in determining the former, still holds back from accepting the utilitarian justification of punishment on the grounds that justice requires that punishment be proportional to the offense, and that utilitarianism is unable to account for this. Cf. *The Right and the Good,* pp. 61–62. I do not claim that utilitarianism can account for this requirement as Sir David might wish, but it happens, nevertheless, that if utilitarian considerations are followed penalties will be proportional to offenses in this sense: the order of offenses according to seriousness can be paired off with the order of penalties according to severity. Also the absolute level of penalties will be as low as possible. This follows from the assumption that people are rational (i.e., that they are able to take into account the "prices" the state puts on actions), the utilitarian rule that a penal system should provide a motive for preferring the less serious offense, and the principle that punishment as such is an evil. All this was carefully worked out by Bentham in *The Principles of Morals and Legislation,* chs. xiii–xv.

3

Therapy, Not Punishment

Karl Menninger

Since ancient times criminal law and penology have been based upon what is called in psychology the pain-pleasure principle. There are many reasons for inflicting pain—to urge an animal to greater efforts, to retaliate for pain received, to frighten, or to indulge in idle amusement. Human beings, like all animals, tend to move away from pain and toward pleasure. Hence the way to control behavior is to reward what is "good" and punish what is "bad." This formula pervades our programs of childrearing, education, and social control of behavior.

With this concept three out of four readers will no doubt concur.

"Why, of course," they will say. "Only common sense. Take me for example. I know the speed limit and the penalty. Usually I drive moderately because I don't want to get a ticket. One afternoon I was in a hurry; I had an appointment, I didn't heed the signs. I did what I knew was forbidden and I got caught and received the punishment I deserved. Fair enough. It taught me a lesson. Since then I drive more slowly in that area. And surely people are deterred from cheating on their income taxes, robbing banks, and committing rape by the fear of punishment. Why, if we didn't have these crime road blocks we'd have chaos!"

This sounds reasonable enough and describes what most people think— *part of the time*. But upon reflection we all know that punishments and the threat of punishments do *not* deter *some* people from doing forbidden things. Some of them take a chance on not being caught, and this chance is a very good one, too, better than five to one for most crimes. Not even

---

Originally published as "Verdict Guilty—Now What?" *Harpers Magazine* (August 1959): 60–64. Reprinted by permission of the author.

the fear of possible death, self-inflicted, deters some speedsters. Exceeding the speed limit is not really regarded as criminal behavior by most people, no matter how dangerous and self-destructive. It is the kind of a "crime" which respectable members of society commit and condone. This is not the case with rape, bank-robbing, check-forging, vandalism, and the multitude of offenses for which the prison penalty system primarily exists. And from these offenses the average citizen, including the reader, is deterred by quite different restraints. For most of us it is our conscience, our self-respect, and our wish for the good opinion of our neighbors which are the determining factors in controlling our impulses toward misbehavior.

Today it is no secret that our official, prison-threat theory of crime control is an utter failure. Criminologists have known this for years. When pocket-picking was punishable by hanging, in England, the crowds that gathered about the gallows to enjoy the spectacle of an execution were particularly likely to have their pockets picked by skillful operators who, to say the least, were not deterred by the exhibition of "justice." We have long known that the perpetrators of most offenses are never detected; of those detected, only a fraction are found guilty and still fewer serve a "sentence." Furthermore, we are quite certain now that of those who do receive the official punishment of the law, many become firmly committed thereby to a continuing life of crime and a continuing feud with law enforcement officers. Finding themselves ostracized from society and blacklisted by industry, they stick with the crowd they have been introduced to in jail and try to play the game of life according to this set of rules. In this way society skillfully converts individuals of borderline self-control into loyal members of the underground fraternity.

The science of human behavior has gone far beyond the common sense rubrics which dictated the early legal statutes. We know now that one cannot describe rape or bank-robbing or income-tax fraud simply as pleasure. Nor, on the other hand, can we describe imprisonment merely as pain. Slapping the hand of a beloved child as he reaches to do a forbidden act is utterly different from the institutionalized process of official punishment. The offenders who are chucked into our county and state and federal prisons are not anyone's beloved children; they are usually unloved children, grown-up physically but still hungry for human concern which they never got or never get in normal ways. So they pursue it in abnormal ways—abnormal, that is, from *our* standpoint.

WHY OUR CRIME THERAPY HAS FAILED

What might deter the reader from conduct which his neighbors would not like does not necessarily deter the grown-up child of vastly different background. The latter's experiences may have conditioned him to believe that the chances of winning by undetected cheating are vastly greater than the probabilities of fair treatment and opportunity. He knows about the official threats and the social disapproval of such acts. He knows about the hazards and the risks. But despite all this "knowledge," he becomes involved in waves of discouragement or cupidity or excitement or resentment leading to episodes of social offensiveness.

These episodes may prove vastly expensive both to him and to society. But sometimes they will have an aura of success. Our periodicals have only recently described the wealth and prominence for a time of a man described as a murderer. Konrad Lorenz, the great psychiatrist and animal psychologist, has beautifully described in geese what he calls a "triumph reaction." It is sticking out of the chest and flapping of the wings after an encounter with a challenge. All of us have seen this primitive biological triumph re-action—in some roosters, for example, in some businessmen and athletes and others—*and* in some criminals.

In general, though, the gains and goals of the social offender are not those which most men seek. Most offenders whom we belabor are not very wise, not very smart, not even very "lucky." It is not the successful criminal upon whom we inflict our antiquated penal system. It is the unsuccessful criminal, the criminal who really doesn't know how to commit crimes, and who gets caught. Indeed, until he is caught and convicted a man is technically not even called a criminal. The clumsy, the desperate, the obscure, the friendless, the defective, the diseased—these men who commit crimes that do not come off—are bad actors, indeed. But they are not the professional criminals, many of whom occupy high places. In some instances the crime is the merest accident or incident or impulse, expressed under unbearable stress. More often the offender is a persistently perverse, lonely, and resentful individual who joins the only group to which he is eligible—the outcasts and the antisocial.

And what do we do with such offenders? After a solemn public cere-mony we pronounce them enemies of the people, and consign them for arbitrary periods to institutional confinement on the basis of laws written many years ago. Here they languish until time has ground out so many weary months and years. Then with a planlessness and stupidity only surpassed by that of their original incarceration they are dumped back upon society, regardless of whether any change has taken place in them for the better and with every assurance that changes have taken place in them for the worse. Once more they enter the unequal tussle with society. Proscribed for employment by most concerns, they are expected to invent a new way to make a living to survive without any further help from society.

Intelligent members of society are well aware that the present system is antiquated, expensive, and disappointing, and that we are wasting vast quantities of manpower through primitive methods of dealing with those who transgress the law. In 1917 the famous Wickersham report of the New York State Prison Survey Committee recommended the abolition of jails, the institution of diagnostic clearing houses or classification centers, the development of a diversified institutional system and treatment program, and the use of indeterminate sentences. *Forty-two years have passed.* How little progress we have made! In 1933 the American Psychiatric Association, the American Bar Association, and the American Medical Association officially and jointly recommended psychiatric service for every criminal and juvenile court to assist the court and prison and parole officers with all offenders.

That was twenty-six years ago! Have these recommendations been carried out anywhere in the United States? With few exceptions offenders continue to be dealt with according to old-time instructions, written by men now dead who knew nothing about the present offender, his past life, the misunderstandings accumulated by him, or the provocation given to him.

The sensible, scientific question is: What kind of treatment could be instituted that would deter him or be most likely to deter him? Some of these methods are well known. For some offenders who have the money or the skillful legal counsel or the good luck to face a wise judge go a different route from the prescribed routine. Instead of jail and deterioration, they get the sort of re-education and re-direction associated with psychiatric institutions and the psychiatric profession. Relatively few wealthy offenders get their "treatment" in jail. This does not mean that justice is to be bought, or bought off. But it does mean that some offenders have relatives and friends who *care* and who try to find the best possible solution to the problem of persistent misbehavior, which is NOT the good old jail-and-penitentiary and make-'em-sorry treatment. It is a reflection on the democratic ideals of our country that these better ways are so often—indeed, *usually*—denied to the poor, the friendless, and the ignorant.

SCIENCE VERSUS TRADITION

If we were to follow scientific methods, the convicted offender would be detained indefinitely pending a decision as to whether and how and when to reintroduce him successfully into society. All the skill and knowledge of modern behavioral science would be used to examine his personality assets, his liabilities and potentialities, the environment from which he came, its effects upon him, and his effects upon it.

Having arrived at some diagnostic grasp of the offender's personality, those in charge can decide whether there is a chance that he can be redirected into a mutually satisfactory adaptation to the world. If so, the most suitable techniques in education, industrial training, group administration, and psychotherapy should be selectively applied. All this may be best done extramurally or intramurally. It may require maximum "security" or only minimum "security." If, in due time, perceptible change occurs, the process should be expedited by finding a suitable spot in society and industry for him, and getting him out of prison control and into civil status (with parole control) as quickly as possible.

The desirability of moving patients out of institutional control swiftly is something which we psychiatrists learned the hard way, and recently. Ten years ago, in the state hospital I know best, the average length of stay was five years; today it is three months. Ten years ago few patients were discharged in under two years; today 90 per cent are discharged within the first year. Ten years ago the hospital was overcrowded; today it has eight times the turnover it used to have; there are empty beds and there is no waiting list.

But some patients do not respond to our efforts, and they have to remain in the hospital, or return to it promptly after a trial home visit. And if the *prisoner,* like some of the psychiatric patients, cannot be changed by genuine efforts to rehabilitate him, we must look *our* failure in the face, and provide for his indefinitely continued confinement, regardless of the technical reasons for it. This we owe society for its protection.

There will be some offenders about whom the most experienced are mistaken, both ways. And there will be some concerning whom no one knows what is best. There are many problems for research. But what I have outlined is, I believe, the program of modern penology, the program now being carried out in some degree in California and a few other states, and in some of the federal prisons.

This civilized program, which would save so much now wasted money, so much unused manpower, and so much injustice and suffering, is slow to spread. It is held back by many things—by the continued use of fixed sentences in many places; by unenlightened community attitudes toward the offender whom some want tortured; by the prevalent popular assumption that burying a frustrated individual in a hole for a short time will change his warped mind, and that when he is certainly worse, he should be released because his "time" has been served; by the persistent failure of the law to distinguish between crime as an accidental, incidental, explosive event, crime as a behavior pattern expressive of chronic unutterable rage and frustration, and crime as a business or elected way of life. Progress is further handicapped by the lack of interest in the subject on the part of lawyers, most of whom are proud to say that they are not concerned with criminal law. It is handicapped by the lack of interest on the part of members of my own profession. It is handicapped by the mutual distrust of lawyers and psychiatrists.

The infestation or devil-possession theory of mental disease is an outmoded, pre-medieval concept. Although largely abandoned by psychiatry, it steadfastly persists in the minds of many laymen, including, unfortunately, many lawyers.

On the other hand, most lawyers have no really clear idea of the way in which a psychiatrist functions or of the basic concepts to which he adheres. They cannot understand, for example, why there is no such thing (for psychiatrists) as "insanity." Most lawyers have no conception of the meaning or methods of psychiatric case study and diagnosis. They seem to think that psychiatrists can take a quick look at a suspect, listen to a few anecdotes about him, and thereupon be able to say, definitely, that the awful "it"—the dreadful miasma of madness, the loathsome affliction of "insanity"—is present or absent. Because we all like to please, some timid psychiatrists fall in with this fallacy of the lawyers and go through these preposterous antics.

AS THE PSYCHIATRIST SEES IT

It is true that almost any offender—like anyone else—when questioned for a short time, even by the most skillful psychiatrist, can make responses and display behavior patterns which will indicate that he is enough like the rest of us to be called "sane." But a barrage of questions is not a psychiatric examination. Modern scientific personality study depends upon various specialists—physical, clinical, and sociological as well as psychological. It takes into consideration not only static and presently observable factors, but dynamic and historical factors, and factors of environmental interaction and change. It also looks into the future for correction, re-education, and prevention.

Hence, the same individuals who appear so normal to superficial observation are frequently discovered in the course of prolonged, intensive scientific study to have tendencies regarded as "deviant," "peculiar," "unhealthy," "sick," "crazy," "senseless," "irrational," "insane."

But now you may ask, "Is it not possible to find such tendencies in any individual if one looks hard enough? And if this is so, if we are all a little crazy or potentially so, what is the essence of your psychiatric distinctions? Who is it that you want excused?"

And here is the crux of it all. We psychiatrists don't want *anyone* excused. In fact, psychiatrists are much more concerned about the protection of the public than are the lawyers. I repeat; psychiatrists don't want anyone excused, certainly not anyone who shows antisocial tendencies. We consider them all responsible, which lawyers do not. And we want the prisoner to take on that responsibility, or else deliver it to someone who will be concerned about the protection of society and about the prisoner, too. We don't want anyone excused, but neither do we want anyone stupidly disposed of, futilely detained, or prematurely released. We don't want them tortured, either sensationally with hot irons or quietly by long-continued and forced idleness. In the psychiatrist's mind nothing should be done in the name of punishment, though he is well aware that the offender may regard either the diagnostic procedure or the treatment or the detention incident to the treatment as punitive. But this is in *his* mind, not in the psychiatrist's mind. And in our opinion it should not be in the public's mind, because it is an illusion.

It is true that we psychiatrists consider that all people have potentialities for antisocial behavior. The law assumes this, too. Most of the time most people control their criminal impulses. But for various reasons and under all kinds of circumstances some individuals become increasingly disorganized or demoralized, and then they begin to be socially offensive. The man who does criminal things is less convincingly disorganized than the patient who "looks" sick, because the former more nearly resembles the rest of us, and seems to be indulging in acts that we have struggled with and controlled. So we get hot under the collar about the one and we call him "criminal" whereas we pityingly forgive the other and call him "lunatic." But a surgeon uses the same principles of surgery whether he is dealing with a "clean" case, say some cosmetic surgery on a face, or a "dirty" case which is foul-smelling and offensive. What we are after is results and the emotions of the operator must be under control. Words like "criminal" and "insane" have no place in the scientific vocabulary any more than pejorative adjectives like "vicious," "psychopathic," "bloodthirsty," etc. The need is to find all the *descriptive* adjectives that apply to the case, and this is a scientific job— not a popular exercise in name-calling. Nobody's insides are very beautiful; and in the cases that require social control there has been a great wound and some of the insides are showing.

Intelligent judges all over the country are increasingly surrendering the onerous responsibility of deciding in advance what a man's conduct will be in a prison and how rapidly his wicked impulses will evaporate there. With more use of the indeterminate sentence and the establishment of scientific diagnostic centers, we shall be in a position to make progress in the science of *treating* antisocial trends. Furthermore, we shall get away from the present legal smog that hangs over the prisons, which lets us detain with heartbreaking futility some prisoners fully rehabilitated while others, whom the prison officials know full well to be dangerous and unemployable, must be released, *against our judgment,* because a judge far away (who has by this time forgotten all about it) said that five years was enough. In my frequent visits to prisons I am always astonished at how rarely the judges who have prescribed the "treatment" come to see whether or not it is effective. What if doctors who sent their seriously ill patients to hospitals never called to see them!

THE END OF TABOO

As more states adopt diagnostic centers directed toward getting the prisoners *out* of jail and back to work, under modern, well-structured parole systems, the taboo on jail and prison, like that on state hospitals, will begin to diminish. Once it was a lifelong disgrace to have been in either. Lunatics, as they were cruelly called, were feared and avoided. Today only the ignorant retain this phobia. Cancer was then considered a *shameful* thing to have, and victims of it were afraid to mention it, or have it correctly treated, because they did not want to be disgraced. The time will come when offenders, much as we disapprove of their offenses, will no longer be unemployable untouchables.

To a physician discussing the wiser treatment of our fellow men it seems hardly necessary to add that under no circumstances should we kill them. It was never considered right for doctors to kill their patients, no matter how hopeless their condition. True, some patients in state institutions have undoubtedly been executed without benefit of sentence. They were a nuisance, expensive to keep and dangerous to release. Various people took it upon themselves to put an end to the matter, and I have even heard them boast of it. The Hitler regime had the same philosophy.

But in most civilized countries today we have a higher opinion of the rights of the individual and of the limits to the state's power. We know, too, that for the most part the death penalty is inflicted upon obscure, impoverished, defective, and friendless individuals. . . .

Capital punishment is, in my opinion, morally wrong. It has a bad effect on everyone, especially those involved in it. It gives a false sense of security to the public. It is vastly expensive. Worst of all it beclouds the entire issue of motivation in crime, which is so importantly relevant to the question of what to do for and with the criminal that will be most constructive to society as a whole. Punishing—and even killing—criminals may yield a kind of grim gratification; let us all admit that there are times when we are so shocked at the depredations of an offender that we persuade ourselves that this is a man the Creator didn't intend to create, and that we had better help correct the mistake. But playing God in this way has no conceivable moral or scientific justification.

Let us return in conclusion to the initial question: "Verdict guilty—now what?" My answer is that now we, the designated representatives of the society which has failed to integrate this man, which has failed him in some way, hurt him and been hurt by him, should take over. It is *our* move. And our move must be a constructive one, an intelligent one, a purposeful one—not a primitive, retaliatory, offensive move. We, the agents of society, must move to end the game of tit-for-tat and blow-for-blow in which the offender has foolishly and futilely engaged himself and us. We are not driven, as he is, to wild and impulsive actions. With knowledge comes power, and with power there is no need for the frightened vengeance of the old penology. In its place should go a quiet, dignified, therapeutic program for the rehabilitation of the disorganized one, if possible, the protection of society during his treatment period, and his guided return to useful citizenship, as soon as this can be effected.

4

Punishment v. Rehabilitation

Richard Wasserstrom

There is a view, held most prominently but by no means exclusively by persons in psychiatry, that we ought never punish persons who break the law and that we ought instead to do something much more like what we do when we treat someone who has a disease. According to this view, what we ought to do to all such persons is to do our best to bring it about that they can and will function in a satisfactory way within society. The functional equivalent to the treatment of a disease is the rehabilitation of an offender, and it is a rehabilitative system, not a punishment system, that we ought to have if we are to respond, even to criminals, in anything like a decent, morally defensible fashion.

Karl Menninger has put the proposal this way:

> If we were to follow scientific methods, the convicted offender would be detained indefinitely pending a decision as to whether and how to reintroduce him successfully into society. All the skill and knowledge of modern behavior science would be used to examine his personality assets, his liabilities and potentialities, the environment from which he came, its effects upon him, and his effects upon it.
>
> Having arrived at some diagnostic grasp of the offender's personality, those in charge can decide whether there is a chance that he can be redirected into a mutually satisfactory adaptation to the world. If so, the most suitable techniques in education, industrial training, group administration, and psychotherapy should be selectively applied. All this may be best done extramurally or intramurally. It may require maximum "security" or only minimum "security." If, in due time, perceptible change occurs, the process

From *Philosophy and Social Issues: Five Studies* by Richard Wasserstrom. Copyright © 1980 by University of Notre Dame Press. Reprinted by permission.

should be expedited by finding a suitable spot in society and industry for him, and getting him out of prison control and into civil status (with parole control) as quickly as possible.[1]

It is important at the outset to see that there are two very different arguments which might underlie the claim that the functional equivalent of a system of treatment is desirable and in fact always ought to be preferred to a system of punishment.

The first argument fixes upon the desirability of such a system over one of punishment in virtue of the fact that, because no offenders are responsible for their actions, no offenders are ever justifiably punished. The second argument is directed towards establishing that such a system is better than one of punishment even if some or all offenders are responsible for their actions. A good deal of the confusion present in discussions of the virtues of a system of treatment results from a failure to get clear about these two arguments and to keep the two separate. The first is superficially the more attractive and ultimately the less plausible of the two. Each, though, requires its own explication and analysis.

One way in which the first argument often gets stated is in terms of the sickness of offenders. It is, so the argument begins, surely wrong to punish someone for something that he or she could not help, for something for which he or she was not responsible. No one can help being sick. No one ought, therefore, ever be punished for being sick. As the Supreme Court has observed: "Even one day in prison would be cruel and unusual punishment for the 'crime' of having a common cold."[2] Now, it happens to be the case that everyone who commits a crime is sick. Hence, it is surely wrong to punish anyone who commits a crime. What is more, when a response is appropriate, the appropriate response to sickness is treatment. For this reason what we ought to do is to treat offenders, not punish them.

One difficulty with this argument is that the relevance of sickness to the rightness or wrongness of the punishment of offenders is anything but obvious. Indeed, it appears that the conclusion depends upon a non sequitur just because we seldom, if ever, seek to punish people for being sick. Instead we punish them for actions they perform. On the surface, at least, it would seem that even if someone is sick, and even if the person cannot help being sick, this in no way implies that none of his or her actions could have been other than what it was. Thus, if the argument against ever punishing the guilty criminal is to be at all persuasive, it must be shown that for one reason or another, the sickness which afflicts all criminals must affect their actions in such a way that they are thereby prevented ever from acting differently. Construed in this fashion, the argument is at least coherent and responsive. Unfortunately, there is now no reason to be persuaded by it.

It might be persuasive were there any reason to believe that all criminal acts were, for example, instances of compulsive behavior; if, that is, we thought it likely to be true that all criminals were in some obvious and distinguishable sense afflicted by or subjected to irresistible impulses which compelled them to break the law. For there are people who do seem to be subjected to irresistible impulses and who are thereby unable to keep themselves from, among other things, committing crimes. And it is surely troublesome if not clearly wrong to punish them for these actions. Thus, the kleptomaniac or the person who is truly already addicted to narcotics does seem to be suffering from something resembling a sickness and, moreover, to be suffering from something which makes it very difficult if not impossible for such a person to control the actions so compelled. Pity not blame seems appropriate, as does treatment rather than punishment.[3]

Now, the notion of compulsive behavior is not without difficulties of its own. How strong, for instance, does a compulsion have to be before it cannot be resisted? Would someone be a kleptomaniac only if such an individual would steal an object even though a policeman were known by the person to be present and observing every move? Is there anything more that is meant by compulsive behavior than the fact that it is behavior which is inexplicable or unaccountable in terms of the motives and purposes people generally have? More importantly, perhaps, why do we and why should we suppose that the apparently "motiveless" behavior must be the product of compulsions which are less resistible than those to which we all are at times subjected? As has been observed, ". . . it is by no means self-evident that [a wealthy] person's yearnings for valueless [items] are inevitably stronger or more nearly irresistible than the poor man's hunger for a square meal or for a pack of cigarettes."[4]

But while there are problems such as these, the more basic one is simply that there is no reason to believe that all criminal acts are instances of compulsive behavior. Even if there are persons who are victims of irresistible impulses, and even if we ought always to treat and never to punish such persons, it surely does not follow that everyone who commits a crime is doing a compulsive act. And because this is so, it cannot be claimed that all criminals ought to be exempted from punishment—treated instead—because they have a sickness of this sort.

It might be argued, though, that while compulsive behavior accounts only for some criminal acts, there are other sicknesses which account for the remainder. At this juncture the most ready candidate to absorb the remaining cases is that of insanity. The law, for example, has always been willing to concede that a person ought never be punished if the person was so sick or so constituted that he or she did not know the nature or quality of the act, or if this were known, that the person did not know that the act was wrong. And more recently, attempts have been made, sometimes successfully, to expand this exemption to include any person whose criminal action was substantially the product of mental defect or disease.[5]

Once again, though, the crucial point is not the formulation of the most appropriate test for insanity, but the fact that it is far from evident, even under the most "liberal" test imaginable, that it would be true that everyone who commits a crime would be found to be sick and would be found to have been afflicted with a sickness which in some sense rendered the action in question unavoidable. Given all of our present knowledge, there is simply every reason to suppose that some of the people who do commit crimes are neither subject to irresistible impulses, incapable of knowing what they are doing, nor suffering from some other definite mental disease. And, if this is so, then it is a mistake to suppose that the treatment of criminals is on this ground always to be preferred to their punishment.

There is, though, one final version of the claim that every criminal action is excusable on grounds of the sickness of the actor. And this version does succeed in bringing all the remaining instances of criminality, not otherwise excusable, within the catgeory of sickness. It does so only by making the defining characteristic or symptom of mental illness the commission of an illegal act. All criminals, so this argument goes, who are not insane or subject to irresistible impulses are sociopaths—people afflicted with that mental illness which manifests itself exclusively through the commission of antisocial acts. This sickness, like any other sickness, should be treated rather than punished.

Once this stage of the discussion is reached, it is important to be aware of what has happened. In particular, there is no longer the evidentiary claim that all criminal acts are caused by some sickness. Instead there is the bare assertion that this must be so—an assertion, moreover, of a somewhat deceptive character. The illness which afflicts these criminals *is simply* the criminal behavior itself. The disease which is the reason for not punishing the action is identical with the action itself. At this point any attempt to substantiate or disprove the existence of a relationship between sickness and crime is ruled out of order. The presence of mental illnesses of these kinds cannot, therefore, be reasons for not punishing, or for anything else.

Thus, even if it is true that we ought never to punish and that we ought always to treat someone whose criminal action was unavoidable because the product of some mental or physical disease—even if we concede all this—it has yet to be demonstrated, without begging the question, that all persons who commit crimes are afflicted with some disease or sickness of this kind. And, therefore, if it is always wrong to punish people, or if it is always preferable to treat them, then an argument of a different sort must be forthcoming.

In general form that different argument is this: The legal system ought to abandon its attempts to assess responsibility and punish offenders and it ought instead to focus solely on the question of how most appropriately the legal system can deal with, i.e., rehabilitate if possible, the person presently before the court—not, however, because everyone is sick, but because no good comes from punishing even those who are responsible.

One such proponent of this view is Lady Barbara Wootton.[6] Her position is an ostensibly simple one. What she calls for is the "elimination" of responsibility. The state of mind, or *mens rea,* of the actor at the time he or she committed the act in question is no longer to be determinative— in the way it now is—of how he or she shall be dealt with by society. Rather, she asserts, when someone has been accused of violating the law we ought to have a social mechanism that will ask and answer two distinct questions: Did the accused in fact do the act in question? If he or she did, given all that we know about this person (including his or her state of mind), what is the appropriate form of social response to him or her?

Lady Wootton's proposal is for a system of social control that is thoroughly forward-looking, and in this sense, rehabilitative in perspective. With the elimination of responsibility comes the elimination of the need by the legal system to distinguish any longer between wickedness and disease. And with the eradication of this distinction comes the substitution of a forward-looking, treatment system for the backward-looking, punitive system of criminal law.

The mental state or condition of the offender will continue to be important but in a different way. "Such conditions . . . become relevant, not to the question of determining the measure of culpability but to the choice of the treatment most likely to be effective in discouraging him from offending again. . . ."[7]

> . . . one of the most important consequences must be to obscure the present rigid distinction between the penal and the medical institution. . . . For purposes of convenience offenders for whom medical treatment is indicated will doubtless tend to be allocated to one building, and those for whom medicine has nothing to offer to another; but *the formal distinction between prison and hospital will become blurred, and, one may reasonably expect, eventually obliterated altogether. Both will be simply "places of safety" in which offenders receive the treatment which experience suggests is most likely to evoke the desired response.*[8]

Thus, on this view even if a person was responsible when he or she acted and blameworthy for having so acted, we still ought to behave toward him or her in roughly the same way that we behave toward someone who is sick—we ought, in other words, to do something very much like treating him or her. Why? Because this just makes more sense than punishment. The fact that he or she was responsible is simply not very relevant. It is wrong of course to punish people who are sick; but even with those who are well, the more humane and civilized approach is one that concerns itself solely with the question of how best to effect the most rapid and complete rehabilitation or "cure" of the offender. The argument is not that no one is responsible or blameworthy; instead, it is that these descriptions are simply irrelevant to what, on moral grounds, ought to be the only significant considerations, namely, what mode of behavior toward the offender is most apt to maximize the likelihood that he or she will not in the future commit those obnoxious or dangerous acts that are proscribed by the law. The only goal ought to be rehabilitation (in this extended sense of "rehabilitation"), the only issue how to bring about the rehabilitation of the offender.

The moral good sense of this approach can be perceived most clearly, so the argument goes on, when we contrast this thoroughly forward-looking point of view with punishment. For if there is one thing which serves to differentiate any form of punishment from that of treatment, it is that punishment necessarily permits the possibility and even the desirability that punishment will be imposed upon an offender even though he or she is fully "cured"—even though there is no significant likelihood that he or she will behave improperly in the future. And, in every such case in which a person is punished—in every case in which the infliction of the punishment will help the offender not at all (and may in fact harm him or her immeasurably)—the act of punishment is, on moral grounds, seriously offensive. Even if it were true that some of the people who commit crimes are responsible and blameworthy, and even if it were the case that we had meaningful techniques at our disposal for distinguishing those who are responsible from those who are not—still, every time we inflict a punishment on someone who will not be benefited by it, we commit a seriously immoral act. This claim, or something like it, lies, I think, at the base of the case which can be made against the punishment even of the guilty. For it is true that any system of punishment does require that some people will be made to suffer even though the suffering will help them not at all. It is this which the analogue to a system of treatment, a rehabilitative system such as Lady Wootton's, expressly prevents, and it is in virtue of this that such a system might be thought preferable.[9]

There are, I think, both practical and theoretical objections to a proposal such as this. The practical objections concern, first, the possibility that certain "effective" treatments may themselves be morally objectionable, and, second, the possibility that this way of viewing offenders may create a world in which we all become indifferent to the characteristics that distinguish those who are responsible from those who are not. The ease, for example, with which someone like Menninger tends to see the criminal not as an adult but as a "grown-up child"[10] says something about the ease with which a kind of paternalistic manipulativeness could readily pervade a system composed of "places of safety."[11]

These are, though, contingent rather than necessary worries. A system organized in accordance with this rehabilitative ideal could have a view that certain therapies were impermissible on moral grounds, just as it could also treat all of the persons involved with all of the respect they deserved as persons. Indeed, it is important when comparing and contrasting proposals for rehabilitative systems with punishment to make certain that the comparisons are of things that are comparable. There are abuses present in most if not all institutional therapeutic systems in existence today, but there are also abuses present in most if not all institutional penal systems in existence today. And the practical likelihood of the different abuses is certainly worth taking seriously in trying to evaluate the alternatives. What is not appropriate, however, is to contrast either an ideal of the sort proposed by Wootton or Menninger with an existing penal one, or an ideal, just penal system with an existing therapeutic one.[12]

These matters to one side, one of the chief theoretical objections to a proposal of the sort just described is that it ignores the whole question of general deterrence. Were we to have a system such as that envisioned by Lady Wootton or Menninger, we would ask one and only one question of each person who violated the law: What is the best, most efficacious thing to do to this individual to diminish substantially the likelihood that he or she will misbehave in this, or similar fashion, again? If there is nothing at all that need be done in order for us to be quite confident that he or she will not misbehave again (perhaps because the person is extremely contrite, or because we are convinced it was an impulsive, or otherwise unlikely-to-be-repeated act), then the logic of this system requires that the individual be released forthwith. For in this system it is the future conduct of the actor, and it alone, that is the only relevant consideration. There is simply no room within this way of thinking to take into account the achievement of general deterrence. H. L. A. Hart has put the matter this way in explaining why the *reform* (when any might be called for) of the prisoner cannot be the general justifying aim of a system of punishment.

> The objection of assigning to Reform this place in punishment is not merely that punishment entails suffering and reform does not; but that Reform is essentially a remedial step for which ex hypothesi there is an opportunity only at the point where the criminal law has failed in its primary task of securing society from the evil which breach of the law involves. Society is divisible at any moment into two classes: (i) those who have actually broken a given law and (ii) those who have not yet broken it but may. *To take Reform as the dominant objective would be to forego the hope of influencing the second—and in relation to the more serious offenses— numerically much greater class. We should thus subordinate the prevention of first offenses to the prevention of recidivism.*[13]

A system of punishment will on this view find its justification in the fact that the announcement of penalties and their infliction upon those who break the laws induces others to obey the laws. The question why punish anyone at all *is* answered by Hart. We punish because we thereby deter potential offenders from becoming actual offenders. For Hart, the case for punishment as a general social practice or institution rests on the prevention of crime; it is not to be found either in the inherent appropriateness of punishing offenders or in the contingently "corrective" or rehabilitative powers of fines or imprisonments on some criminals.

Yet, despite appearances, the appeal to general deterrence is not as different as might be supposed from the appeal to a rehabilitative ideal. In both cases, the justification for doing something (or nothing) to the offender rests upon the good consequences that will ensue. General deterrence just as much as rehabilitation views what should be done to offenders as a question of *social control.* It is a way of inducing those who can control their behavior to regulate it in such a way that it will conform to the dictates of the law. The disagreement with those who focus upon rehabilitation is only over the question of whose behavioral modification justifies the imposition of deprivations upon the criminals. Proponents of general deterrence say it is the modification of the behavior of the noncriminals that matters; proponents of rehabilitation say it is the modification of the behavior of the criminals that is decisive. Thus, a view such as Hart's is less a justification of punishment than of a system of threats of punishment. For if the rest of society could be convinced that offenders would be made to undergo deprivations that persons would not wish to undergo we would accomplish all that the deterrent theory would have us achieve through our somewhat more visible applications of these deprivations to offenders. This is so because it is the belief that punishment will follow the commission of an offense that deters potential offenders. The actual punishment of persons is on this view necessary in order to keep the threat of punishment credible. . . .

NOTES

1. Menninger, "Therapy, Not Punishment," reprinted in Murphy (ed.), *Punishment and Rehabilitation* (Belmont, Calif.: Wadsworth Publishing Co., 1973), p. 136. [Chapter 3 in this volume.]

2. *Robinson* v. *California,* 370 U.S. 660 (1962).

3. The Supreme Court has worried about this problem in, for example, the case of chronic alcoholism, in *Powell* v. *Texas,* 392 U.S. 514 (1968). The discussion in this and related cases is neither very clear nor very illuminating.

4. Barbara Wootton, *Social Science and Social Pathology* (London: G. Allen & Unwin, 1959), p. 235.

5. See, e.g., *Durham* v. *United States,* 214 F. 2d 862 (D.C. Cir., 1954); *United States* v. *Brawner,* 471 F. 2d 969 (D.C. Cir., 1972); and Model Penal Code § 4.01.

6. Barbara Wootton, *Crime and the Criminal Law* (London: Stevens, 1963).

7. Ibid., p. 77.

8. Ibid., pp. 79–80 (emphasis added).

9. There are some additional, more practical arguments that might be offered in support of such a proposal.

To begin with, by making irrelevant the question of whether the actor was responsible when he or she acted, the operation of the criminal law could be greatly simplified. More specifically, by "eliminating" the issue of responsibility we thereby necessarily eliminate the requirement that the law continue to attempt to make those terribly difficult judgments of legal responsibility which our system of punishment requires to be made. And, as a practical matter, at least, this is no small consideration. For surely there is no area in which the techniques of legal adjudication have functioned less satisfactorily than in that of determining the actor's legal responsibility as of the time he violated the law. The attempts to formulate and articulate satisfactory and meaningful criteria of responsibility; the struggles to develop and then isolate specialists who can meaningfully and impartially relate these criteria to the relevant medical concepts and evidence; and the difficulties encountered in requiring the traditional legal fact-finding mechanism—the jury—ultimately to resolve these issues— all of these bear impressive witness, it could plausibly be claimed, for the case for ceasing to make the effort.

In addition, it is no doubt fair to say that most people do not like to punish others. They may, indeed, have no objection to the punishment of others; but the actual task of inflicting and overseeing the infliction of an organized set of punishments is distasteful to most. It is all too easy, therefore, and all too typical, for society to entrust the administration of punishments to those who, if they do not actually enjoy it, at least do not find it unpleasant. Just as there is no necessary reason for punishments ever to be needlessly severe, so there is no necessary reason for those who are charged with the duty of punishing to be brutal or unkind. Nonetheless, it is simply a fact that it is difficult, if not impossible, to attract sensitive, kindly or compassionate persons to assume this charge. No such analogous problem, it might be argued, attends the call for treatment.

10. "What might deter the reader from conduct which his neighbors would not like does not necessarily deter the grown-up child of vastly different background. . . .

"It is not the successful criminal upon whom we inflict our antiquated penal system. It is the unsuccessful criminal, the criminal who really doesn't know how to commit crimes and who gets caught. . . . The clumsy, the desperate, the obscure, the friendless, the defective, the diseased—these men who commit crimes that do not come off—are bad actors, indeed. But they are not the professional criminals, many of whom occupy high places." Menninger, "Therapy, Not Punishment," supra note 1 [see p. 43 of this volume].

11. These are discussed persuasively and in detail by Morris in his important article, "Persons and Punishment," *The Monist* 52 (1968): 476–90.

12. I think that Morris at times indulges in an improper comparison of the two. Ibid.

13. H. L. A. Hart, *The Concept of Law* (Oxford: Clarendon Press, 1961), p. 181 (emphasis added).

5

Persons and Punishment

Herbert Morris

"They acted and looked . . . at us, and around in our house, in a way that had about it the feeling—at least for me—that we were not people. In their eyesight we were just things, that was all."

Malcolm X

"We have no right to treat a man like a dog."

Governor Maddox of Georgia

Alfredo Traps in Durrenmatt's tale discovers that he has brought off, all by himself, a murder involving considerable ingenuity. The mock prosecutor in the tale demands the death penalty "as reward for a crime that merits admiration, astonishment, and respect." Traps is deeply moved; indeed, he is exhilarated, and the whole of his life becomes more heroic, and, ironically, more precious. His defense attorney proceeds to argue that Traps was not only innocent but incapable of guilt, "a victim of the age." This defense Traps disavows with indignation and anger. He makes claim to the murder as his and demands the prescribed punishment—death.

The themes to be found in this macabre tale do not often find their way into philosophical discussions of punishment. These discussions deal with large and significant questions of whether or not we ever have the right to punish, and if we do, under what conditions, to what degree, and in what manner. There is a tradition, of course, not notable for its present vitality, that is closely linked with motifs in Durrenmatt's tale of crime and punishment. Its adherents have urged that justice requires a person be punished

---

Reprinted, with changes, from *The Monist* 52 (October 1968): 475–94, by permission of the publisher.

if he is guilty. Sometimes—though rarely—these philosophers have expressed themselves in terms of the criminal's *right to be punished*. Reaction to the claim that there is such a right has been astonishment combined, perhaps, with a touch of contempt for the perversity of the suggestion. A strange right that no one would ever wish to claim! With that flourish the subject is buried and the right disposed of. In this paper the subject is resurrected.

My aim is to argue for four propositions concerning rights that will certainly strike some as not only false but preposterous: first . . . that we have a right to punishment [and] that this right derives from a fundamental human right to be treated as a person. . . .

1. When someone claims that there is a right to be free, we can easily imagine situations in which the right is infringed and easily imagine situations in which there is a point to asserting or claiming the right. With the right to be punished, matters are otherwise. The immediate reaction to the claim that there is such a right is puzzlement. And the reasons for this are apparent. People do not normally value pain and suffering. Punishment is associated with pain and suffering. When we think about punishment we naturally think of the strong desire most persons have to avoid it, to accept, for example, acquittal of a criminal charge with relief and eagerly, if convicted, to hope for pardon or probation. Adding, of course, to the paradoxical character of the claim of such a right is difficulty in imagining circumstances in which it would be denied one. When would one rightly demand punishment and meet with any threat of the claim being denied?

So our first task is to see when the claim of such a right would have a point. I want to approach this task by setting out two complex types of institutions both of which are designed to maintain some degree of social control. In the one a central concept is punishment for wrongdoing and in the other the central concepts are control of dangerous individuals and treatment of disease.

Let us first turn attention to the institutions in which punishment is involved. The institutions I describe will resemble those we ordinarily think of as institutions of punishment; they will have, however, additional features we associate with a system of just punishment.

Let us suppose that men are constituted roughly as they now are, with a rough equivalence in strength and abilities, a capacity to be injured by each other and to make judgments that such injury is undesirable, a limited strength of will, and a capacity to reason and to conform conduct to rules. Applying to the conduct of these men are a group of rules, ones I shall label 'primary', which closely resemble the core rules of our criminal law, rules that prohibit violence and deception and compliance with which provides benefits for all persons. These benefits consist in noninterference by others with what each person values, such matters as continuance of life and bodily security. The rules define a sphere for each person, then, which is immune from interference by others. Making possible this mutual benefit is the assumption by individuals of a burden. The burden consists in the exercise of self-restraint by individuals over inclinations that would, if satisfied, directly interfere or create a substantial risk of interference with others in proscribed ways. If a person fails to exercise self-restraint even though he might have and gives in to such inclinations, he renounces a burden which others have voluntarily assumed and thus gains an advantage which others, who have restrained themselves, do not possess. This system, then, is one in which the rules establish a mutuality of benefit and burden and in which the benefits of noninterference are conditional upon the assumption of burdens.

Connecting punishment with the violation of these primary rules, and making public the provision for punishment, is both reasonable and just. First, it is only reasonable that those who voluntarily comply with the rules be provided some assurance that they will not be assuming burdens which others are unprepared to assume. Their disposition to comply voluntarily will diminish as they learn that others are with impunity renouncing burdens they are assuming. Second, fairness dictates that a system in which benefits and burdens are equally distributed have a mechanism designed to prevent a maldistribution in the benefits and burdens. Thus, sanctions are attached to noncompliance with the primary rules so as to induce compliance with the primary rules among those who may be disinclined to obey. In this way the likelihood of an unfair distribution is diminished.

Third, it is just to punish those who have violated the rules and caused the unfair distribution of benefits and burdens. A person who violates the rules has something others have—the benefits of the system—but by renouncing what others have assumed, the burdens of self-restraint, he has acquired an unfair advantage. Matters are not even until this advantage is in some way erased. Another way of putting it is that he owes something to others, for he has something that does not rightfully belong to him. Justice—that is, punishing such individuals—restores the equilibrium of benefits and burdens by taking from the individual what he owes, that is, exacting the debt. It is important to see that the equilibrium may be restored in another way. Forgiveness—with its legal analogue of a pardon—while not the righting of an unfair distribution by making one pay his debt is, nevertheless, a restoring of the equilibrium by forgiving the debt. Forgiveness may be viewed, at least in some types of cases, as a gift after the fact, erasing a debt, which, had the gift been given before the fact, would not have created a debt. But the practice of pardoning has to proceed sensitively, for it may endanger in a way the practice of justice does not, the maintenance of an equilibrium of benefits and burdens. If all are indiscriminately pardoned less incentive is provided individuals to restrain their inclinations, thus increasing the incidence of persons taking what they do not deserve.

There are also in this system we are considering a variety of operative principles compliance with which provides some guarantee that the system of punishment does not itself promote an unfair distribution of benefits and burdens. For one thing, provision is made for a variety of defenses, each one of which can be said to have as its object diminishing the chances of forcibly depriving a person of benefits others have if that person has not derived an unfair advantage. A person has not derived an unfair advantage if he could not have restrained himself or if it is unreasonable to expect him to behave otherwise than he did. Sometimes the rules preclude punishment of classes of persons such as children. Sometimes they provide a defense if on a particular occasion a person lacked the capacity to conform his conduct to the rules. Thus, someone who in an epileptic seizure strikes another is excused. Punishment in these cases would be punishment of the innocent, punishment of those who do not voluntarily renounce a burden others have assumed. Punishment in such cases, then, would not equalize but rather cause an unfair distribution in benefits and burdens.

Along with principles providing defenses there are requirements that the rules be prospective and relatively clear so that persons have a fair opportunity to comply with the rules. There are, also, rules governing, among other matters, the burden of proof, who shall bear it and what it shall be, the prohibition on double jeopardy, and the privilege against self-incrimination. Justice requires conviction of the guilty, and requires their punishment, but in setting out to fulfill the demands of justice we may, of course, because we are not omniscient, cause injustice by convicting and punishing the innocent. The resolution arrived at in the system I am describing consists in weighing as the greater evil the punishment of the innocent. The primary function of the system of rules was to provide individuals with a sphere of interest immune from interference. Given this goal, it is determined to be a greater evil for society to interfere unjustifiably with an individual by depriving him of good than for the society to fail to punish those that have unjustifiably interfered.

Finally, because the primary rules are designed to benefit all and because the punishments prescribed for their violation are publicized and the defenses respected, there is some plausibility in the exaggerated claim that in choosing to do an act violative of the rules an individual has chosen to be punished. This way of putting matters brings to our attention the extent to which, when the system is as I have described it, the criminal "has brought the punishment upon himself" in contrast to those cases where it would be misleading to say "he has brought it upon himself," cases, for example, where one does not know the rules or is punished in the absence of fault.

To summarize, then: first, there is a group of rules guiding the behavior of individuals in the community which establish spheres of interest immune from interference by others; second, provision is made for what is generally regarded as a deprivation of some thing of value if the rules are violated; third, the deprivations visited upon any person are justified by that person's having violated the rules; fourth, the deprivation, in this just system of punishment, is linked to rules that fairly distribute benefits and burdens and to procedures that strike some balance between not punishing the guilty and punishing the innocent, a class defined as those who have not voluntarily done acts violative of the law, in which it is evident that the evil of punishing the innocent is regarded as greater than the nonpunishment of the guilty.

At the core of many actual legal systems one finds, of course, rules and procedures of the kind I have sketched. It is obvious, though, that any ongoing legal system differs in significant respects from what I have presented here, containing 'pockets of injustice'.

I want now to sketch an extreme version of a set of institutions of a fundamentally different kind, institutions proceeding on a conception of man which appears to be basically at odds with that operative within a system of punishment.

Rules are promulgated in this system that prohibit certain types of injuries and harms.

In this world we are now to imagine when an individual harms another his conduct is to be regarded as a symptom of some pathological condition in the way a running nose is a symptom of a cold. Actions diverging from some conception of the normal are viewed as manifestations of a disease in the way in which we might today regard the arm and leg movements of an epileptic during a seizure. Actions conforming to what is normal are assimilated to the normal and healthy functioning of bodily organs. What a person does, then, is assimilated, on this conception, to what we believe today, or at least most of us believe today, a person undergoes. We draw a distinction between the operation of the kidney and raising an arm on request. This distinction between mere events or happenings and human actions is erased in our imagined system.[1]

There is, however, bound to be something strange in this erasing of a recognized distinction, for, as with metaphysical suggestions generally, and I take this to be one, the distinction may be reintroduced but given a different description, for example, 'happenings with X type of causes' and 'happenings with Y type of causes'. Responses of different kinds, today legitimated by our distinction between happenings and actions, may be legitimated by this new manner of description. And so there may be isomorphism between a system recognizing the distinction and one erasing it. Still, when this distinction is erased certain tendencies of thought and responses might naturally arise that would tend to affect unfavorably values respected by a system of punishment.

Let us elaborate on this assimilation of conduct of a certain kind to symptoms of a disease. First, there is something abnormal in both the case of conduct, such as killing another, and a symptom of a disease such as an irregular heart beat. Second, there are causes for this abnormality in action such that once we know of them we can explain the abnormality as we now can explain the symptoms of many physical diseases. The abnormality is looked upon as a happening with a causal explanation rather than an action for which there were reasons. Third, the causes that account for the abnormality interfere with the normal functioning of the body, or, in the case of killing, with what is regarded as a normal functioning of an individual. Fourth, the abnormality is in some way a part of the individual, necessarily involving his body. A well going dry might satisfy our three foregoing conditions of disease symptoms, but it is hardly a disease or the symptom of one. Finally, and most obscure, the abnormality arises in some way from within the individual. If Jones is hit with a mallet by Smith, Jones may reel about and fall on James who may be injured. But this abnormal conduct of Jones is not regarded as a symptom of disease. Smith, not Jones, is suffering from some pathological condition.

With this view of man the institutions of social control respond, not with punishment, but with either preventive detention, in case of 'carriers', or therapy in the case of those manifesting pathological symptoms. The logic of sickness implies the logic of therapy. And therapy and punishment differ widely in their implications. In bringing out some of these differences I want again to draw attention to the important fact that while the distinctions we now draw are erased in the therapy world, they may, in fact, be reintroduced but under different descriptions. To the extent they are, we really have a punishment system combined with a therapy system. I am concerned now, however, with what the implications would be were the world indeed one of therapy and not a disguised world of punishment and therapy, for I want to suggest tendencies of thought that arise when one is immersed in the ideology of disease and therapy.

First, punishment is the imposition upon a person who is believed to be at fault of something commonly believed to be a deprivation where that deprivation is justified by the person's guilty behavior. It is associated with resentment, for the guilty are those who have done what they have no right to do by failing to exercise restraint when they might have and where others have. Therapy is not a response to a person who is at fault. We respond to an individual, not because of what he has done, but because of some condition from which he is suffering. If he is no longer suffering from the condition, treatment no longer has a point. Punishment, then, focuses on the past; therapy on the present. Therapy is normally associated with compassion for what one undergoes, not resentment for what one has illegitimately done.

Second, with therapy, unlike punishment, we do not seek to deprive the person of something acknowledged as a good, but seek rather to help and to benefit the individual who is suffering by ministering to his illness in the hope that the person can be cured. The good we attempt to do is not a reward for desert. The individual suffering has not merited by his disease the good we seek to bestow upon him but has, because he is a creature that has the capacity to feel pain, a claim upon our sympathies and help.

Third, we saw with punishment that its justification was related to maintaining and restoring a fair distribution of benefits and burdens. Infliction of the prescribed punishment carries the implication, then, that one has 'paid one's debt' to society, for the punishment is the taking from the person of something commonly recognized as valuable. It is this conception of 'a debt owed' that may permit, as I suggested earlier, under certain conditions, the nonpunishment of the guilty, for operative within a system of punishment may be a concept analogous to forgiveness, namely pardoning. Who it is that we may pardon and under what conditions—contrition with its elements of self-punishment no doubt plays a role—I shall not go into though it is clearly a matter of the greatest practical and theoretical interest. What is clear is that the conceptions of 'paying a debt' or 'having a debt forgiven' or pardoning have no place in a system of therapy.

Fourth, with punishment there is an attempt at some equivalence between the advantage gained by the wrongdoer—partly based upon the seriousness of the interest invaded, partly on the state of mind with which the wrongful act was performed—and the punishment meted out. Thus, we can understand a prohibition on 'cruel and unusual punishments' so that disproportionate pain and suffering are avoided. With therapy attempts at proportionality make no sense. It is perfectly plausible giving someone who kills a pill and treating for a lifetime within an institution one who has broken a dish and manifested accident proneness. We have the concept of 'painful treatment'. We do not have the concept of 'cruel treatment'. Because treatment is regarded as a benefit, though it may involve pain, it is natural that less restraint is exercised in bestowing it, than in inflicting punishment. Further, protests with respect to treatment are likely to be assimilated to the complaints of one whose leg must be amputated in order for him to live, and, thus, largely disregarded. To be sure, there is operative in the therapy world some conception of the "cure being worse than the disease," but if the disease is manifested in conduct harmful to others, and if being a normal operating human being is valued highly, there will naturally be considerable pressure to find the cure acceptable.

Fifth, the rules in our system of punishment governing conduct of individuals were rules violation of which involved either direct interference with others or the creation of a substantial risk of such interference. One could imagine adding to this system of primary rules other rules proscribing preparation to do acts violative of the primary rules and even rules proscribing thoughts. Objection to such suggestions would have many sources but a principal one would consist in its involving the infliction of punishment on too great a number of persons who would not, because of a change of mind, have violated the primary rules. Though we are interested in diminishing violations of the primary rules, we are not prepared to punish too many individuals who would never have violated the rules in order to achieve this aim. In a system motivated solely by a preventive and curative ideology there would be less reason to wait until symptoms manifest themselves in socially harmful conduct. It is understandable that we should wish at the earliest possible stage to arrest the development of the disease. In the punishment system, because we are dealing with deprivations, it is understandable that we should forbear from imposing them until we are quite sure of guilt. In the therapy system, dealing as it does with benefits, there is less reason for forbearance from treatment at an early stage.

Sixth, a variety of procedural safeguards we associate with punishment have less significance in a therapy system. To the degree objections to double jeopardy and self-incrimination are based on a wish to decrease the chances of the innocent being convicted and punished, a therapy system, unconcerned with this problem, would disregard such safeguards. When one is out to help people there is also little sense in urging that the burden of proof be on those providing the help. And there is less point to imposing the burden of proving that the conduct was pathological beyond a reasonable doubt. Further, a jury system which, within a system of justice, serves to make accommodations to the individual situation and to introduce a human element, would play no role or a minor one in a world where expertise is required in making determinations of disease and treatment.

In our system of punishment an attempt was made to maximize each individual's freedom of choice by first of all delimiting by rules certain spheres of conduct immune from interference by others. The punishment associated with these primary rules paid deference to an individual's free choice by connecting punishment to a freely chosen act violative of the rules, thus giving some plausibility to the claim, as we saw, that what a person received by way of punishment he himself had chosen. With the world of disease and therapy all this changes and the individual's free choice ceases to be a determinative factor in how others respond to him. All those principles of our own legal system that minimize the chances of punishment of those who have not chosen to do acts violative of the rules tend to lose their point in the therapy system, for how we respond in a therapy system to a person is not conditioned upon what he has chosen but rather on what symptoms he has manifested or may manifest and what the best therapy for the disease is that is suggested by the symptoms.

Now, it is clear, I think, that were we confronted with the alternatives I have sketched, between a system of just punishment and a thoroughgoing system of treatment, a system, that is, that did not reintroduce concepts appropriate to punishment, we could see the point in claiming that a person has a right to be punished, meaning by this that a person had a right to all those institutions and practices linked to punishment. For these would provide him with, among other things, a far greater ability to predict what would happen to him on the occurrence of certain events than the therapy system. There is the inestimable value to each of us of having the responses of others to us determined over a wide range of our lives by what we choose rather than what they choose. A person has a right to institutions that respect his choices. Our punishment system does; our therapy system does not.

Apart from those aspects of our therapy model which would relate to serious limitations on personal liberty, there are clearly objections of a more profound kind to the mode of thinking I have associated with the therapy model.

First, human beings pride themselves in having capacities that animals do not. A common way, for example, of arousing shame in a child is to compare the child's conduct to that of an animal. In a system where all actions are assimilated to happenings we are assimilated to creatures—indeed, it is more extreme than this—whom we have always thought possessed of less than we. Fundamental to our practice of praise and order of attainment is that one who can do more—one who is capable of more and one who does more—is more worthy of respect and admiration. And we have thought of ourselves as capable where animals are not of making, of creating, among other things, ourselves. The conception of man I have outlined would provide us with a status that today, when our conduct is assimilated to it in moral criticism, we consider properly evocative of shame.

Second, if all human conduct is viewed as something men undergo, thrown into question would be the appropriateness of that extensive range of peculiarly human satisfactions that derive from a sense of achievement. For these satisfactions we shall have to substitute those mild satisfactions attendant upon a healthy well-functioning body. Contentment is our lot if we are fortunate; intense satisfaction at achievement is entirely inappropriate.

Third, in the therapy world nothing is earned and what we receive comes to us through compassion, or through a desire to control us. Resentment is out of place. We can take credit for nothing but must always regard ourselves—if there are selves left to regard once actions disappear— as fortunate recipients of benefits or unfortunate carriers of disease who must be controlled. We know that within our own world human beings who have been so regarded and who come to accept this view of themselves come to look upon themselves as worthless. When what we do is met with resentment, we are indirectly paid something of a compliment.

Fourth, attention should also be drawn to a peculiar evil that may be attendant upon regarding a man's actions as symptoms of disease. The logic of cure will push us toward forms of therapy that inevitably involve changes in the person made against his will. The evil in this would be most apparent in those cases where the agent, whose action is determined to be a manifestation of some disease, does not regard his action in this way. He believes that what he has done is, in fact, 'right' but conception of 'normality' is not the therapeutically accepted one. When we treat an illness we normally treat a condition that the person is not responsible for. He is 'suffering' from some disease and we treat the condition, relieving the person of something preventing his normal functioning. When we begin treating persons for actions that have been chosen, we do not lift from the person something that is interfering with his normal functioning but we change the person so that he functions in a way regarded as normal by the current therapeutic community. We have to change him and his judgments of value. In doing this we display a lack of respect for the moral status of individuals, that is, a lack of respect for the reasoning and choices of individuals. They are but animals who must be conditioned. I think we can understand and, indeed, sympathize with a man's preferring death to being forcibly turned into what he is not.

Finally, perhaps most frightening of all would be the derogation in status of all protests to treatment. If someone believes that he has done something right, and if he protests being treated and changed, the protest will itself be regarded as a sign of some pathological condition, for who would not wish to be cured of an affliction? What this leads to are questions of an important kind about the effect of this conception of man upon what we now understand by reasoning. Here what a person takes to be a reasoned defense of an act is treated, as the action was, on the model of a happening of a pathological kind. Not just a person's acts are taken from him but also his attempt at a reasoned justification for the acts. In a system of punishment a person who has committed a crime may argue that what he did was right. We make him pay the price and we respect his right to retain the judgment he has made. A conception of pathology precludes this form of respect.

It might be objected to the foregoing that all I have shown—if that—is that if the only alternatives open to us are a *just* system of punishment or the mad world of being treated like sick or healthy animals, we do in fact have a right to a system of punishment of this kind. But this hardly shows that we have a right *simpliciter* to punishment as we do, say, to be free. Indeed, it does not even show a right to a just system of punishment, for surely we can, without too much difficulty, imagine situations in which the alternatives to punishment are not this mad world but a world in which we are still treated as persons and there is, for example, not the pain and suffering attendant upon punishment. One such world is one in which there are rules but response to their violation is not the deprivation of some good but forgiveness. Still another type of world would be one in which violation of the rules were responded to by merely comparing the conduct of the person to something commonly regarded as low or filthy, and thus, producing by this mode of moral criticism, feelings of shame rather than feelings of guilt.

I am prepared to allow that these objections have a point. While granting force to the above objections I want to offer a few additional comments with respect to each of them. First, any existent legal system permits the punishment of individuals under circumstances where the conditions I have set forth for a just system have not been satisfied. A glaring example of this would be criminal strict liability which is to be found in our own legal system. Nevertheless, I think it would be difficult to present any system we should regard as a system of punishment that would not still have a great advantage over our imagined therapy system. The system of punishment we imagine may more and more approximate a system of sheer terror in which human beings are treated as animals to be intimidated and prodded. To the degree that the system is of this character it is, in my judgment, not simply an unjust system but one that diverges from what we normally understand by a system of punishment. At least some deference to the choice of individuals is built into the idea of punishment. So there would be some truth in saying we have a right to any system of punishment if the only alternative to it was therapy.

Second, people may imagine systems in which there are rules and in which the response to their violation is not punishment but pardoning, the legal analogue of forgiveness. Surely this is a system to which we would claim a right as against one in which we are made to suffer for violating the rules. There are several comments that need to be made about this. It may be, of course, that a high incidence of pardoning would increase the incidence of rule violations. Further, the difficulty with suggesting pardoning as a general response is that pardoning presupposes the very responses that it is suggested it supplant. A system of deprivations, or a practice of deprivations on the happening of certain actions, underlies the practice of pardoning and forgiving, for it is only where we possess the idea of a wrong to be made up or of a debt owed to others, ideas we acquire within a world in which there have been deprivations for wrong acts, that we have the idea of pardoning for the wrong or forgiving the debt.

Finally, if we look at the responses I suggested would give rise to feelings of shame, we may rightly be troubled with the appropriateness of this response in any community in which each person assumes burdens so that each may derive benefits. In such situations might it not be that individuals have a right to a system of punishment so that each person could be assured that inequities in the distribution of benefits and burdens are unlikely to occur and if they do, procedures exist for correcting them? Further, it may well be that, everything considered, we should prefer the pain and suffering of a system of punishment to a world in which we only experience shame on the doing of wrong acts, for with guilt there are relatively simple ways of ridding ourselves of the feeling we have, that is, gaining forgiveness or taking the punishment, but with shame we have to bear it until we no longer are the person who has behaved in the shameful way. Thus, I suggest that we have, wherever there is a distribution of benefits and burdens of the kind I have described, a right to a system of punishment.

I want also to make clear in concluding this section that I have argued, though very indirectly, not just for a right to a system of punishment, but for a right to be punished once there is in existence such a system. Thus, a man has the right to be punished rather than treated if he is guilty of some offense. And, indeed, one can imagine a case in which, even in the face of an offer of a pardon, a man claims and ought to have acknowledged his right to be punished.

2. The primary reason for preferring the system of punishment as against the system of therapy might have been expressed in terms of the one system treating one as a person and the other not. In invoking the right to be punished, one justifies one's claim by reference to a more fundamental right. I want now to turn attention to this fundamental right and attempt to shed light—it will have to be little, for the topic is immense—on what is meant by 'treating an individual as a person'.

When we talk of not treating a human being as a person or 'showing no respect for one as a person' what we imply by our words is a contrast between the manner in which one acceptably responds to human beings and the manner in which one acceptably responds to animals and inanimate objects. When we treat a human being merely as an animal or some inanimate object our responses to the human being are determined, not by his choices, but ours in disregard of or with indifference to his. And when we 'look upon' a person as less than a person or not a person, we consider the person as incapable of rational choice. In cases of not treating a human being as a person we interfere with a person in such a way that what is done, even if the person is involved in the doing, is done not by the person but by the user of the person. In extreme cases there may even be an elision of a causal chain so that we might say that X killed Z even though Ys hand was the hand that held the weapon, for Ys hand may have been entirely in Xs control. The one agent is in some way treating the other as a mere link in a causal chain. There is, of course, a wide range of cases in which a person is used to accomplish the aim of another and in which the person used is less than fully free. A person may be grabbed against his will and used as a shield. A person may be drugged or hypnotized and then employed for certain ends. A person may be deceived into doing other than he intends doing. A person may be ordered to do something and threatened with harm if he does not and coerced into doing what he does not want to. There is still another range of cases in which individuals are not used, but in which decisions by others are made that affect them in circumstances where they have the capacity for choice and where they are not being treated as persons.

But it is particularly important to look at coercion, for I have claimed that a just system of punishment treats human beings as persons; and it is not immediately apparent how ordering someone to do something and threatening harm differs essentially from having rules supported by threats of harm in case of noncompliance.

There are affinities between coercion and other cases of not treating someone as a person, for it is not the coerced person's choices but the coercer's that are responsible for what is done. But unlike other indisputable cases of not treating one as a person, for example using someone as a shield, there is some choice involved in coercion. And if this is so, why does the coercer stand in any different relation to the coerced person than the criminal law stands to individuals in society?

Suppose the person who is threatened disregards the order and gets the threatened harm. Now suppose he is told, "Well, you did after all bring it upon yourself." There is clearly something strange in this. It is the person doing the threatening and not the person threatened who is responsible. But our reaction to punishment, at least in a system that resembles the one I have described, is precisely that the person violating the rules brought it upon himself. What lies behind these different reactions?

There exist situations in the law, of course, which resemble coercion situations. There are occasions when in the law a person might justifiably say "I am not being treated as a person but being used" and where he might properly react to the punishment as something "he was hardly responsible for." But it is possible to have a system in which it would be misleading to say, over a wide range of cases of punishment for noncompliance, that we are using persons. The clearest case in which it would be inappropriate to so regard punishment would be one in which there was explicit agreement in advance that punishment should follow on the voluntary doing of certain acts. Even if one does not have such conditions satisfied, and obviously such explicit agreements are not characteristic, one can see significant differences between our system of just punishment and a coercion situation.

First, unlike the case with one person coercing another 'to do his will', the rules in our system apply to all, with the benefits and burdens equally distributed. About such a system it cannot be said that some are being subordinated to others or are being used by others or gotten to do things by others. To the extent that the rules are thought to be to the advantage of only some or to the extent there is a maldistribution of benefits and burdens, the difference between coercion and law disappears.

Second, it might be argued that at least any person inclined to act in a manner violative of the rules stands to all others as the person coerced stands to his coercer, and that he, at least, is a person disadvantaged as others are not. It is important here, I think, that he is part of a system in which it is commonly agreed that forbearance from the acts proscribed by the rules provides advantages for all. This system is the accepted setting; it is the norm. Thus, in any coercive situation, it is the coercer who deviates from the norm, with the responsibility of the person he is attempting to coerce, defeated. In a just punishment situation, it is the person deviating from the norm, indeed he might be a coercer, who is responsible, for it is the norm to restrain oneself from acts of that kind. A voluntary agent diverging in his conduct from what is expected or what the norm is, on general causal principles, is regarded as the cause of what results from his conduct.

There is, then, some plausibility in the claim that, in a system of punishment of the kind I have sketched, a person chooses the punishment that is meted out to him. If, then, we can say in such a system that the rules provide none with advantages that others do not have, and further, that what happens to a person is conditioned by that person's choice and not that of others, then we can say that it is a system responding to one as a person.

We treat a human being as a person provided: first, we permit the person to make the choices that will determine what happens to him and second, when our responses to the person are responses respecting the person's choices. When we respond to a person's illness by treating the illness it is neither a case of treating or not treating the individual as a person. When we give a person a gift we are neither treating him or not treating him as a person, unless, of course, he does not wish it, chooses not to have it, but we compel him to accept it.

3. This right to be treated as a person is a fundamental human right belonging to all human beings by virtue of their being human. . . .

If the right is one that we possess by virtue of being human beings, we are immediately confronted with an apparent dilemma. If, to treat another as a person requires that we provide him with reasons for acting and avoid force or deception, how can we justify the force and deception we exercise with respect to children and the mentally ill? If they, too, have a right to be treated as persons are we not constantly infringing their rights? One way out of this is simply to restrict the right to those who satisfy the conditions of being a person. Infants and the insane, it might be argued, do not meet these conditions, and they would not then have the right. Another approach would be to describe the right they possess as a prima facie right to be treated as a person. This right might then be outweighed by other considerations. This approach generally seems to me, as I shall later argue, inadequate.

I prefer this tack. Children possess the right to be treated as persons but they possess this right as an individual might be said in the law of property to possess a future interest. There are advantages in talking of individuals as having a right though complete enjoyment of it is postponed. Brought to our attention, if we ascribe to them the right, is the legitimacy of their complaint if they are not provided with opportunities and conditions assuring their full enjoyment of the right when they acquire the characteristics of persons. More than this, all persons are charged with the sensitive task of not denying them the right to be a person and to be treated as a person by failing to provide the conditions for their becoming individuals who are able freely and in an informed way to choose and who are prepared themselves to assume responsibility for their choices. There is an obligation imposed upon us all, unlike that we have with respect to animals, to respond to children in such a way as to maximize the chances of their becoming persons. This may well impose upon us the obligation to treat them as persons from a very early age, that is, to respect their choices and to place upon them the responsibility for the choices to be made. There is no need to say that there is a close connection between how we respond to them and what they become. It also imposes upon us all the duty to display constantly the qualities of a person, for what they become they will largely become because of what they learn from us is acceptable behavior. . . .

NOTE

1. "When a man is suffering from an infectious disease, he is a danger to the community, and it is necessary to restrict his liberty of movement. But no one associates any idea of guilt with such a situation. On the contrary, he is an object of commiseration to his friends. Such steps as science recommends are taken to cure him of his disease, and he submits as a rule without reluctance to the curtailment of liberty involved meanwhile. The same method in spirit ought to be shown in the treatment of what is called 'crime.'"

Bertrand Russell, *Roads to Freedom* (London: George Allen and Unwin Ltd., 1918), p. 135.

"We do not hold people responsible for their reflexes—for example, for coughing in church. We hold them responsible for their operant behavior—for example, for whispering in church or remaining in church while coughing. But there are variables which are responsible for whispering as well as coughing, and these may be just as inexorable. When we recognize this, we are likely to drop the notion of responsibility altogether and with it the doctrine of free will as an inner causal agent."

B. F. Skinner, *Science and Human Behavior* (New York: Macmillan, 1953), pp. 115–16.

"Basically, criminality is but a symptom of insanity, using the term in its widest generic sense to express unacceptable social behavior based on unconscious motivation flowing from a disturbed instinctive and emotional life, whether this appears in frank psychoses, or in less obvious form in neuroses and unrecognized psychoses. . . .

If criminals are products of early environmental influences in the same sense that psychotics and neurotics are, then it should be possible to reach them psychotherapeutically."

Benjamin Karpman, "Criminal Psychodynamics," *Journal of Criminal Law and Criminology* 47 (1956): 9.

"We, the agents of society, must move to end the game of tit-for-tat and blow-for-blow in which the offender has foolishly and futilely engaged himself and us. We are not driven, as he is, to wild and impulsive actions. With knowledge comes power, and with power there is no need for the frightened vengeance of the old penology. In its place should go a quiet, dignified, therapeutic program for the rehabilitation of the disorganized one, if possible, the protection of society during the treatment period, and his guided return to useful citizenship, as soon as this can be effected."

Karl Menninger, "Therapy, Not Punishment," *Harper's Magazine* (August 1959), pp. 63–64 [see p. 49 of this volume].

6

Playing Fair with Punishment*

Richard Dagger

In his influential essay "Are There Any Natural Rights?" H. L. A. Hart appealed to a "mutuality of restrictions" to account for the obligation to obey the law. As Hart put it, "when a number of persons conduct any joint enterprise according to rules and thus restrict their liberty, those who have submitted to these restrictions when required have a right to a similar submission from those who have benefited by their submission."[1] As developed by John Rawls and others. Hart's "mutuality of restrictions" acquired a new name—the principle of fairness (or fair play)—and soon played a leading part in discussions not only of legal obligation, but of legal punishment as well.[2] For if considerations of fairness or reciprocity account for the obligation to obey the law, as the principle's proponents argued, then they should presumably justify the punishment of those who fail to fulfill this obligation.

Now, nearly forty years after the publication of Hart's essay, the principle of fair play figures prominently in a lively debate on the question of whether there is or can be a general obligation to obey the law, with advocates and critics of the principle vigorously arguing their cases.[3] Punishment remains the center of an equally lively debate, but in this case the principle of fairness seems no longer to play a significant role. Indeed, critics have raised so many serious objections that they seem to have overwhelmed those who once regarded the principle of fair play as the best justification of punishment. These

First published in *Ethics: An International Journal of Social, Political and Legal Philosophy* 103, no. 3 (1993). Reprinted by permission of the author and the University of Chicago Press.

*Although he is an apostate in these matters. I am indebted to Jeffrie Murphy for a number of stimulating conversations on topics relating to obligation, fair play, and punishment. I am also grateful for the thoughtful comments of Alan Ryan, an anonymous reviewer, and two anonymous *Ethics* associate editors.

objections, however, are not as damaging as they appear. Or so I shall argue in this article, which attempts to restore the principle of fair play to a central place in discussions of the justification of punishment.

Before I examine the objections to the principle, it is first necessary to explain briefly how fair play provides a justification of punishment. This, in turn, requires a few words about what counts as a justification of punishment. Here I follow Stanley Benn's observation that any attempt to justify punishment must supply a justification at two different levels, for both the institution of punishment and its application in particular instances must be justified.[4] This distinction is important, as Benn noted, because what serves as a satisfactory justification at one level may be entirely unsatisfactory at the other. If we want to provide a justification for legal punishment, then, we must answer two distinct questions: (1) What justifies punishment *as a social practice*? and (2) What justifies *punishing particular persons*? The principle of fair play is an especially attractive theory of punishment, I shall argue, because it offers plausible and compelling answers to both these questions. I shall also suggest that there is a third question—How should we punish those who commit crimes?—that fair play cannot answer without help from other sources.

I

As it applies to punishment, the principle of fair play begins with a conception of society as a cooperative endeavor secured by coercion. To think of society in this way is to recognize that the individuals who compose a society enjoy a number of benefits available only because of the cooperation of their fellows. The social order enables us to work together for common purposes and to pursue in peace our private interests. But we can do these things only when others, through their cooperation, help to maintain this order. This has two important implications. The first is that rules or conventions of some sort become necessary, for we need to know what the required acts of cooperation are. The second is that those who enjoy the benefits of society owe their own cooperation to the other members of society. Because the cooperation of others makes these benefits available to me, fairness demands that I help provide these benefits for them by cooperating in turn. When other things are equal, then, I owe it to the others to obey the rules; if I fail to do so, I take unfair advantage of them.

There are, however, two complications. One is that we are sometimes required to do things for the sake of cooperation that we find unpleasant or burdensome—paying taxes, driving within the speed limit, respecting the persons or property of others, and so on. In all but the smallest and most closely knit societies, moreover, it is often possible to receive the benefits without bearing the burdens of cooperation. This is due to the second complicating feature of the social order—that it provides public goods. One of these, perhaps the most important, is the rule of law. Like other public goods, the rule of law provides benefits for those who do not cooperate as well as for those who do. Under these circumstances the rational course of action for each individual is to withhold cooperation—to be a free rider—whenever cooperation is unpleasant.

This is where punishment enters the picture. Even if people want to cooperate by obeying the rules of the social order, they will find it unwise to do so when there is widespread disobedience. In some circumstances, where the sense of community is especially strong, the threat of coercion may not be necessary to ensure cooperation. But these circumstances are not likely to obtain in the legal systems of modern states. With the aid of the institution of punishment, however, we can provide a guarantee that "those who would voluntarily obey shall not be sacrificed to those who would not."[5]

This is to say that punishment as a practice is justified because it is necessary to the maintenance of the social order. As long as the social order is itself just, or reasonably so, and as long as we cannot trust everyone to obey its rules, we may use punishment to secure its survival. To justify the institution of punishment is not to justify its applications to particular cases, however. Hence Benn's second question must be asked: Whom may we punish?

The answer again follows from the conception of society as a cooperative venture secured by coercion. In this case, though, the relationship between the individuals who compose the society is more important than its security. This is because these individuals are under an obligation to one another to obey the laws of their society. According to the principle of fair play, anyone who takes part in a cooperative practice and accepts the benefits it provides is obligated to bear his or her share of the burdens of the practice. In the case of the legal order this means that everyone who profits from others' obedience to the law is under an obligation to reciprocate by obeying the law in turn. As Jeffrie Murphy once put it, "in order to enjoy the benefits that a legal system makes possible, each man must be prepared to make an important sacrifice—namely, the sacrifice of obeying the law even when he does not desire to do so. Each man calls on others to do this, and it is only just or fair that he bear a comparable burden when his turn comes."[6]

The problem is that people do not always act justly or fairly, especially when they can be free riders or gain in some other way from their unfair actions. As we have seen, one of the purposes of punishment is to discourage us from taking unfair advantage of those who, through their obedience to the law, enable us to enjoy the benefits of the social order. For some, the mere threat of punishment will not be a sufficient deterrent; and in these cases punishment itself is justified.

Punishment is justified, *ceteris paribus,* because the persons who disobey the law fail to meet their obligations to the other members of society. In this sense every crime is a crime of unfairness, whatever else it may be. Criminals act unfairly when they take advantage of the opportunities the legal order affords them without contributing to the preservation of that order. In doing so, they upset the balance between benefits and burdens at the heart of the notion of justice. Justice requires that this balance be restored, and this can only be achieved through punishment or pardon. As Herbert Morris has argued, "A person who violates the rules has something others have—the benefits of the system—but by renouncing what others have assumed, the burdens of self-restraint, he has acquired an unfair advantage. Matters are not even until this advantage is in some way erased. . . . [H]e owes something to others, for he has something that does not rightfully belong to him. Justice—that is, punishing such individuals—restores the equilibrium of benefits and burdens by taking from the individual what he owes, that is, exacting the debt."[7]

This, according to the advocates of fair play, is how we must justify punishing particular individuals. But we must be careful to note what this implies. If we hold that punishment is a means to the end of restoring equilibrium between benefits and burdens, then we must also hold that punishment is warranted only when this equilibrium has been disturbed. We are presuming, in other words, that benefits and burdens were in balance before the person we intend to punish upset matters by breaking the law. And this means that punishment is justified only when there is a just balance of benefits and burdens to begin with—when the social order is just, or reasonably so.[8]

When the social order does come reasonably close to balancing the costs and rewards of cooperation, however, punishment is justified as an institution and society is justified in punishing those who break the law. At both the levels Benn distinguished, then, the principle of fair play provides a justification for punishment.

II

Nevertheless, the attempt to ground punishment in fair play has been the subject of serious criticism by a number of philosophers. Society may well have a right to punish those who break its laws, they say, but this right cannot follow from the principle of fair play. The philosophers who make this complaint typically acknowledge that fair play or reciprocity is an attractive and plausible foundation for punishment. Yet they proceed to argue that closer inspection reveals serious flaws in this foundation. Exactly what those flaws are is the subject of some disagreement—indeed, they sometimes criticize one another's criticisms—but among them the critics have uncovered six principal reasons for rejecting fair play.[9] None of the six provides a conclusive objection to the fair play account of punishment, however, as I shall now try to show. Indeed, these criticisms often rest on a misunderstanding of the nature of the benefits and burdens involved in fair play.

First Objection: Neither Prohibit nor Punish

The first complaint is that the principle of fair play can justify neither prohibiting nor punishing those who break the law. This is because the principle, as Morris elaborates it, requires that a just balance be maintained between the benefits and burdens of social cooperation. Lawbreakers upset this balance by taking benefits that do not belong to them and by shirking burdens that do. To restore the proper balance, society must remove the extra benefit from the offender while reimposing the burdens of social co-operation—that is, obeying the law. But this need not mean that the offender must be punished. As Herbert Fingarette insists, restoring the balance and punishing the offender are quite different from one another.

> On [Morris's] view, provided the books are ultimately balanced, I would seem to have two equally legitimate options—paying my debts earlier in cash, or paying later in punishment. But surely that's not the intent of the law *prohibiting* stealing. The intent is precisely to *deny* us a legitimate alternative to paying the storekeeper for what we take. And even if I restore the balance by returning the stolen goods, and by paying back any incidental losses incurred by the storekeeper, it still remains intelligible and important—not only in principle but in the practice of the law— to ask whether I should *also* be punished. So Morris's kind of view . . . fails to account for law as prohibition, and . . . to make intelligible the question of punishment as something over and above the equitable distribution of burdens and benefits.[10]

This criticism rests on a misconception of the relationship between reciprocity and punishment. There is, to be sure, a distinction between restoring the balance and punishing offenders. If a payroll clerk mistakenly pays an employee more than he or she is supposed to, the clerk may have to retrieve the money from the employee, or take it out of the employee's next pay check, in order to balance the books. This need not involve punishment, either of the clerk or the other employee. But balancing the books in this case does not require a balance of benefits and burdens, which makes it very different from the kind of case Morris has in mind. The clerk and the other employee do not stand in the same relation to one another as the law-abiding citizen (the storekeeper in Fingarette's example) and the lawbreaker (the thief). To restore the balance between the second set is to preserve or restore the balance between the benefits and burdens of cooperation under the rule of law. Indeed, when the thief steals from the storekeeper, he upsets the balance not only with regard to her, but to all law-abiding citizens.

The benefit that the thief gains, in other words, is not simply whatever he steals from the storekeeper. This can be repaid, as Fingarette says, without punishment. Instead, the benefit is to be understood as the double advantage of not obeying the law when it suits one's purposes while also enjoying the advantages of the rule of law provided by the law-abiding citizens. This benefit cannot be repaid simply by forcing the thief not to break the law again—that would leave the "books" unbalanced. So, to restore the balance, the lawbreaker must be punished. The whole point of the principle, then, is to secure a cooperative practice such as the rule of law by prohibiting actions that will undermine the practice and by punishing those who nevertheless do them. The first criticism simply fails to see this.[11]

Second Objection: Sufficient, but Not Necessary

The second criticism holds that acting unfairly may be a sufficient warrant for legal punishment, but it cannot be necessary. There are many people who deserve to be punished, on this view, not because they have acted unfairly, but because they have done something far worse. Put in terms of the distinction between acts that are *mala prohibita* [prohibited evils] and those that are *mala in se* [evil in themselves], the point of this criticism is that some misdeeds should be punished because they take unfair advantage of others, thus falling into the first category, while other and more serious crimes deserve punishment because they are intrinsically wrong. Rape, murder, and other forms of assault are wrong, and they ought to be proscribed; but we cannot explain their wrongness in terms of a violation of fair play or a lack of reciprocity. As R. A. Duff says, "Such talk of the criminal's unfair advantage implies that obedience to the law is a burden for us all: but is this true of such *mala in se*? Surely many of us do not find it a *burden* to obey the laws against murder and rape, or need to *restrain* ourselves from such crimes: how then does the murderer or rapist gain an unfair advantage over the rest of us, by evading a burden of self-restraint which we accept?"[12] The problem with fair play, then, is that it justifies punishment in some cases, but not in all—and not in the cases in which punishment seems most obviously deserved.

There is something to this charge. Rape and murder and other acts of violence are wrong for reasons that have nothing to do with fairness. But this is not to say that considerations of reciprocity play no part in our condemnation and punishment of those who are guilty of such crimes. All crimes, I have said, are in some sense crimes of unfairness. They may be *more than* crimes of unfairness, as rape, robbery, and murder surely are, but they must be *at least* crimes of this sort.

This is true whenever the rule of law is in effect. Murders and rapes and other vicious acts may take place when it is not, of course, but then the character of the offense is different. In such circumstances the offense may be taken to be a private matter involving only the offender and the victim; or it may be regarded as an offense against family honor, or perhaps against the gods or the proper order of things. But it cannot be an offense against the public, or society, unless there is some sense that the members of society are bound together under the rule of laws that it is wrong, *ceteris paribus,* to violate. Nor can the offender suffer legal punishment unless the rule of law obtains. He may suffer revenge, or the punishment of the gods, but not punishment under the law.

The contrast between these two attitudes toward offenses and offenders is one of the themes of Aeschylus's *Oresteia.* So, too, is the advantage of living under the rule of law. In place of the blood feuds and ceaseless quarrels of the lawless life, the rule of law at least promises us the chance to live under rules made and enforced by impartial authorities. To achieve the security and freedom thus promised, we must be willing to forgo the private "punishment" of those who have, we believe, injured us. When we do this, we recognize that an injury to one person is not only an injury to her and her kin, but an offense against the law itself—and therefore a wrong done to all those who make the rule of law possible.

It is in this sense, that all crimes (under the rule of law) are crimes of unfairness. The robber, the rapist, and the murderer do terrible things to the specific victims of their crimes, and the charge of unfairness does not capture this. But what gives society, rather than the victim or his or her kin, the right to punish is the criminals' violation of fairness and reciprocity. The criminals want the security and freedom afforded by the rule of law, but they are not willing to grant this same security and freedom to their victims. They enjoy the benefits of cooperation without bearing a full share of its burdens. When they commit their crimes, therefore, they wrong all the law-abiding members of society. For this crime of unfairness they may properly be punished, as well as for the additional wrong they have done to their particular victims. All crimes (under the rule of law) are crimes of unfairness, in short, even if some are much more than that.

Third Objection: What Benefit? What Burden?

In rejecting the foregoing criticisms I have relied in part on the claim that the critics misunderstand the nature of the benefits and burdens involved in a cooperative practice governed by fair play. But what exactly are these benefits and burdens? Is there really a balance to be struck between them? Can we really justify the practice and infliction of punishment by appeal to such notions? Not according to the third criticism, which holds that the principle of fair play offers no coherent and plausible account of benefits and burdens.

The problem stems, again, from the difficulty of seeing how some crimes are to be analyzed in terms of an unfair distribution of benefits and burdens. To return to Duff's example, it is easy enough to see how the would-be rapist or murderer will find compliance with the laws against rape or murder burdensome; but those who are never tempted to commit one of these crimes will not feel the restrictions of these laws at all. Insofar as rape is defined as unlawful carnal knowledge of a female by a male, moreover, it seems that a man cannot benefit from its proscription, at least not in the same way a woman can. For that matter, the man who wants to commit rape, or the person who wants to be cruel to animals, may derive no benefit at all from laws against these acts.[13] There are, it seems, laws that provide no benefit to some people and laws that impose no burden on some people. That being so, it must be impossible to balance benefits and burdens in these cases. Does this mean that these laws should be eliminated? No, because these laws are among those most of us consider most important. It means, instead, that the principle of fair play cannot provide the ground for a justification of criminal punishment.

This criticism is effective only if we take the benefits and burdens in question to be the benefits provided and burdens imposed by obedience to particular laws. But this is not what the principle of fair play requires. The benefits and burdens in question are those that follow from obedience to the laws of a cooperative *practice*—in this case, the rule of law in a reasonably just society.[14] When these circumstances obtain, everyone engaged in the practice is free to act, to enjoy his or her rights, with a security that would otherwise be impossible. This is a benefit everyone shares. But everyone also shares the burden of self-restraint. The freedom one gains as a result of the cooperation of others, in other words, must be balanced by a restriction on one's freedom, on one's right to act, in order to make freedom under law possible. Everyone thus receives the same benefit—freedom under law— and bears the same burden—obedience to the law. Rights and obligations are in balance, furthermore, for every person in the practice has a right to the cooperation of the others and an obligation to cooperate in turn.

This balance is upset when someone breaks the law. In some cases the lawbreaker may have good, even public-spirited reasons for disobedience. In most cases, however, the lawbreaker seeks a double benefit for himself. He seeks to enjoy the benefits of freedom under law, that is, while enjoying freedom from the burden of obedience as well. If he succeeds, the lawbreaker achieves an excess of freedom over the law-abiding members of society.[15] He enjoys the benefit of cooperation, then, without bearing its burden. It is in this sense that the balance of benefits and burdens is upset.

The offender achieves this, furthermore, by doing what he cannot want everyone else to do. This is the Kantian aspect of reciprocity that Murphy has emphasized.[16] The lawbreaker is typically someone who wants the advantages of the rule of law, but who is unwilling to make the sacrifice of self-restraint. By taking advantage of the obedience of others to enjoy benefits for himself, he treats the law-abiding citizens as means to his own ends.

Fourth Objection: How to Punish?

The fourth criticism is that fair play cannot provide a satisfactory basis for punishment because it cannot tell us how, or to what extent, we are to punish offenders. If all crimes are (at least) crimes of unfairness, then does it follow that all criminals are to suffer the same punishment? If so, we shall have no way to account for the different degrees of seriousness we attach to different crimes.

One possible escape from this difficulty is to look for some sense of proportionality in the principle of fair play. Beginning with the notion that the principle requires us to restore the balance of benefits and burdens under the rule of law, one might say that those who commit the most serious offenses throw the distribution of benefits and burdens further out of balance than those who commit petty crimes. To restore the balance, then, the murderer must be punished more severely than the robber, who must be punished more severely than the thief, and so on.

The trouble with this defense of fair play, as Richard Burgh argues, is that it requires us to look not only to the gravity of the crime in question, but to the benefits and burdens involved. If the benefit the criminal receives is relief from the burden of self-restraint, with the extra freedom this brings, we must then find some way of understanding what the force of the burden of obeying the law is. "Now," Burgh says, "one way of understanding this burden is to see it in terms of the strength of the inclination to commit the crime. The stronger the inclination, the greater the burden one undertakes in obeying the law. Hence, if the strength of the inclination to commit one crime is stronger than another, a greater advantage will be derived from committing that crime. If the basis of desert is the removing of the advantage, then the person who commits the crime will be deserving of more punishment.[17] The consequences of such a policy, Burgh continues, are surely unacceptable. The crimes we ordinarily consider the most serious are the ones that most people are least inclined to commit, while the ones most people are most inclined to commit are usually regarded as the least serious. But this will change if we base punishment on the strength of the inclination to break the law. As Burgh puts it, "insofar as we think of the burden of self-restraint in terms of the strength of inclination to violate the law, it probably follows that a greater burden is renounced with regard to tax fraud than with respect to murder." Accepting the principle of fair play thus seems to entail the surrender of "the rather central intuition that punishment must be proportional to the gravity of the crime. In fact, if this analysis yields the result that the tax evader deserves a greater punishment than the murderer, then I think most would be inclined to reject the analysis."[18]

As Burgh says, "one way of understanding" the burden of obedience is in terms of the strength of the inclination to commit a particular crime. This is not the only way to understand this burden, however, nor is it the right way. Here, as with my response to the second criticism, the key is to distinguish between the burden of obeying a particular law and the burden of obeying the law in general. Reciprocity does not mean that everyone must benefit from and feel the burden of each and every law. On the contrary, it is the system of laws—law as a cooperative practice—from which each must benefit, and to which each must contribute by bearing the burden of cooperation. Cooperation will not always be burdensome; if it were, the practice would probably collapse. But there are times for almost all of us when we would like to have the best of both worlds—that is, the freedom we enjoy under the rule of law plus freedom from the burden of obeying laws. Because the rule of law is a public good, it is sometimes possible to do this—up to the point, at least, where disobedience is widespread enough to threaten the breakdown of law. Punishment is the device we use to prevent this from happening.

This way of understanding the burden of obedience saves fair play from Burgh's criticism. Still, it does not address the more general point, namely, Does fair play tell us how, or to what extent various offenders are to be punished? The answer is that it does not. Fair play tells us *that* those who take unfair advantage of the cooperating members of a cooperative practice should be punished—allowing, of course, for the possibility of overriding considerations. But it does not tell us *how* they should be punished. Nor should it.

The principle of fair play enables us to see how certain actions constitute offenses against society because those who engage in these actions take advantage of the law-abiding citizens who make the rule of law possible. From this point of view, as I have said, all crimes are crimes of unfairness. From this point of view, furthermore, that is all that they are. The murderer and the tax cheater are on a par in this respect. Both are guilty of taking unfair advantage of those who obey the law, and both should be punished accordingly. Exactly how they should be punished is something fair play cannot tell us. That will depend upon the circumstances of the society in question, and perhaps even on the circumstances of the individuals in question, since what counts as an efficacious punishment at one place and time may not count at another. But the murderer and tax cheater should be punished to the same extent for their crimes of unfairness.

This is not to say that the murderer and the tax cheater should receive the same punishment *tout court*. For the murderer has committed two crimes, in a sense, but the tax cheater only one. The murderer has simultaneously committed a crime of unfairness (a *malum prohibitum*) *and* a crime against her particular victim (a *malum in se*). For these two offenses, as it were, she must suffer two punishments. The first serves to discharge her debt to society by restoring the balance of benefits and burdens under the rule of law. The second punishment must be justified and established on other grounds.[19]

It is true, then, that the principle of fair play does not tell us everything we need to know about punishment. But this does not mean that it is unsatisfactory as a grounding principle. On the contrary, it simply means that reciprocity must be supplemented by other considerations—for example, deterrence, reform, moral education, restitution—when it is time to decide how exactly to punish wrongdoers. But it is important to notice that none of these other considerations provides a satisfactory account of society's right to punish. For that we must rely on the principle of fair play.

Fifth Objection: Restitution or Compensation, Not Punishment

A different kind of objection tries to sever the connection between fair play and punishment. In this case the complaint is that fair play or reciporcity may provide a sound foundation for a system of criminal justice, but such a system will not include punishment. If the point of criminal justice is to maintain the balance of benefits and burdens on the part of those who live under the rule of law, the argument goes, then it is by no means clear that punishment is necessary to secure or restore this balance. "For it remains to be seen," as Richard Wasserstrom argues, "how it is that *punishing* the wrongdoer constitutes a taking of the wrongfully appropriated benefit away from him or her. . . . [C]ompensation or restitution to the victim by the wrongdoer, not his or her punishment, appears to be the natural and direct way to restore the balance in respect to wrongful appropriation of something that belonged to the victim."[20] All crimes may be (at least) crimes of unfairness, in other words, and society may have a right to respond to these crimes, but there is no reason to believe that punishment is the proper response.

Although I do not want to insist that punishment should be the sole response to crime, I do want to resist the conclusion that it is not *a* proper response. There are two primary reasons for taking this position.

First, there is no entirely suitable substitute for punishment. Restitution and compensation to victims both have their place, as I have argued elsewhere, but they work best when they are regarded as forms of or supplements to punishment.[21] Pure (as opposed to punitive) restitution promises to restore the balance of benefits and burdens between the criminal and his or her direct victims, or the victims' beneficiaries; it offers little, however, to the indirect or secondary victims who must endure the anxiety, frustration, and insurance costs that accompany crime.[22] Nor can pure restitution deal adequately with those offenses, such as tax evasion or violation of anti-pollution statutes, in which there are no specific victims to be identified for purposes of restitution. Requiring some form of community service may be the appropriate response to crimes of this sort, but community service is usually taken to be a form of punitive restitution.

As for compensation to the victims of crime, another set of problems arises. Compensation may help to restore the victims to their previous condition in some sense, but it falls far short of restoring the balance of benefits and burdens under the rule of law. For if compensation is made from public funds, then it is principally the law-abiding who are responsible for compensating the victims for their losses and suffering. This simply imposes an additional burden on those who are already bearing the indirect costs of crime, thereby throwing the benefits and burdens of the rule of law farther out of balance.[23] Another tactic might be to pay a reward of some sort to people who obey the law. This might serve to secure the benefits of the rule of law without resorting to punishment. In this case, however, everyone would be taxed to provide these rewards to people who either would obey the laws anyhow or who obey only to gain the reward. But in this case those who would willingly obey the law would find themselves paying what amounts to extortion to those who would otherwise break it—and that hardly counts as restoring the balance.

These problems lead me to believe that there are no entirely suitable substitutes for punishment. Punishment provides something that these other approaches necessarily lack—which brings me to my second reason for believing that is a proper response to criminal wrongdoing. Punishment rests on the notion that certain actions are wrong, either as *mala in se* or *mala prohibita*. That is why we must draw a distinction, to return to Fingarette's argument, between restoring the balance and punishing offenders. We may restore the balance, as I suggested earlier, without implying that anyone is guilty of criminal intent or misconduct. If a payroll clerk mistakenly pays an employee too much, then steps should be taken to correct the mistake and prevent its happening again. If the clerk and the other employee are working together to steal from their employer, however, simply restoring the balance in the sense of regaining the money is not a sufficient response. These criminals have wronged both their employer and, I have argued, the law-abiding people who make it possible for them to enjoy the benefits of the rule of law. Steps must be taken to make the offenders and others aware of the wrong they have done. These actions are necessary to restore the benefits and burdens under the rule of law. Making restitution to the employer is not enough to restore the balance between the offenders and the law-abiding members of society. To do that, some form of punishment—some form that affirms the belief that it is wrong to take advantage of those whose cooperation makes the rule of law possible—seems necessary.

Punishing offenders is a way of restoring the balance in these cases because it responds to a disruption of the equality that everyone is supposed to enjoy in the eyes of the law. Insofar as people are members of a society governed by the rule of law, that is, they all should have the same rights and obligations. All should be equal and alike as subjects of the law, no matter how different and unequal they are in other respects. The criminal, however, sets himself apart. By taking advantage of the cooperation of others to advance his own interests, he says in effect that others are less important than he. He wants them to bear the burdens of cooperation while he receives only benefits. In Kantian language, he treats others as mere means to his ends; he fails to show respect for their dignity as persons. Such an attitude threatens the rule of law. It must be condemned in order to maintain equality in the eyes of the law. The balance to be restored, then, is the balance between people qua equal subjects of the law. Punishing those who upset this equality is the closest we can come to restoring the balance in this sense.

Sixth Objection: Does the Law Play Fair?

This leads us to the final objection. In this case the complaint is that the notion of fair play simply fails to capture important features of law and punishment. The belief that we should obey the law because we owe obedience to the cooperating members of society may make sense in some circumstances, according to the objection, but not in all. Laws that prohibit certain forms of sexual relations seem to have nothing to do with fairness, for instance. Should two consenting adults who find themselves behind closed doors really refrain from engaging in proscribed sexual activity on the grounds that disobeying the law would be taking unfair advantage of others? Do considerations of fairness even play a part in this and similar cases? If they do not, as it appears, then fairness cannot provide the foundation for the rule of law and the practice of punishment.[24]

This in a way is the other side of the second objection, which holds that fair play cannot account for rape, robbery, murder, and other acts that are *mala in se*. In this case the complaint is that fairness or reciprocity requires people to obey, on utterly inappropriate grounds, laws that probably ought not to be laws in the first place. This is a forceful objection. Yet we may admit its force without abandoning the principle of fair play. In fact, it is possible to respond to this objection in a way that strengthen the case for fair play. This response involves three steps.

First, we should notice once again that all crimes must be, on the fair play theory, crimes of unfairness. But this does not mean, as we have seen, that actions are or should be criminal only if they are ordinarily understood to be unfair. Some actions should be outlawed because they are unfair, others because they are wrong in some other way. The principle of fair play, however, is concerned with the overall balance of benefits and burdens in society, especially the benefits and burdens involved in the rule of law. If we live in a society that may be reasonably regarded as a cooperative venture under the rule of law, then fairness requires us to obey the law, even if the particular law in question seems to have nothing to do with fairness.

The second step in the response is to recall that this general obligation to obey the law is defeasible. It holds only when one's society is reasonably just, and even then it may be overridden by more pressing moral considerations. No society will be perfectly just, so it is always possible that an unjust law will be on the books of a reasonably just society. That may be the case now with laws prohibiting certain kinds of sexual conduct, for instance. If so, a person may well conclude that he or she may, or even should, disobey the laws in question. Or there may be other laws that are not in themselves unjust, but seem to require pointless obedience—such as stopping at a red light in the early morning hours when it is clear that there is no one else on the road. Here again there is an obligation to obey, but it is a relatively weak obligation, and it may therefore be overridden more easily than, say, the obligation to pay one's taxes.[25]

But how are we to distinguish just laws from unjust, or weak obligations from strong? The answer, at least in part, is to look to considerations of fairness and reciprocity. This forms the third step in the response to the final objection. Those laws that have the strongest force are those that are most essential to the maintenance of a cooperative venture under the rule of law. Laws that place unfair burdens on some or give unfair benefits to others serve to undermine cooperation and the rule of law, so they cannot be just. In the case of private, consensual sexual conduct, for example, laws proscribing certain activities seem to place an unfair burden on some people—namely, the burden of repressing their sexual inclinations and activities while others are legally free to pursue theirs. Other things being equal, such laws are neither just nor in harmony with the principle of fair play. Until they are abolished, those who are affected by these laws have reason to believe that their obligation to obey them is of little force.

III

It seems, in sum, that the principle of fair play does a better job of accounting for crime and punishment than its critics suspect. Indeed, if the arguments I have presented are correct, the principle's ability to meet the six objections considered in this article strongly suggests that it provides the basis for the practice of punishment. The principle does not tell us everything we need to know about punishment—it does not tell us exactly how to punish every offender, as I have noted, or what the fitting punishment is for every crime— but it does provide the foundation from which we can go on to address these matters.

The principle of fair play, then, provides plausible answers to Benn's two questions about the justification of punishment—What justifies punishment as a practice? What justifies punishing particular individuals?—and it provides a partial answer to a third. If this is not reason enough to recognize fair play as the true or the best philosophical account of punishment, it is surely reason to restore it to a central place in the debate over punishment's justification.

NOTES

1. H. L. A. Hart, "Are There Any Natural Rights?" in *Human Rights,* ed. A. I. Melden (Belmont, Calif.; Wadsworth, 1970), p. 70. Hart's essay originally appeared in *Philosophical Review* 64 (1955): 175–91. For an earlier, but less influential, statement of this view, see C. D. Broad, "On the Function of False Hypotheses in Ethics," *International Journal of Ethics* 26 (1915–16): 377–97.

2. John Rawls, "Legal Obligation and the Duty of Fair Play," in *Law and Philosophy,* ed. Sidney Hook (New York: New York University Press, 1964).

3. Important criticisms of the fair play theory of legal obligation include M. B. E. Smith, "Is There a Prima Facie Obligation to Obey the Law?" *Yale Law Journal* 82 (1973): 950–76; Robert Nozick, *Anarchy, State, and Utopia* (New York: Basic, 1974), pp. 90–95; and A. John Simmons, *Moral Principles and Political Obligations* (Princeton, N.J.: Princeton University Press, 1979), chap. 5. For defenses, see, inter alia: Richard Arneson, "The Principle of Fairness and Free-Rider Problems," *Ethics* 92 (1982): 616–33; Richard Dagger, "Rights, Boundaries, and the Bonds of Community: A Qualified Defense of Moral Parochialism," *American Political Science Review* 79 (1985): 436–47, esp. pp. 443–46; and George Klosko, *The Principle of Fairness and Political Obligation* (Lanham, Md.: Rowman & Littlefield, 1992).

4. Stanley Benn, "An Approach to the Problems of Punishment," *Philosophy* 33 (1958): 325–41.

5. H. L. A. Hart, *The Concept of Law* (Oxford: Clarendon Press, 1961), p. 193.

6. Jeffrie Murphy, "Three Mistakes about Retributivism," *Analysis* 31 (1971): 166–69, p. 166; also see his *Retribution, Justice, and Therapy* (Dordrecht: D. Reidel, 1979), p. 77. For Murphy's more recent doubts about the adequacy of this principle, see his "Retributivism, Moral Education, and the Liberal State," *Criminal Justice Ethics* 4 (1985): 3–11, esp. pp. 6–7, and his review of George Sher's *Desert* in *Philosophical Review* 99 (April 1990): 280–83.

7. Herbert Morris, "Persons and Punishment," *Monist* 52 (1968): 475–501, p. 478.

8. On the connection between punishment and social justice, see Jeffrie Murphy, "Marxism and Retribution," *Philosophy and Public Affairs* 2 (1973): 217–43; also see Murphy, *Retribution, Justice, and Therapy,* pp. 93–115.

9. For a criticism of criticisms, see Richard Burgh, "Do the Guilty Deserve Punishment?" *Journal of Philosophy* 79 (1982): 193–213.

10. Herbert Fingarette, "Punishment and Suffering," *Proceedings and Addresses*

of the American Philosophical Association 50 (1977): 499–525, p. 502; emphasis in original.

11. See Burgh, "Do the Guilty Deserve Punishment?" p. 203, n. 18, for a related criticism of Fingarette's argument.

12. R. A. Duff, *Trials and Punishments* (Cambridge: Cambridge University Press, 1986), p. 213; emphasis in original. See also Richard Wasserstrom, *Philosophy and Social Issues* (Notre Dame, Ind.: University of Notre Dame Press, 1980), pp. 143–46.

13. As Burgh says in "Do the Guilty Deserve Punishment?" p. 205.

14. Burgh, ibid., recognizes this, but argues that this "retreat to a second-order set of benefits, viz., those received from obedience to law in general" must fail because it entails "that all offenders are, regardless of the offense they committed, deserving of the same punishment" (p. 206). I respond to this . . . , under "Fourth Objection."

15. Here I follow George Sher, *Desert* (Princeton, N.J.: Princeton University Press, 1987), pp. 78–80.

16. See esp. Jeffrie G. Murphy, "Kant's Theory of Criminal Punishment," in Murphy, *Retribution, Justice, and Therapy,* pp. 82–92.

17. Burgh, "Do the Guilty Deserve Punishment?" p. 209.

18. Ibid., pp. 209–210. For a related criticism, see David Dolinko, "Some Thoughts about Retributivism," *Ethics* 101 (1991): 537–59, esp. pp. 546–49.

19. This should help to alleviate at least part of Murphy's concern about the phrase *debt to society.* "The idiom of owing and paying a debt is misleading," he says, "in that it tends to obscure the fact that (i) criminal 'debts' differ from ordinary debts in that we have an antecedent moral obligation not to incur them and (ii) undergoing punishment for (say) murder, unlike paying the final installment on a loan, can hardly be said to make things all right again, to make the world morally as it was before" (*Retribution, Justice, and Therapy,* p. 78). On my analysis, the criminal's punishment for the crime of unfairness repays the debt to society. This does not "make the world morally as it was before"—perhaps nothing can do that— but that is asking for more than a debt to society can entail.

20. Wasserstrom, *Philosophy and Social Issues,* p. 145; emphasis in original.

21. I make a case for restitution as an especially valuable form of punishment in "Restitution, Punishment, and Debts to Society," in *Victims, Offenders, and Alternative Sanctions,* ed. J. Hudson and B. Galaway (Lexington, Mass.: Lexington Books, 1980), pp. 11–18, and in "Restitution: Pure or Punitive?" *Criminal Justice Ethics* 10 (1991): 29–39.

22. In addition to the articles cited in the previous note, see Franklin Miller, "Restitution and Punishment: A Reply to Barnett," *Ethics* 88 (1978): 358–60; and Margaret Holmgren, "Punishment as Restitution: The Rights of the Community," *Criminal Justice Ethics* 2 (1983): 36–49, for this and other criticisms of pure restitution.

23. For a scheme in which all crime victims are to receive compensation from those criminals who are apprehended and convicted, see Mane Hajdin, "Criminals as Gamblers: A Modified Theory of Pure Restitution," *Dialogue* 26 (1987): 77–86. I criticize Hajdin's proposal in "Restitution: Pure or Punitive?" esp. pp. 33–35.

24. Jeffrie Murphy raises this objection in his review of Sher's *Desert.*

25. In this and the succeeding paragraph I draw on George Klosko, "The Moral Force of Political Obligations," *American Political Science Review* 84 (1990): 1235–50.

Part Two

Capital Punishment

7

Punishment of the Innocent

Michael L. Radelet, Hugo Adam Bedau, and Constance E. Putnam

At about half past eight on the evening of Monday, October 23, 1989, the telephone rang at Officer Gary McLaughlin's desk. He picked it up immediately, answering, "State Police, Boston." From the other end of the line he heard a man's voice: "My wife's been shot. I've been shot." Thus began a thirteen-minute, life-or-death conversation between Officer McLaughlin and the caller.

McLaughlin quickly learned that the man on the line, using a car phone as he sat behind the steering wheel, was Charles Stuart. Half an hour earlier Stuart and his wife, Carole, had been at Brigham and Women's Hospital attending a birthing clinic. Carole DiMaiti Stuart was pregnant with their first child. Now, slumped down on the seat next to her husband, she bled profusely; a bullet had been fired point-blank into her face. Stuart himself had been shot in the stomach. Minutes later a patrol car arrived, and the young couple was on its way to the hospital emergency room.

When the police arrived at the crime scene, so did the media. Starting with the eleven o'clock news on television that night, the media flooded the country with stories and pictures of the crime and its victims. For several days the nation's attention was fixed on their fate. Carole Stuart died, as did the couple's premature child delivered by Caesarean section. For countless Americans, the brutal attack on a young couple about to become parents—

attractive, white, professional, still in their twenties—was a nightmare suddenly made real.

Right behind the police and the news media came the politicians. In 1989 Massachusetts was one of fourteen states in the nation that did not punish any kind of murder with the death penalty. The day after Carole Stuart's death, the chairman of the Massachusetts State GOP, Raymond Shamie, flanked by his party's gubernatorial candidates, held a news conference at the State House urging speedy enactment of death penalty legislation. Representative John H. Flood, a Democrat seeking his party's nomination for governor, filed a death penalty bill in the legislature. Attorney General Francis X. Bellotti, also a Democrat and a rival for the gubernatorial nomination, said he would himself willingly pull the switch of the electric chair on the killer. At Carole Stuart's funeral, a thousand people—led by Governor Michael Dukakis—paid their last respects.

Under considerable public pressure to solve the crime, the police promptly began their search for the murderer. Charles Stuart, out of danger and recovering from his stomach wound, was able to provide some help. He described the gunman as 6 feet tall, black, and about thirty years old. Not much, but still something for the police to go on. The next day Stuart eleborated on his description of the killer, and the police circulated the information. So did the Boston papers. By Wednesday evening, two days after the crime, Police Commissioner Francis Roache could report to the media that Stuart's description, along with fingerprint evidence from his automobile, was yielding good leads. "We have reduced our list of suspects to a chosen few," he said.

The police concentrated their attention on the Mission Hill district near the hospital. Mission Hill is on the border between the Fenway—part of Boston's middle-class, still-fashionable Back Bay—and Roxbury, where some of the city's poorest neighborhoods are found. Not normally a setting for street violence of the sort found in Boston's less well integrated areas, Mission Hill was soon overrun with law-enforcement officers. Residents felt besieged as platoons of police swept through the area, looking for the black killer. Search efforts were concentrated on the public-housing projects in the district, home mainly to blacks and other minorities.

On November 10, two weeks after the Stuart murder, police in the Boston suburb of Burlington arrested a Willie Bennett on a traffic offense. Less than three days later, he was arraigned by the authorities in Brookline—a mile or so from the Mission Hill district where the Stuart murder had occurred—for armed robbery of a video store. Bennett, who had a previous criminal record, was thirty-nine years old and black. Just after Christmas, the Boston police showed a photograph of Bennett to Charles Stuart; they also arranged a line-up with Bennett in it for Stuart to review. He promptly fingered Bennett as the man who looked "most like" the killer of his wife.

Thus, within six weeks of the crime, it appeared the police had their man. The newspapers applauded and turned to other stories.

Shortly thereafter, the case was suddenly turned inside out. On the morning of January 5, 1990, readers of the *Boston Globe* were stunned when they saw bold headlines: "STUART DIES IN JUMP OFF TOBIN BRIDGE AFTER POLICE ARE TOLD HE KILLED HIS WIFE." Incredible though it seemed, it was true. Apparently from well before the murder, Stuart had carefully woven a fabric of lies as he plotted the death of his pregnant wife. For reasons still not altogether clear, he, too, was dead, an apparent suicide.

The news that Stuart himself might have been the killer led Willie Bennett to say that his life had "been ruined and no one is willing to take responsibility." His anger and bitterness were understandable. Through an improbable pattern of bad luck, he had come very close to being indicted for a crime he had nothing to do with.

Why? Because he had an arrest record in other cases, including armed robbery. Because the police were under intense pressure to solve the crime. Because Bennett more or less fit the description provided by a seemingly unimpeachable eyewitness to the crime. And, above all, because the public— clamoring for some way to express its indignation—found him a plausible target.

There seems to be no doubt about Willie Bennett's complete innocence. Fortunately, the truth—or enough of it—emerged in time to spare him not only a trial for murder but all of the possible undeserved consequences of such a trial. Bad as Bennett's ordeal was, the system did not come close to convicting him. And it is, of course, erroneous *conviction,* not merely wrongful *arrest,* that is the crucial threshold to undeserved punishment— whether years in prison or death in the execution chamber. Crossing that threshold from accusation and indictment to a guilty verdict is one of the gravest steps the system can take. Only two steps are more serious: actually sentencing the defendant to death, and carrying out the execution.

The Willie Bennett case marks one end of the spectrum on which miscarriages of justice in capital cases occur. The case of James Adams marks the other. On May 10, 1984, Adams was executed in Florida for murder. (As Adams was being executed in the electric chair in Florida State Prison and as death penalty opponents stood in silent vigil across the street, an unidentified man drove by in a pickup truck, and with a thumbs-up gesture shouted, "Fry the nigger!") No national publicity surrounded this case, which had stretched out over a decade. It had begun on the morning of November 12, 1973, with the murder of Edgar Brown in Ft. Pierce, Florida. Brown was found badly beaten, allegedly during the course of a robbery in his home. A 61-year-old rancher and former deputy sheriff, Brown died the next day. Adams was promptly arrested, tried, and convicted.

During the penalty phase of his trial, the State called only one witness, a Tennessee sheriff, who testified that Adams had escaped from prison there after conviction for rape. Adams's public defender called no witnesses, and the jury spent a mere five minutes deliberating over the sentence. Four months and three days after the crime, St. Lucie County Circuit Judge Wallace Sample, concurring with the jury's recommendation, sentenced James Adams to death.

Barely more than a week before the execution, Adam's appellate attorneys, led by West Palm Beach public defenders Richard Burr and Craig Barnard, filed with Governor Bob Graham their second request for execution clemency. In their application, the lawyers presented for the first time facts relating to Adams's background and the circumstances surrounding his conviction, asserting:

> We believe, as strongly as human beings can believe, that the life of James Adams is in your hands today solely because he is a poor black Southerner. . . . The outcome of Mr. Adams's every involvement in the criminal justice system since 1955 has been influenced by his race or by the race of the victims of his alleged crimes.

Adams's first encounter with the law had come in 1955 when he was convicted of assault and battery. In 1957 he and his brother were convicted of petit larceny (they had stolen a pig for their family's dinner table), and Adams was sentenced to one year in jail. He was not provided with counsel in connection with either of these two convictions. During his incarceration for stealing the pig, he was once beaten unconscious with a bat by a jailer and severely beaten on other occasions as well. He suffered dizzy spells, blackouts, and blurred vision as a result of these beatings, and he bore their marks until his death.

In October 1962, Adams was convicted of rape. The records of this conviction did not become available to the attorneys fighting for Adams's life until December 1983. No blacks had been included among the five hundred persons on the list from which jurors at his trial were selected. In addition, the white victim had repeatedly referred to her assailant as a "nigger." Despite the lack of any physical evidence of rape—it was simply her word against his—Adams was convicted. He was sentenced to ninety-nine years in prison.

Under decisions of the United States Supreme Court, Adams's first two convictions ought to have been ruled unconstitutional because he had been denied the assistance of counsel. Racial discrimination in the selection of the jury made the rape conviction also constitutionally defective. Nonetheless, all three convictions were cited by the prosecution as aggravating factors in the sentencing phase of Adams's Florida trial, and they no doubt played a role in the jury's decision to recommend a death sentence.

After Adams had served nine years of his prison sentence for rape, the Tennessee Board of Probation and Paroles found his behavior "exemplary" and recommended to the governor that his sentence be commuted to time served. The governor refused, on the ground that the district attorney who had prosecuted Adams objected. A year later, the Board of Probation and Paroles decided not to recommend release, because the district attorney still opposed such a move.

At the time, Adams was not being housed as one might think a convicted rapist would be: he was a "trusty" at a correctional facility for teenaged girls. As part of his job he had access to state-owned vehicles. When he was told that he would not be released until the prosecutor dropped his objections, Adams—heartbroken (he had done all he could to earn release)—drove off in one of the prison trucks. Ten months later he was arrested for murder in Florida.

The killer had entered Edgar Brown's unoccupied home on the morning of Novementer 12, 1973. Sometime later Brown returned home, where he was attacked and beaten with a fireplace poker. Adams's car had been parked in the driveway, and it was seen traveling to and from the victim's home. One witness, Willie Orange, positively identified Adams as the driver of the car; a second witness, John Thompkins, "thought" Adams was the driver. The car was located later that day at a shop where it had been left for the repainting job Adams had been planning for months. Adams claimed his car had been driven that morning, at 10:00 or 10:15 A.M. (one half hour before the assault) by a friend, Vivian Nickerson, and another man, Kenneth Crowell. According to Adams, while they were off in his car—precisely at the time of the homicide—he was at the Nickerson home playing cards.

The victim, it was known, always carried between $700 and $1500 in cash; no cash was found in his wallet after the assault. When Adams was arrested, he had only $185 with him. He also had a credible explanation for the source of this money: His employer had recently lent him $200. The State offered no explanation of what it thought had happened to the other $500 to $1300 that Brown would have been carrying and that had in all likelihood been taken by his killer. One bill in Adams's possession had a dried patch of O-positive blood on it, consistent with the blood of the victim—and that of 45 percent of the rest of the population.

The one person who had a chance to identify the killer at Brown's home was Foy Hortman. He testified that he drove up to the house shortly after Brown had returned home and heard a woman shout from inside, "In the name of God, don't do it!" He then saw and briefly spoke with someone leaving the house, but failed to identify Adams as that person. More than that, he testified that the person he spoke with was blacker than Adams and, unlike Adams, had no mustache. On the day of the homicide, Hortman viewed a police line-up that included Adams and said he was positive that none of the men was the person he had seen leaving the Brown house. Nonetheless, at trial Hortman testified that Adams "may or may not have been" the person at the scene. (A logician would call that remark a tautology, but the jury appears to have been influenced by it.)

John Thompkins testified that he thought it was James Adams he had seen driving a car to the victim's home shortly before the homicide. "It had to be (Adams)," Thompkins said, "because he throwed up his hand at me, because everybody that passed there don't hardly wave at you unless you know him." Not a very precise or damning statement, yet the State relied heavily on it.

Willie Orange, on the other hand, did positively identify Adams as driving the car away from the Brown home. His was the sole testimony that placed Adams near the crime scene. Perhaps not so incidentally, it later turned out that Orange believed Adams was having an affair with his wife. During the clemency hearing, three witnesses were located who had heard Orange stating before the trial that he was going to testify against Adams because of this affair. One witness quoted Orange as saying before the trial, "I'm going to send him [Adams] because he's been going with my wife." A polygraph administered to Orange to support Adams's appeal for clemency in 1984, while hardly conclusive, indicated that Orange was being deceptive when he testified at the trial.

Vivian Nickerson, the person Adams said had access to his car at the time of the homicide, was fifteen years old. She was very large for her age and had a strikingly masculine appearance. In fact, she resembled James Adams, and her height, size, and complexion fit Hortman's eyewitness description better than Adams's did. It is possible that she was the person Hortman saw leaving the victim's house. If she was, that would explain another loose end not tied up by the State's theory of the crime: Hers could have been the woman's voice Hortman testified he had heard coming from inside the house. Yet no photos of Vivian Nickerson were shown to Hortman, and he never saw her in a police line-up.

Interestingly enough, Nickerson was called by Adams to corroborate his alibi at trial. She was a reluctant witness, however, and ended up hurting his case. By claiming that he had not arrived at her house until 11:00 A.M., she undermined his testimony. In a pretrial deposition, given under oath, she had stated that Adams reached her house prior to 10:30 and that she had then borrowed his car. In other words, contrary to what she claimed during the trial, Nickerson when deposed had said that Adams was at her house and that she was driving his car at the time of the crime. This inconsistency was by no means a minor one; unfortunately, Adams's defense counsel never confronted Nickerson with the contradiction.

The most significant blow to the State's case against Adams arose from evidence not presented at trial. En route to the hospital in an ambulance with her husband, Mrs. Brown found strands of hair clasped in his hand—hair presumably pulled from the head of his assailant. The State's crime laboratory compared these hairs with samples of Adams's hair and determined that although the hair was "very dark brown, Negroid, [and] curly," Adams was definitely not its source. This report, however, was not released until three days after Adams had been sentenced. Even then, when it could have been used to support a request for a new trial, it was not given to the defense attorneys.

In their 1984 clemency papers, Adams's attorneys succinctly stated their case as follows:

> In sum, had all of the evidence raising doubt about Mr. Adams's guilt been submitted to the jury, there would have been at least a reasonable doubt about Mr. Adams's guilt. The evidence would have shown that the only person who had an opportunity to observe the perpetrator was "positive" that Mr. Adams was not that person. The evidence would have shown that Willie Orange's identification of Mr. Adams as the person driving away from Brown's house was wholly unbelievable because of his stated motive to "get" James Adams. The evidence would have shown that a specimen of hair asserted by the investigating deputy to have been recovered from the hand of Mr. Brown in the ambulance after the assault against him could not have come from James Adams. . . . Had the jury been told about Vivian Nickerson's sworn testimony less than two months before James Adams's trial which unequivocally corroborated Mr. Adams's testimony that he was continuously at Ms. Nickerson's house from before the homicide until well after the homicide, the jury would have been more likely to suspect Vivian Nickerson as the perpetrator than James Adams.

No doubt due process of law failed rather badly in the Adams case, and these deficiencies played a critical role in his conviction and death sentence. But was Adams truly innocent? Did he deserve to be acquitted on the ground that he had no involvement in the murder of Edgar Brown, even though members of the trial jury—given the evidence before them—believed otherwise? Adams's postconviction attorneys, Burr and Barnard, thought so. We think so. But from the moment Adams was executed, it became virtually impossible to resolve the issue one way or the other. There is no legal forum in which the innocence of the dead can be officially confirmed, or even satisfactorily investigated. The court of public opinion—such as it is—is the only recourse, and James Adams was too obscure, too bereft of friends and supporters with time and money, to have his claim of innocence tested and vindicated posthumously in that forum.

Once Adams was dead, his attorneys had to turn their full attention to the plight of other death row clients. Time spent reinvestigating the circumstances of the Edgar Brown murder in the hope of vindicating the late James Adams was time denied to clients still alive but facing the electric chair. No newspaper editor or team of reporters, no investigative journalist, has seen fit (so far as we know) to reopen the Adams case. Instead, a giant question mark continues to haunt his execution, a question mark that will probably never be removed. A rare case? Perhaps, but not unique. We know of nearly two dozen cases in this century where the evidence similarly suggests that the wrong person was convicted of murder or rape, sentenced to death, and executed. . . .

8

A General History of
Capital Punishment in America

Information Plus

THE COLONIAL PERIOD

Since the first European settlers arrived in America the death penalty has
been accepted as just punishment for a variety of offenses. The English
Penal Code, which applied to the British colonies, listed fourteen capital
offenses, but actual practice varied from colony to colony. In the Massachusetts Bay Colony, thirteen crimes warranted the death penalty: idolatry,
witchcraft, blasphemy, rape, statutory rape, kidnapping, perjury in a trial
involving a possible death sentence, rebellion, murder, assault in sudden
anger, adultery, and buggery (sodomy). In the statue each crime was accompanied by an appropriate biblical quotation justifying the capital punishment.
Later, arson, treason, and grand larceny were added.

On the other hand, the Quakers adopted much milder laws. The Royal
Charter for South Jersey (1646) did not permit capital punishment for any
crime and there was no execution until 1691. In Pennsylvania, William Penn's
Great Act of 1682 limited the death penalty to treason and murder. Most
states, however, followed the much harsher British codes.

THE FIRST ABOLITIONIST OF THE DEATH PENALTY

Although the Founding Fathers commonly accepted the death penalty, many early Americans opposed capital punishment. In the late eighteenth century, Dr. Benjamin Rush (1745–1813), considered to be the founder of the American abolitionist movement, decried capital punishment. He attracted the support of Benjamin Franklin, and it was at Franklin's home in Philadelphia that Rush became one of the first Americans to propose a "House of Reform," a prison where criminals could be detained until they learned to change their antisocial behavior. Consequently, in 1790, the Walnut Street Jail was built in Philadelphia, the primitive seed from which the American penal system grew.

Dr. Rush published numerous pamphlets, the most noted of which was "Inquiry into the Justice and Policy of Punishing Murder by Death." Rush argued that the biblical support given capital punishment was questionable and that the threat of hanging did not deter crime and, in fact, might increase it. Reflecting the philosophy of the Enlightenment, Rush believed the state exceeded its granted powers when it executed a citizen. In addition to Franklin, Rush attracted many other Pennsylvanians to his cause, including Pennsylvania's Attorney General, William Bradford. As a result, Pennsylvania repealed the death penalty for all crimes, except first-degree murder.

THE ABOLITIONIST MOVEMENT

Rush's proposals attracted many followers and numerous abolitionst petitions were presented in states such as Ohio, New Jersey, New York, and Massachusetts, but no state reversed its laws. The second quarter of the nineteenth century was a time of reform in America and capital punishment opponents rode the tide of righteousness and indignation created by the anti-saloon and anti-slavery advocates. Abolitionist societies sprang up, most notably along the Atlantic coast, and, in 1845, the American Society for the Abolition of Capital Punishment was founded. In the late 1840s, Horace Greeley, the editor and founder of the *New York Tribune* and a leading advocate of most abolitionist causes, became a leader in the crusade against the death penalty. Finally, in 1846, the Territory of Michigan abolished the death penalty and replaced it with life imprisonment. The law took effect the following year, making Michigan, for all practical purposes, the first English-speaking jurisdiction in the world to abolish the death penalty for common crimes. (It retained it for treason.) In 1852, Rhode Island included even treason when it outlawed hanging, as did Wisconsin a year later. Most states began limiting the number of capital crimes and, in fact, outside the South, murder and treason became the only acts warranting capital punishment.

Opponents of the death penalty initially benefited from abolitionist sentiment, but as the Civil War neared, concern about the death penalty was lost amidst the growing anti-slavery movement. It was not until after the Civil War that Maine and Iowa abolished the death penalty, but almost immediately their legislatures reversed themselves and reinstated it. In 1887, Maine again reversed itself and abolished capital punishment.

Meanwhile, the federal government, following considerable debate, reduced the number of federal crimes punishable by death to three—treason, murder, and rape. In no instance was it to be mandatory. Colorado also abolished capital punishment, but apparently against the will of many of its citizens. At least twice they lynched convicted murderers and, in response, Colorado restored the penalty.

A DECLINE IN ABOLITIONIST FORTUNES

At the turn of the century, death penalty abolitionists again rode the tide of American reformism as the Progressives (liberal reformers) tried to correct the deficiencies of the American system. Between 1907 and 1917, nine states and Puerto Rico outlawed capital punishment, but the momentum failed to last. By 1921, five states had reinstated it. The Prohibition Era, characterized by frequent disdain for law and order, almost destroyed the abolitionist movement. Only the determined efforts of the famed Clarence Darrow, the "attorney for the damned"; Lewis E. Lawes, the abolitionist warden of Sing-Sing Prison (New York); and the American League to Abolish Capital Punishment, founded in 1927, prevented the movement's complete collapse. Nonetheless, of the sixteen states and jurisdictions (includes Puerto Rico) that outlawed capital punishment after 1845, only seven—Michigan, Rhode Island, Wisconsin, Maine, North Dakota, Minnesota, and Puerto Rico—had no major death penalty statute coming into the 1950s. In fact, between 1917 and 1957 no state abolished the death penalty.

The movement made a mild comeback in the mid–1950s and the issue was discussed in several state legislatures. Nonetheless, only the (then) territories of Alaska and Hawaii (1957) abolished the death penalty. The movement's singular success in Delaware (1958) was reversed only three years later (1961), a major disappointment for the opponents of the death penalty. Nonetheless, the abolitionists were able to recover during the Civil Rights movement of the 1960s. Michigan (1963, for treason), Oregon (1964), Iowa (1965), and West Virginia (1965) all abolished capital punishment, while many other states sharply reduced the number of crimes warranting the death penalty.

RESOLVING THE CONSTITUTIONAL ISSUES

Until the 1960s, there was legally no question that the death penalty was acceptable under the United States Constitution. Then, in 1963, Justice Arthur Goldberg (who was joined by Justices Douglas and Brennan) wrote a dissent in a rape case in which the defendant had been sentenced to death (*Rudolph* v. *Alabama* [375 US 889, 1963]), in which he raised the question of the legality of the death penalty. The filing of a large number of cases in the late 1960s led to an implied moratorium on the carrying out of the death penalty which lasted until 1977, when the state of Utah executed a convicted murderer.

Beginning in 1972 with *Furman* v. *Georgia* (408 US 238) and the accompanying cases, the Supreme Court has been defining and refining what is and is not acceptable under the U.S. Constitution. With the replacement of Chief Justice Warren Burger and his later replacement by Chief Justice William Rehnquist, the court majority has generally interpreted the death penalty as worthy of extra attention because of the seriousness of the consequences, but most assuredly acceptable punishment for murder. There can be little question that the High Court position reflects that of the American public.

The Supreme Court's strongest opponents of capital punishment, Justices Brennan and Marshall, both of whom believed capital punishment should be abolished, have retired. Supreme Court appointments under the Reagan administration generally supported capital punishment and Bush's appointments to replace Brennan and Marshall, Souter and Thomas, generally support capital punishment. In February 1994, Justice Blackmun was the sole dissent from the Court's refusal to hear the appeal of a Texas prisoner who was scheduled to be executed on February 23, 1994, arguing that "no sentence of death may be constitutionally imposed. . . ." Consequently, some opponents of capital punishment have begun to focus on using state consitutions to fight capital punishment in states where capital punishment is permissible.

WORLDWIDE TREND

The *de facto* moratorium between 1967 and 1977 paralleled a general worldwide movement, especially among Western nations, toward the abolition of capital punishment. While the United States resumed executions during the late 1970s, most of the Western world was either formally or informally abolishing it. Today, among the Western democratic nations with which the United States traditionally compares itself, only the United States imposes the death penalty. (There are technical exceptions—Israel, for example, despite continuing conflict, maintains the death penalty for "crimes against mankind," but has only executed Adolf Eichmann, while some countries still maintain the death penalty for treason—although no Western democracy has actually been imposing it.)

GETTING LEGAL ASSISTANCE

Although there are thousands of prisoners on death row, only a handful are executed every year. Those opposing the death penalty sometimes interpret this as the nation introducing a *de facto* ban on capital punishment or use it to emphasize the erratic (and perhaps unfair) nature of the punishment with so few actually having to suffer death. Supporters attribute the small number actually executed to the tying up of the court system with appeals which often drag on for years and years. If appeals were not lodged under what many death penalty supporters consider shaky procedural grounds, there would be more executions and the penalty would be less freakish and unfair.

With the growing number of inmates on death row, it has become increasingly difficult to get lawyers to help the condemned prisoners file appeals. Most of this work is done *pro bono* (for free), and even lawyers dedicated to making sure these prisoners receive all their legal rights cannot be expected to spend all of their time working for nothing. Lawyers defending condemned prisoners often receive the case within a few months or weeks of the scheduled execution and, knowing little about the case, search the case for what are often considered "technicalities" in order to gain delays and stays of execution so they can then handle the case properly.

In 1985, the state of Florida created a special office to assist death row inmates to make sure they receive all their rights. The few lawyers assigned to that office have been swamped with the appeals of the hundreds of prisoners awaiting execution in that state. While there have been instances of major law firms (mainly located in the Northeast) helping to provide legal assistance, most prisoners are dependent on volunteers, usually supplied by the American Bar Association (ABA) and the American Civil Liberties Union (ACLU).

JAMMING THE COURT DOCKETS

The Supreme Court has become increasinly impatient with the issue. The High Court's 1987 ruling in *McCleskey* v. *Kemp* (481 US 279) (when the Court decreed that broad-based scientific findings of racial discrimination had to apply to the particular case being considered) has been judged, by many observers, as the last systemic challenge to the death penalty on federal constitutional grounds—that the death penalty was a violation of the prisoner's constitutional rights of either equal protection or the issue of cruel and unusual punishment. With the growing conservative majority on the Supreme Court, this is unlikely to change. This situation has forced lawyers defending condemned prisoners to stress procedural grounds. Currently, it takes about seven years from the imposition of the death sentence until execution. Most of that time is filled with appeals.

EXECUTING THE INNOCENT

The changing emphasis away from constitutional issues has also led some to investigate the actual issue of guilt and innocence. While the overwhelming majority of those sentenced to death are unquestionably guilty of murder, a small fraction have been wrongly convicted. Hugo Bedau of Tufts University (MA) and Michael Radelet of the University of Florida, in *Miscarriages of Justice in Potentially Capital Cases* (1985), counted, since the turn of the century, 343 cases in which a defendant facing a possible death penalty was wrongfully convicted. Of these, 137 were sentenced to death and 25 were actually executed. Sixty-one served more than ten years in jail and seven died in prison.

James Marquart and Jonathan Sorensen, both of Sam Houston State University (TX), in an unpublished study, traced the lives of 558 death row inmates whose executions were commuted to prison terms by the 1972 Supreme Court decisions. Four were later released as innocent, four others murdered again while in prison, and another, following his release, killed again before committing suicide. The researchers claim that "executing all of them would not have greatly protected society. We would have executed nearly 600 convicts to protect us from five. And we would have killed four innocent people in the process."

Over the past decade, two Texas cases, one Florida case, and one Alabama case have involved individuals wrongly sent to death row. Such findings and incidents continue to raise the issue of whether it is better to house thousands of guilty murderers for life rather than risk executing a handful of innocent people.

THE COST OF AN EXECUTION

Some abolitionists have been advocating life imprisonment without chance of parole as an alternative to the death sentence. (According to the Bureau of Justice Statistics, the average murderer sentenced to life with a chance of parole serves 85.3 months—1987, *Time Served in Prison and on Parole, 1984,* WDC.) While the Gallup Poll still found a majority of Americans

(53 percent) continuing to favor the death penalty over life without parole (35 percent), this alternative may come about simply because it has become so expensive to execute a prisoner.

A study of the California system suggested a minimum cost of $500,000 per case (including all capital cases, not just those executed). One of New York State estimated the cost per capital case of $1.8 million, while a Maryland study figured about $750,000 per case. While introducing life imprisonment without parole would probably require a huge prison construction program, costing about $55,000 per cell, the Bureau of Justice Statistics estimates that it costs $11,302 per inmate to operate a confinement facility (*1984 Census of State Adult Correctional Facilities,* WDC, 1987).

A 1991 study of the Texas criminal justice system estimated the cost of appealing capital murder at $2,316,655. Some expenses include $265,640 for the trial; $294,240 for the state appeals; $113,608 for federal appeals (over six years); and $135,875 for death row housing. In contrast, the cost of housing a prisoner in a Texas maximum security prison single cell for 40 years is estimated at $750,000.

The cost of executing a convicted murderer can also be counted ways other than dollars. A Texas spokesperson for VOTERS (Victims Organized to Ensure Rights and Safety) commented that only in rare cases does the organization support the death penalty over a life sentence without parole. Because the process of conviction and appeal is so long and difficult, the family of the murder victim is required to relive their nightmare many times at each appeal, each hearing, and each scheduled execution date.

Supporters of the death penalty, however, point out that, while they advocate proper review of the cases, both the lengthy time and the high expense result from innumerable appeals, many over "technicalities" which have little or nothing to do with the question of guilt or innocence, and do little more than jam up the nation's court system. If these "frivolous" appeals were eliminated, the procedure would neither take so long nor cost so much.

PUBLIC AND PRIVATE EXECUTIONS

Early arguments for capital punishment centered around the issue of deterrence. Therefore, executions were held in public to inhibit anyone contemplating the same deed as the condemned. Many of these executions were held in a circus atmosphere causing many to oppose such a public display. In 1830, the State of New York recommended that executions take place in private, but it still remained the decision of the local sheriff. Five years later the state legislature prohibited public executions.

The idea caught on slowly and, even where executions were confined to jail courtyards, it was often not difficult to find a perch from which to watch the hanging. By the end of the century, private executions had become standard, although many public executions still took place. The last public hanging was in 1936, in Owensboro, Kentucky, where a black man was hanged before 20,000 spectators. The holiday atmosphere, recorded on wire service photographs, caused such a reaction that the Kentucky legislature banned public executions two years later.

Today all states limit the number of witnesses, although in celebrated cases, such as the Rosenbergs in 1953 and Caryl Chessman in 1960, the audience, swelled by reporters, grew to several dozen. The idea of private executions was introduced to appease abolitionists, but today many opponents of capital punishment support the idea of returning to public executions. They feel that private executions hide the act from the public and make it more acceptable, and some have even recommended televised executions.

9

The Crusade against Capital Punishment

J. Gordon Melton

Capital punishment has arisen in the twentieth century as one easily isolated issue in the complex and continuing question of reform of the criminal justice system. Prior to the eighteenth century, there was a unanimous opinion that society needed the death penalty to keep lawlessness from growing beyond all bounds (just as torture was considered appropriate in the treatment of criminals). Then, in the 1760s, a single voice (that of Italian philosopher and economist Cesare Beccaria) was raised against torture and the death penalty, and within a few years other voices joined what became a small chorus that was heard across Europe and North America. The small group invited society and the church to align themselves with the new cause of eliminating capital punishment from the criminal justice system.

At first, only a few religious groups known for their pacifism responded to the new crusade. It would not be until the 1950s, after decades of reflection by social scientists and church ethicists on the problems of crime and reform of the criminal justice system, that mainline Christian religious organizations would begin to seriously consider adopting the abolitionist position on the death penalty for both practical and theological reasons. In the process they had to significantly revise Western religious and ethical tradition, which had accepted and believed in the practice. However, over the generation from 1956 to the 1980s, the majority of the larger religious bodies (i.e., the Christian churches) in North America would adopt an abolitionist position.

To date, the great majority of religious groups, especially the more conservative Christian churches, have simply not spoken on the issue. While some churches refuse to take stands on what are perceived to be political or social issues, the silence of most should not be taken as an absence of opinion. Many groups have simply seen no need to comment on an issue that the Bible (and the almost unanimous opinion of church teaching through the centuries) so plainly supports. The death penalty is upheld, even commanded, in the Mosaic Code (legal codes found in the first five books of the Bible) and the Hebrew Bible and is not refuted in the Christian New Testament. Paul's Epistle to the Romans implies that the state has power to enact whatever laws it might choose that are not contrary to God's laws. Hence, while the acceptance and/or toleration of capital punishment may never be formalized into an official document by most churches, it is implied in statements such as the following from the Church of God (Jerusalem Acres), which explains how Christians are expected to live in "Conformity to Civil Laws":

> According to the New Testament, the Christian is obligated to be conformable to the civil powers of the nation in which he lives, as long as the laws of the nation do not conflict with the ordinances and commandments of the Holy Scriptures or with the Christian worship and service to God. The words of Jesus in Matthew 22:17-21 lay the foundation for the teachings of the church on this issue. When confronted by the Pharisees and Herodians with the question, "Is it lawful to give tribute to Caesar, or not?" Jesus answered, "Render unto Caesar the things that are Caesar's; and unto God the things that are God's." This self-explanatory statement of Jesus is sufficient proof for The Church of God that matters that are not directly related to God and the worship of His name may be controlled by civil governments. Members of the church are therefore responsible to render unto civil governments the respect and dues that pertain unto them (Matt. 5:25, 26).
>
> Peter confirmed this to be the position of the early church on this issue in I Peter 2:13, 14. "Submit yourself to every ordinance of man for the Lord's sake: whether it be to the king, as supreme; or unto governors, as unto them that are sent by him for the punishment of evil doers, and for the praise of them that do well." Peter declared that the purpose for which civil authorities are established is to praise those who do well and punish evildoers; therefore, the Christian is to submit himself to the ordinances and laws of civil governments. In Acts 5:29,30 Peter also confirmed the second part of the position that Jesus set forth regarding civil obedience. In situations where the edicts of governments interfere with the preaching of the Word of God or require the believer to violate the laws of God, Peter declared, "We ought to obey God rather than men."
>
> Paul established the same teaching among the Gentiles with his instruction to Titus: "Put them in mind to be subject to principalities and powers, to obey magistrates, to be ready unto every good work" (Titus 3:1). In Romans 13 he declared that civil authorities were even ministers of God in the sense that those powers that are in authority are controlled by God and in the sense that civil governments are established by God for the purpose of providing public safety by punishing those who violate the universal laws

of public morality. "For rulers are not a terror to good works, but to the evil . . . for he is the minister of God to thee for good. But if thou do that which is evil, be afraid; for he beareth not the sword in vain: for he is the minister of God, a revenger to execute wrath upon him that doeth evil. For this cause pay ye tribute also: for they are God's ministers, attending continually upon this very thing. Render therefore to all their dues: tribute to whom tribute is due; custom to whom custom; fear to whom fear; honor to whom honor" (Rom. 13:3, 4, 6, 7). Paul quoted the words of Jesus regarding taxation as a conclusion to his assertion that Christians should be obedient to the civil authorities that are over them for protection.

The Church of God encourages the conformity of its members to the laws of the lands in which they live that are made for the public good and do not violate the commandments of God.

THE RISE OF OPPOSITION TO CAPITAL PUNISHMENT

The modern crusade to eliminate the death penalty is generally acknowledged to have begun with Beccaria (1738–1794). In 1764, he published his *Essay on Crimes and Punishments* at a time when the basic trend of Western society was to increase the number of offenses punishable by death. Based upon his extensive survey of penal law, Beccaria concluded that, under normal circumstances, the state should do away with both torture and capital punishment. Capital punishment, he argued, was allowable in times of unrest to prevent a revolution, but in normal peaceful circumstances, it could only be justified if it served as a deterrence to crime. Throughout the ages, however, the death penalty had not been a deterrence to crime, even the crime of murder. This belief that the death penalty prevented further homicides had been (and to some extent remains) the bedrock of arguments for its continuance.

In his several works touching on capital punishment, Beccaria presented most of the additional arguments still used today by opponents of the death penalty. First, long-term imprisonment is as effective, if not more so, as the death penalty in preventing further crime. Second, the commission of a homicide by the state (i.e., in executing a criminal) merely increases the level of violence rather than teaching citizens not to murder. Third, the death penalty is final and unchangeable. If a person is punished and later proven innocent, capital punishment offers no opportunity to correct the action of the justice system.

Beccaria's arguments quickly spread through Europe, especially among individuals who had embraced the philosophical tenets of the Enlightenment, and his work is generally credited with initiating the trend in reducing the number of crimes punishable by death and in some countries eliminating the death penalty altogether. In England, the arguments were championed by Sir Samuel Romilly and Jeremy Bentham. Developing many of the same arguments as Beccaria, Bentham wrote eloquently against the death penalty.

Romilly took Beccaria's and Bentham's arguments into Parliament and began to lobby for the restriction of the death penalty. His first success came in 1808 when, to his happy surprise, he had the death penalty abolished for the crime of picking pockets. (That same year in America, the pacifist Quakers helped establish the first association dedicated to the abolition of the death penalty.) While Romilly was unable to get the substantial reforms he sought due to opposition in the House of Lords he opened the issue for the next generation.

In 1819, the year after Romilly's death, a Select Committee under the leadership of Sir James Mackintosh was established by the House of Commons to study the death penalty. As a result, a number of crimes were removed from the list requiring the death penalty, and over the following decades even more were removed. It should be noted that Romilly, Mackintosh, and their supporters had developed a very pragmatic argument to eliminate the death penalty—it had become the punishment of so many relatively minor offenses that juries would not bring in guilty verdicts even in cases of obvious guilt. The work of these early leaders to curtail the number of crimes punishable by death started a trend that continues even today.

CAPITAL PUNISHMENT IN NINETEENTH-CENTURY AMERICA

English-language translations of Beccaria's writings had an immediate impact in Quaker Pennsylvania. A century earlier, William Penn had established a precedent for the Pennsylvania colony in the Great Act of 1682, limiting the death penalty to those convicted of premeditated murder. Far ahead of his time, Penn used his personal power to keep the law in place, but the very year of his death (1718), the Crown forced contemporary British law (which included thirteen capital offenses) on the colony. That there was no rise in flagrant crime during the 36 years of the Great Act became an argument in later years for abolitionists.

In 1776, just twelve years after Beccaria's essay was published, Pennsylvania's Quaker community mobilized what strength it could to organize the Philadelphia Society for the Relieving of Distressed Prisoners. However, events in Concord and Lexington, Massachusetts, that same year took precedence, and the society soon died out. Not long after the Revolutionary War ended, though, the Philadelphia Society for Alleviating the Miseries of Public Prisons was formed. Among its most outstanding members was Benjamin Rush, whose 1787 paper, "An Enquiry into the Effects of Public Punishments upon Criminals and upon Society," contained the first reasoned argument in America favoring the abolition of the death penalty. The paper created a storm of controversy, which led Rush to produce an expanded work, *Considerations on the Injustice and Impolite of Punishing Murder by Death* (1792). Important to the body of this second effort was a substantial portion devoted to a Christian view of the death penalty.

The following year, William Bradford, the Pennsylvania attorney general (and later United States attorney general), published his attack upon the death penalty. While not arguing for its total elimination, he presented a strong case for its limitation to the most severe cases. In 1794 he was able, for the first time, to persuade the Pennsylvania legislature to make a distinction between first-degree (i.e., premeditated) and second-degree murder, and limit the death penalty to the former.

The Philadelphia society became the center from which reform of capital punishment laws (usually placed within the larger context of general reform of penal codes and jail conditions) permeated the United States during the rest of the century, though there was considerably more progress in prison reform than in efforts to abolish the death penalty. It was not until 1847 that Michigan became the first state to do away with the death penalty altogether, and only two others, Rhode Island and Wisconsin, dropped it prior to the Civil War.

SCIENTIFIC PRISON REFORM

Due to the introduction of a new idea into the capital punishment debate, the decades following the Civil War were a period of hope for abolitionists. This new idea, a "scientific" perspective, emphasized the rehabilitation of criminals rather than a single-minded interest in retributive punishment. Among those leading the way in this new approach was Zebulon R. Brockway, who introduced the concept of indeterminant sentencing. Under Brockway's procedures, a convicted criminal would be sentenced to a minimum and a maximum amount of prison time; the exact period to be served would then be determined based on later evaluations. This type of sentencing led to the creation of probation. As a result of this new perspective, the National Prison Association was formed in 1870.

Scientific penology also seemed to provide a context for a new evaluation of the death penalty. In 1878, abolitionists heartily supported the International Penitentiary Congress that convened in Stockholm, Sweden, but overall they were unsuccesful in getting states to drop the death penalty. Several states, including Kansas, Iowa, and Colorado, did experiment in dropping it for brief periods. Legislation of the death penalty showed a marked tendency to echo the ephemeral emotions of the public and often followed this cyclical pattern: An eloquent and impassioned plea for abolishing the death penalty would lead to its consideration and even enactment by a legislature; then, in the wake of a particularly heinous crime, the death penalty would be reinstated. Such was the case in Maine, which had abolished the death penalty in 1836 in large part due to the efforts of Tobias Purrington and Thomas C. Upham. The *de facto* prohibition of the death penalty was formally enacted in 1872, but six years later, when a prison official was attacked by an insane convict, public opinion forced the return of capital punishment.

The cause of the abolitionists was continually raised and debated into the early decades of the twentieth century, with each hard-earned victory countered by a defeat. States would abolish capital punishment and some years later return it to the legal statutes. A particularly bad year was 1917, when four states reinstituted death penalty codes. That reduced the number of states in the abolitionist camp to a mere eight.

THE INFLUENCE OF CLARENCE DARROW

In the early twentieth century, the abolitionist cause saw the rise of one of its most eloquent spokespersons, Unitarian-turned-agnostic lawyer Clarence Darrow (1857–1938). Champion of despised people and unpopular causes, Darrow found both themes coming together in his work as a defense attorney and an advocate of the abolition of the death penalty. His 1924 defense of Richard Loeb and Nathan Leopold, Jr., who had confessed to the murder of a young boy, led to their receiving a sentence of life imprisonment rather than death. This case also seemed to revitalize the flagging abolitionist movement. In 1925, the League for the Abolition of Capital Punishment was formed in New York, and in February 1926 it launced its national campaign in New York City just twenty-four hours before Darrow addressed Congress on the issue.

The efforts of the league were further spurred by the case involving Italian immigrants Nicola Sacco and Bartolomeo Venzetti, who, in spite of considerable evidence of their innocence, were convicted of killing two men during a robbery and sentenced to death. Their conviction led to the formation of the Massachusetts Council for the Abolition of the Death Penalty and led the wife of Herbert B. Ehrmann, one of the defendants' lawyers, to dedicate her life to the overthrow of capital punishment.

Darrow's perspective on crime and punishment grew out of his understanding of what sociologists and scientific penologists had to say about the social and psychological correlates of crime. In his maturity, Darrow accepted the idea of basic social determinism and rejected the notion of individual free will. Without free will, there could of course be no individual moral responsibility. Humans turned to crime because society made them that way, not because of any free choices on their part. For criminals, crime was inevitable. Darrow worked to eliminate the widespread belief in moral responsibility, which he considered a great social evil, since it was this belief which allowed society to justify taking vengeance upon wrongdoers. Instead of punishing its criminals,

Darrow believed society should attempt to reform them. Correctional institutions should be modeled more on hospitals and schools than on jails.

Darrow hoped that once society came to understand that criminals were drive by their emotions and desires, which in turn were dominated by heredity and environmental forces largely beyond their control, it would respond with love and compassion rather than vengeance. He preached an ethic of "nonresistance" and flatly rejected the idea of the *lex talionis* (i.e., an eye for an eye, and a tooth for a tooth). He opposed force and violence at all levels and believed that love and mercy, not moral indignation, were needed. Criminals were the products of an unjust social order and in the end society, not the criminal, was the guilty party. Thus, no one person nor any particular element of society has the right to punish one of its members.

The agnostic Darrow was on occasion presented with the idea that his emphasis upon love and mercy was simply good Christian doctrine. He responded, somewhat candidly, that he wished it were, but that his experience was quite the opposite. Christian ministers of whom he was aware were preaching punishment and vengeance, and there were few Christians outside of the small peace churches who stood with the abolitionists. This situation was to change throughout the twentieth century when many Christian leaders, influenced by social and psychological sciences, began to accept a perspective not far from that of Darrow. This perspective would later mold liberal Protestant and, more recently, Roman Catholic thought.

THE BIBLE AND THE DEATH PENALTY

The traditional religious consensus supporting the death penalty relies on the biblical treatment of the problem, since Christians generally accept the Bible as their authority for faith and practice. In fact, those verses most directly treating the death penalty were from the Old Testament, which Judaism also accepts as its Bible and constituting document. Within the several codes quoted in the books of Exodus, Leviticus, and Numbers are a number dealing with offenses for which death is the prescribed penalty. While few, at least in the twentieth century, have argued that the Mosaic laws should be enacted literally, they form a bulwark of religious belief that God has sanctioned the death penalty. Among the more frequently quoted are verses from Exodus 21 and 22 and Leviticus 20, including Exodus 21:12–17, 23–25, 28–29:

> He that smiteth a man, so that he die, shall be surely put to death. And if a man lie not in wait, but God deliver him into his hand; then I will appoint thee a place whither he shall flee. But if a man come upon his neighbor to slay him with guile: thou shalt take him with guile; thou shalt

take him from mine altar, that he may die. And he that smiteth his father, or his mother, shall be surely put to death. And he that stealeth a man, and selleth him, or if he be found in his hand, he shall surely be put to death. And he that curseth his father, or his mother, shall surely be put to death. . . .

And if any mischief follow, then shalt give life for life, foot for foot, burning for burning, wound for wound, stripe for stripe. . . .

If an ox gore a man or woman . . . if the ox were wont to push with his horn in time past, and if it hath been testified to his owner, and he hath not kept him in, but that he hath killed a man or a woman; the ox shall be stoned, and his owner shall be put to death.

Exodus 22:18–20:

Thou shalt not suffer a witch to live. Whosoever lieth with a beast shall surely be put to death. He that sacrificeth unto any god, save unto the Lord only, he shall be utterly destroyed.

and Leviticus 20:2, 10–16, 27:

Whosoever he be of the children of Israel, or of the strangers that sojourn in Israel, that giveth any of his seed unto Molech; he shall surely be put to death; the people of the land shall stone him with stones. . . .

And the man that committeth adultery with another man's wife, even he that committeth adultery with his neighbor's wife, the adulterer and the adulteress shall surely be put to death. And the man that lieth with his father's wife hath uncovered his father's nakedness; both of them shall surely be put to death; their blood shall be upon them. And if a man lie with his daughter-in-law, both of them shall surely be put to death: they have wrought confusion; their blood shall be upon them. If a man also lie with mankind, as he lieth with a woman, both of them have committed an abomination; they shall surely be put to death; their blood shall be upon them. And if a man take a wife and her mother, it is wickedness: they shall be burnt with fire, both he and they: that there be no wickedness among you. And if a man lie with a beast, he shall surely be put to death: and ye shall slay the beast. And if a woman approach unto any beast, and lie down thereto, thou shalt kill the woman, and the beast; their blood shall be upon them. . . .

A man also or a woman that hath a familiar spirit, or that is a wizard, shall surely be put to death: they shall stone them with stones: their blood shall be upon them.

These are by no means the only references to the sanctioning of capital punishment in ancient Israel, but these are typical of laws that existed during fairly stable periods. In wartime, additional drastic measures were allowed against defeated enemies. In total, ancient Hebrew law prescribed the death penalty for approximately a dozen offenses, ranging from murder and kidnapping for the purpose of selling a person into slavery, to a variety of sexual offenses (adultery, incest, bestiality) and the practice of witchcraft. The primary method of execution was stoning, but particular offenses led to burning (for the crimes of incest and prostitution), beheading (defying royalty), or the use of sword or spear (idolatry).

Within conservative Jewish and Christian communities, these biblical passages form the keystone of any argument favoring capital punishment. While few conservative Christians would argue for the retention of capital punishment for all of the specific cases cited in the passages quoted above, most would argue that the passages from the Hebrew Scriptures do establish the principle that God has ultimately sanctioned the use of capital punishment for particularly offensive crimes.

The Christian New Testament does not comment upon the issue of capital punishment directly, but does make several allusions to it. Among those most cited by supporters of the death penalty are several verses in Paul's writings:

> Let every soul be subject unto the higher powers. For there is no power but of God, the powers that be are ordained of God. Whosoever therefore resisteth the power, resisteth the ordinance of God: and they shall receive unto themselves damnation. For the rulers are not a terror to good works, but to the evil. (Rom. 13:1–3)

Presenting an attitude of general acceptance of the power of government to wield its power against evil, this passage is seen as sanctioning the use of punishments, even the taking of life. It has traditionally been the single most-quoted passage in works which reflect upon a Christian approach to government. Most frequently cited in direct reference to the payment of taxes and service in the armed forces, it has also been used to justify capital punishment.

Another passage often cited is a quotation ascribed to Jesus, "Render therefore unto Caesar the things that are Caesar's; and unto God the things that are God's" (Matt. 22:21). While specifically related to the payment of taxes, it, too, has been cited along with the passage in Romans as granting the secular government a legitimate realm of power that includes the right (if not the mandate) to use deadly force. Additional Christian arguments note that Jesus' acquiescence to and complete lack of protest of the death sentence imposed by Pilate implies a condoning of the state's authority to act in cases which result in the death penalty.

Opponents of the death penalty have also based their arguments on the Bible by highlighting a different set of verses. In general, the passages from the Mosaic law are dismissed as irrelevant in the modern world. Typical is a statement from the Roman Catholic bishops of Tennessee:

Clearly the church has never considered that all of the Jewish laws concerning the death penalty were binding on Christians. In fact, we would be in a genuine dilemma if we considered every verse of the Hebrew Scriptures to be the unequivocal "word of God" for us. How should we regard the dietary laws, the prohibition against wearing a garment woven of both wool and linen, the requirement to have children by a brother's widow or the requirement to build a parapet around the roof of any new house?

Just as most conservative Christians have abandoned the majority of the specifics of the law, including those found in verses immediately adjacent to laws concerning capital punishment, so in like measure advocates of abolishing capital punishment suggest those verses prescribing the death penalty should be abandoned. Instead, concentrated reflection should be directed to the many New Testament passages emphasizing love and compassion, especially to the outcast and prisoner. In relation to capital punishment, for example, the incident of the woman accused of adultery (a capital offense in the Mosaic law) has been considered most illustrative:

And the scribes and the Pharisees brought a woman taken in adultery and having set her in the midst, they said unto him, "Teacher, this woman hath been taken in adultery, in the very act. Now the law Moses commanded us to stone such: what then sayest thou of her?" And this they said trying him, that they might have whereof to accuse him.

But Jesus stooped down, and with his finger wrote on the ground. But when they continued asking him, he lifted himself and said unto them, "He that is without sin among you, let him cast the first stone." And again he stooped down and with his finger wrote on the ground. And they, when they heard it, went out one by one, beginning from the eldest, even unto the last and Jesus was left alone, and the woman, where she was, in the midst. And Jesus lifted up himself, and said unto her, "Woman, where are they? Did no man condemn thee?"

And she said, "No man, Lord."

And Jesus said, "Neither do I condemn thee. Go, and sin no more." (John 8:3–11.)

The story is full of cryptic details (what did Jesus write?) and has provided room for endless speculation. However, more liberal Christians have seen it as indicating that forgiveness should be extended even to a convicted felon otherwise deserving of capital punishment.

As is true on a number of issues, underlying the two distinct Christian approaches to capital punishment are the two approaches to Scripture. Conservatives tend to take a more literal approach and draw from the Bible specific admonitions for ordering life. Liberal Christians tend to place the Bible in the context of an ongoing growth in the understanding of God's will for humanity. They find in the Bible broad principles that must be applied to each generation as new light is shed upon old issues. Clearly the development of modern biblical interpretation within the major denominations has made them open to arguments against capital punishment toward which the more traditional literal interpretation was ill disposed.

CAPITAL PUNISHMENT SINCE WORLD WAR II

As noted previously, the fate of efforts to restrict capital punishment is often determined by some dramatic event, such as a particularly gruesome crime. In the years after World War II, a singularly dramatic event—the case of Caryl Chessman—brought many into the crusade to prohibit the detah penalty.

Chessman was convicted of kidnapping in 1948. He was sentenced to death under the "Lindbergh" law, a law passed in the wake of the kidnapping of the infant son of Charles Lindbergh, which had so aroused public sentiment. Chessman spent the next twelve years on death row at San Quentin while the appeal process was pursued. During this time Chessman seemed to undergo a process of rehabilitation. Without any of the normal assets of wealth, professional training, family, or friends to assist him, and certainly no contacts in influential places, he decided to fight for his life and to establish his innocence.

From his jail cell he began to study law. He wrote his own numerous legal briefs, and on five separate occasions his trek led him to the United States Supreme Court. He also authored four books, including *Cell 2455 Death Row* (1954), *Trial by Ordeal* (1956), *Face of Justice* (1957), and *The Kid Was a Killer* (1960). Two films were made from his extraordinary story, dramatizing how he was led step by step into a life of crime.

With each passing year of his incarceration, Chessman became a public figure. Many people believed he was innocent, and the sympathy for his plight and the demands for clemency generated a new life for the movement to abolish the death penalty. In the last months before his eventual execution, even the governor of California took a stand against capital punishment. It was as a result of the many pleas to stop the execution of Chessman that the first religious groups (outside of the older peace church community) entered a new debate over the legitimacy of the death penalty.

The first church body to go on record against the death penalty seems to have been the Methodist Church (1939–1968) in 1956. Formed by a merger of the Methodist Episcopal Church, the Methodist Protestant Church, and the Methodist Episcopal Church, South, in 1939, the merged body expanded the social creed of the southern church (which had spoken of the "application of the redemptive principle" in the treatment of criminals) to affirm:

> We recommend a continued and more intensive scientific study by Christians, citizens, governmental agencies, and other groups of the punishment of crimes now requiring the death penalty to the end that some method of handling the problem can be found which will protect society and at the same time not offend the sensibility of those who believe capital punishment is contrary to the teachings of Jesus the Christ.

At the Methodist General Conference of 1956 this statement, which recognized the division of opinion that existed on the issue and thus merely called for study, was altered to read simply "we deplore the use of capital punishment." That stance has been reaffirmed by each general conference of the church (now a consituent part of the United Methodist Church) each quadrennium.

The Methodists were quickly followed by the United Church of Canada (1956), the American Baptists (1958), Union of American Hebrew Congregations (1959), the American Ethical Union (1960), and other groups.

Following the execution of Chessman in 1960, very few churches took up the debate, although during the decade a few important voices were added when the United Church of Christ (1962), the Reformed Church in America (1965), and the Lutheran Church in America (1966) each joined the list of those calling for abolition of the death penalty. Toward the end of the decade, the National Council of Churches was able to garner enough votes from its member churches to go on record against capital punishment.

Meanwhile, the turn of events had led to a general decline of the death penalty even in those states where it was still enforced. Through the late 1950s and the 1960s, a significant decline in the number of executions was seen. During the 1950s, there was an average of 70 or more executions annually, down from an average of more than 120 annually in the 1940s. Beginning with 56 in 1960 the number dropped steadily:

1961	42
1962	47
1963	21
1964	15
1965	7
1966	1
1967	2

In 1967, the last executions for a number of years occurred. This informal moratorium occurred while states were awaiting the adjudication of several challenges to the constitutionality of capital punishment, challenges which developed as a result of the significantly large number of blacks and poor people who were sentenced to death.

Meanwhile in Canada a similar story was occurring. Beginning in 1956, a noticeable attack upon capital punishment had begun. It was led by the United Church of Canada, which came out against the death penalty that same year. During the next five years, 60 out of 85 people convicted of murder (which carried a mandatory death sentence) had their sentences commuted to life imprisonment. In an admittedly ambiguous 1960 statement, the Canadian Catholic Conference showed it was leaning toward the abolishment of capital punishment. In 1961, a new law was passed that distinguished between capital and noncapital murder. In 1965, England abolished the death penalty. In 1967, Canada passed a five-year moratorium on the death penalty which was renewed in 1972 with the full support of both the United Church and the Roman Catholics. Finally, in 1976, Canada abolished the death penalty altogether. The law survived in spite of threats to place it back on the books. One especially sensitive issue in Canada has been the safety of law enforcement officials. The deaths of several police officials in the early 1980s led to the most recent cries for the return of the death penalty.

During the 1970s, the debate over the death penalty reached its most intense phase. In a surprising move, the Supreme Court in 1972 ruled on an appeal from Georgia concerning the unconstitutionality of the death penalty. Those who brought the case argued that the death penalty was being applied arbitrarily and with extreme racial bias. The Court accepted the argument and ruled that all state capital punishment laws as they currently existed were unconstitutional. In the case *Furman* v. *Georgia,* the Court said that the arbitrary manner of applying the death penalty violated the Eighth Amendment against cruel and unusal forms of punishment. Somewhat lost in the immediate emotional impact of the ruling was the Court's establishment of guidelines that any law prescribing capital punishment must meet.

Immediately after the ruling, utilizing the Court's guidelines, states began passing new laws. Most of the states that had capital punishment laws reinstituted them, while Rhode Island (which had abandoned capital punishment in 1852) joined the death penalty states by passing a law mandating the death penalty in a few, limited situations. The reintroduction of capital punishment, soon to be accomplished in 35 states, ignited a new debate in the churches. Several religious bodies for the first time identified with the growing abolitionist sentiment, the most important being the Roman Catholic Church. In 1974, through its bishops, the church issued a brief but decisive statement, "The U.S. Catholic Conference goes on record in opposition to capital punishment." At the same time, a number of the more conservative organizations found a need to express their adherence to the more traditional position favoring capital punishment. These included the National Association of Evangelicals (1972), the Lutheran Church-Missouri Synod (1976), and the National Association of Free Will Baptists (1977).

The debate raged for several years but came to a sudden climax in the events of 1976 and 1977. In 1976, the Supreme Court heard five cases on the new laws passed since the *Furman* v. *Georgia* decision. Though striking down the new laws in Louisiana and North Carolina, the Court upheld the new laws in Georgia, Florida, and Texas. Thus, just as Canada finally succeeded in abolishing capital punishment, the United States reinstated it.

Unsuccessful in preventing the reinstitution of state laws calling for capital punishment, the churches moved to prevent their enforcement. Their hopes were dashed by the 1977 execution of Gary Gilmore in Utah. Five more prisoners were executed during the next four years. Twenty-four were executed in 1984. Hundreds now sit on death row across the United States. Particular attention was focused upon Florida where the single largest number of people sentenced to death was concentrated.

Throughout the 1980s, executions have continued in spite of the actions of the churches. On the one hand, church efforts to abolish the death penalty in the United States have been completely unsuccessful, as witnessed by the steady reinstitution of capital punishment in state after state in the late 1970s and the rising number of executions in the 1980s. On the other hand, the actions of the churches and other religious groups opposed to capital punishment have succeeded in limiting the number of crimes for which the death penalty can be prescribed, and there is every reason to believe that their intercession has stopped what could have become a massive wave of executions since 1976.

Churches opposed to the death penalty represented the largest block of organized religion in the United States, but they still represented a minority opinion in the American public. As illustrated by public opinion polls taken at that time, most Americans (including the membership of many of the large churches) favored capital punishment. Conservative churches also favored it. Many of those church bodies that have not identified with the abolitionist cause are strong in the South, where public opinion most strongly favors capital punishment. Included are the National Association of Free Will Baptists (which favors capital punishment) and the 13-million-member Southern Baptist Convention (which has not spoken on the issue).

. . . With state laws in place, few items of legislation pending, and even fewer constitutional challenges to capital punishment before the appeals courts, the churches have been left with almost no capital punishment issue on which to build any immediate emotional intensity. They have instead shifted their attention to prison ministries and efforts to reform the larger criminal justice system.

Someday in the not too distant future, however, the debate over capital punishment will be renewed. It awaits only a new incident or a new insight to again bring it to the fore. When that occurs, the churches will have an asset they did not have when the Chessman case first effectively raised the issue several decades ago. They now have a fairly strong consensus around a well-articulated position. The success of their future actions on this issue will depend upon their ability to win over a voting public still demonstrating a stong belief in capital punishment.

10

On Deterrence and the Death Penalty

Ernest van den Haag

I

If rehabilitation and the protection of society from unrehabilitated offenders were the only purposes of legal punishment the death penalty could be abolished: It cannot attain the first end, and is not needed for the second. No case for the death penalty can be made unless "doing justice," or "deterring others," are among our penal aims. Each of these purposes can justify capital punishment by itself; opponents, therefore, must show that neither actually does, while proponents can rest their case on either.

Although the argument from justice is intellectually more interesting, and, in my view, decisive enough, utilitarian arguments have more appeal: The claim that capital punishment is useless because it does not deter others, is most persuasive. I shall, therefore, focus on this claim. Lest the argument be thought to be unduly narrow, I shall show, nonetheless, that some claims of injustice rest on premises which the claimants reject when arguments for capital punishment are derived therefrom; while other claims of injustice have no independent standing: Their weight depends on the weight given to deterrence.

II

Capital punishment is regarded as unjust because it may lead to the execution of innocents, or because the guilty poor (or disadvantaged) are more likely to be executed than the guilty rich.

Regardless of merit, these claims are relevant only if "doing justice" is one purpose of punishment. Unless one regards it as good, or, at least, better, that the guilty be punished rather than the innocent, and that the equally guilty be punished equally, unless, that is, one wants penalties to be just, one cannot object to them because they are not. However, if one does include justice among the purposes of punishment, it becomes possible to justify any one punishment—even death—on grounds of justice. Yet, those who object to the death penalty because of its alleged injustice, usually deny not only the merits, or the sufficiency, of specific arguments based on justice, but the propriety of justice as an argument: They exclude "doing justice" as a purpose of legal punishment. If justice is not a purpose of penalties, injustice cannot be an objection to the death penalty, or to any other; if it is, justice cannot be ruled out as an argument for any penalty.

Consider the claim of injustice on its merits now. A convicted man may be found to have been innocent; if he was executed, the penalty cannot be reversed. Except for fines, penalties never can be reversed. Time spent in prison cannot be returned. However, a prison sentence may be remitted once the prisoner serving it is found innocent; and he can be compensated for the time served (although compensation ordinarily cannot repair the harm). This, though (nearly) all penalties are irreversible, the death penalty, unlike others, is irrevocable as well.

Despite all precautions, errors will occur in judicial proceedings: The innocent may be found guilty,[1] or the guilty rich may more easily escape conviction, or receive lesser penalties than the guilty poor. However, these injustices do not reside in the penalties inflicted but in their maldistribution. It is not the penalty—whether death or prison—which is unjust when inflicted on the innocent, but its imposition on the innocent. Inequity between poor and rich also involves distribution, not the penalty distributed.[2] Thus injustice is not an objection to the death penalty but to the distributive process— the trial. Trials are more likely to be fair when life is at stake—the death penalty is probably less often unjustly inflicted than others. It requires special consideration not because it is more, or more often, unjust than other penalties, but because it is always irrevocable.

Can any amount of deterrence justify the possibility of irrevocable injustice? Surely injustice is unjustifiable in each actual individual case; it must be objected to whenever it occurs. But we are concerned here with the process that may produce injustice, and with the penalty that would make it irrevocable—not with the actual individual cases produced, but with the general rules which may produce them. To consider objections to a general rule (the provision of any penalties by law) we must compare the likely net result of alternative rules and select the rule (or penalty) likely to produce the least injustice. For however one defines justice, to support it cannot mean less than to favor the least injustice. If the death of innocents because of judicial error is unjust, so is the death of innocents by murder. If some murders could be avoided by a penalty conceivably more deterrent than others—such as the death penalty—then the question becomes: Which penalty will minimize the number of innocents killed (by crime and by punishment)? It follows that the irrevocable injustice sometimes inflicted by the death penalty would not significantly militate against it, if capital punishment deters enough murders to reduce the total number of innocents killed so that fewer are lost than would be lost without it.

In general, the possibility of injustice argues against penalization of any kind only if the expected usefulness of penalization is less important than the probable harm (particularly to innocents) and the probable inequities. The possibility of injustice argues against the death penalty only inasmuch as the added usefulness (deterrence) expected from irrevocability is thought less important than the added harm. (Were my argument specifically concerned with justice, I could compare the injustice inflicted by the courts with the injustice—outside the courts—avoided by the judicial process. I.e., "important" here may be used to include everything to which importance is attached.)

We must briefly examine now the general use and effectiveness of deterrence to decide whether the death penalty could add enough deterrence to be warranted.

III

Does any punishment "deter others" at all? Doubts have been thrown on this effect because it is thought to depend on the incorrect rationalistic psychology of some of its eighteenth- and nineteenth-century proponents. Actually deterrence does not depend on rational calculation, on rationality or even on capacity for it; nor do arguments for it depend on rationalistic psychology. Deterrence depends on the likelihood and on the regularity—not on the rationality—of human responses to danger; and further on the possibility of reinforcing internal controls by vicarious external experiences.

Responsiveness to danger is generally found in human behavior; the danger can, but need not, come from the law or from society; nor need it be explicitly verbalized. Unless intent on suicide, people do not jump from high mountain cliffs, however tempted to fly through the air; and they take precautions against falling. The mere risk of injury often restrains us from doing what is otherwise attractive; we refrain even when we have no direct experience, and usually without explicit computation of probabilities, let alone conscious weighing of expected pleasure against possible pain. One abstains from dangerous acts because of vague, inchoate, habitual and, above all, preconscious fears. Risks and rewards are more often felt than calculated; one abstains without accounting to oneself, because "it isn't done," or because one literally does not conceive of the action one refrains from. Animals as well refrain from painful or injurious experiences presumably without calculation; and the threat of punishment can be used to regulate their conduct.

Unlike natural dangers, legal threats are constructed deliberately by legislators to restrain actions which may impair the social order. Thus legislation transforms social into individual dangers. Most people further transform external into internal danger: They acquire a sense of moral obligation, a conscience, which threatens them, should they do what is wrong. Arising originally from the external authority of rulers and rules, conscience is internalized and becomes independent of external forces. However, conscience is constantly reinforced in those whom it controls by the coercive imposition of external authority on recalcitrants and on those who have not acquired it. Most people refrain from offenses because they feel an obligation to behave lawfully. But this obligation would scarcely be felt if those who do not feel or follow it were not to suffer punishment.

Although the legislators may calculate their threats and the responses to be produced, the effectiveness of the threats neither requires nor depends on calculations by those responding. The predictor (or producer) of effects must calculate; those whose responses are predicted (or produced) need not. Hence, although legislation (and legislators) should be rational, subjects, to be deterred as intended, need not be: They need only be responsive.

Punishments deter those who have not violated the law for the same reasons—and in the same degrees (apart from internalization: moral obligation) as do natural dangers. Often natural dangers—all dangers not deliberately created by legislation (e.g., injury of the criminal inflicted by the crime victim) are insufficient. Thus, the fear of injury (natural danger) does not suffice to control city traffic; it must be reinforced by the legal punishment meted out to those who violate the rules. These punishments keep most people observing the regulations. However, where (in the absence of natural danger) the threatened punishment is so light that the advantage of violating rules tends to exceed the disadvantage of being punished (divided by the risk), the rule is violated (i.e., parking fines are too light). In this case the feeling of obligation tends to vanish as well. Elsewhere punishment deters.

To be sure, not everybody responds to threatened punishment. Nonresponsive persons may be (a) self-destructive or (b) incapable of responding to threats, or even of grasping them. Increases in the size, or certainty, of penalties would not affect these two groups. A third group

(c) might respond to more certain or more severe penalties.[3] If the punishment threatened for burglary, robbery, or rape were a $5 fine in North Carolina, and five years in prison in South Carolina, I have no doubt that the North Carolina treasury would become quite opulent until vigilante justice would provide the deterrence not provided by law. Whether to increase penalties (or improve enforcement) depends on the importance of the rule to society, the size and likely reaction of the group that did not respond before, and the acceptance of the added punishment and enforcement required to deter it. Observation would have to locate the points—likely to differ in different times and places—at which diminishing, zero, and negative returns set in. There is no reason to believe that all present and future offenders belong to the *a priori* nonresponsive groups, or that all penalties have reached the point of diminishing, let alone zero returns.

IV

Even though its effectiveness seems obvious, punishment as a deterrent has fallen into disrepute. Some ideas which help explain this progressive heedlessness were uttered by Lester Pearson, then Prime Minister of Canada, when, in opposing the death penalty, he proposed that instead "the state seek to eradicate the causes of crime—slums, ghettos and personality disorders."[4]

"Slums, ghettos and personality disorders" have not been shown, singly or collectively, to be "the causes" of crime.

(1) The crime rate in the slums is indeed higher than elsewhere; but so is the death rate in hospitals. Slums are no more "causes" of crime, than hospitals are of death; they are locations of crime, as hospitals are of death. Slums and hospitals attract people selectively; neither is the "cause" of the condition (disease in hospitals, poverty in slums) that leads to the selective attraction.

As for poverty which draws people into slums, and, sometimes, into crime, any relative disadvantage may lead to ambition, frustration, resentment and, if insufficiently restrained, to crime. Not all relative disadvantages can be eliminated; indeed very few can be, and their elimination increases the resentment generated by the remaining ones; not even relative poverty can be removed altogether. (Absolute poverty—whatever that may be—hardly affects crime.) However, though contributory, relative disadvantages are not a necessary or sufficient cause of crime: Most poor people do not commit crimes, and some rich people do. Hence, "eradication of poverty" would, at most, remove one (doubtful) cause of crime.

In the United States, the decline of poverty has not been associated with a reduction of crime. Poverty measured in dollars of constant purchasing power, according to present government standards and statistics, was the condition of one-half of all our families in 1920; of one-fifth in 1962; and of less than one-sixth in 1966. In 1967, 5.3 million families out of 49.8 million were poor—one-ninth of all families in the United States. If crime has been reduced in a similar manner, it is a well-kept secret.

Those who regard regard poverty as a cause of crime often draw a wrong inference from a true proposition: The rich will not commit certain crimes—Rockefeller never riots; nor does he steal. (He mugs, but only on T.V.) Yet while wealth may be the cause of not committing (certain) crimes, it does not follow that poverty (absence of wealth) is the cause of committing them. Water extinguishes or prevents fire; but its absence is not the cause of fire. Thus, if poverty could be abolished, if everybody had all "necessities" (I don't pretend to know what this would mean), crime would remain, for, in the words of Aristotle, "the greatest crimes are committed not for the sake of basic necessities but for the sake of superfluities." Superfluities cannot be provided by the government; they would be what the government does not provide.

(2) . . . Ethnic separation, voluntary or forced, obviously has little to do with crime; I can think of no reason why it should.[5]

(3) I cannot see how the state could "eradicate" personality disorders even if all causes and cures were known and available. (They are not.) Further, the known incidence of personality disorders within the prison population does not exceed the known incidence outside—though our knowledge of both is tenuous. Nor are personality disorders necessary, or sufficient causes for criminal offenses, unless these be identified by means of (moral, not clinical) definition with personality disorders. In this case, Mr. Pearson would have proposed to "eradicate" crime by eradicating crime—certainly a sound, but not a helpful idea.

Mr. Pearson's views are part as well of the mental furniture of the former U.S. Attorney General Ramsey Clark, who told a congressional committee that ". . . only the elimination of the causes of crime can make a significant and lasting difference in the incidence of crime." Uncharitably interpreted, Mr. Clark revealed that only the elimination of causes eliminates effects—a sleazy cliché and wrong to boot. Given the genefit of the doubt, Mr. Clark probably meant that the causes of crime are social; and that therefore crime can be reduced "only" by nonpenal (social) measures.

This view suggests a fireman who declines fire-fighting apparatus by pointing out that "in the long run only the elimination of the causes" of fire "can make a significant and lasting difference in the incidence" of fire, and that fire-fighting equipment does not eliminate "the causes"—except that such a fireman would probably not rise to fire chief. Actually, whether fires are checked, depends on equipment and on the efforts of the firemen using it no less than on the presence of "the causes": inflammable materials. So with crimes. Laws, courts, and police actions are no less important in restraining them than "the causes" are in impelling them. If firemen (or attorneys general) pass the buck and refuse to use the means available, we may all be burned while waiting for "the long run" and the "elimination of the causes."

Whether any activity—be it lawful or unlawful—takes place depends on whether the desire for it, or for whatever is to be secured by it, is stronger than the desire to avoid the costs involved. Accordingly people work, attend college, commit crimes, go to the movies—or refrain from any of these activities. Attendance at a theater may be high because the show is entertaining and because the price of admission is low. Obviously the attendance depends on both—on the combination of expected gratification and cost. The wish, motive or impulse for doing anything—the experienced, or expected, gratification—is the cause of doing it; the wish to avoid the cost is the cause of not doing it. One is no more and no less "cause" than the other. (Common speech supports this use of "cause" no less than logic: "Why did you go to Jamaica!" "*Because* it is such a beautiful place." "Why didn't you go to Jamaica" "*Because* it is too expensive."—"Why do you buy this?" "*Because* it is so cheap." "Why don't you buy that?" "*Because* it is too expensive.") Penalties (costs) are causes of lawfulness, or (if too low or uncertain) of unlawfulness, of crime. People do commit crimes because, given their conditions, the desire for the satisfaction sought prevails. They refrain if the desire to avoid the cost prevails. Given the desire, low cost (penalty) causes the action, and high cost restraint. Given the cost, desire becomes the causal variable. Neither is intrinsically more causal than the other. The crime rate increases if the cost is reduced or the desire raised. It can be decreased by raising the cost or by reducing the desire.

The cost of crime is more easily and swiftly changed than the conditions producing the inclination to it. Further, the costs are very largely within the power of the government to change, whereas the conditions producing propensity to crime are often only indirectly affected by government action, and some are altogether beyond the control of the government. Our unilateral emphasis on these conditions and our undue neglect of costs may contribute to an unnecessarily high crime rate.

V

The foregoing suggests the question posed by the death penalty: Is the deterrence added (return) sufficiently above zero to warrant irrevocability (or other, less clear, disadvantages)? The question is not only whether the penalty deters, but whether it deters more than alternatives and whether the difference exceeds the cost of irrevocability. (I shall assume that the alternative is actual life imprisonment so as to exclude the complication produced by the release of the unrehabilitated.)

In some fairly infrequent but important circumstances the death penalty is the only possible deterrent. Thus, in case of acute *coups d'état,* or of acute substantial attempts to overthrow the government, prospective rebels would altogether discount the threat of any prison sentence. They would not be deterred because they believe the swift victory of the revolution will invalidate a prison sentence and turn it into an advantage. Execution would be the only deterrent because, unlike prison sentences, it cannot be revoked by victorious rebels. The same reasoning applies to deterring spies or traitors in wartime. Finally, men who, by virtue of past acts, are already serving, or are threatened, by a life sentence, could be deterred from further offenses only by the threat of the death penalty.[6]

What about criminals who do not fall into any of these (often ignored) classes? Professor Thorsten Sellin has made a careful study of the available statistics: He concluded that they do not yield evidence for the deterring effect of the death penalty.[7] Somewhat surprisingly, Professor Sellin seems to think that this lack of evidence for deterrence is evidence for the lack of deterrence. It is not. It means that deterrence has not been demonstrated statistically—not that nondeterrence has been.

It is entirely possible, indeed likely (as Professor Sellin appears willing to concede), that the statistics used, though the best available, are nonetheless too slender a reed to rest conclusions on. They indicate that the homicide rate does not vary greatly between similar areas with or without the death penalty, and in the same area before and after abolition. However, the similar areas are not similar enough; the periods are not long enough; many social differences and changes, other than the abolition of the death penalty, may account for the variation (or lack of) in homicide rates with and without, before and after abolition; some of these social differences and changes are likely to have affected homicide rates. I am unaware of any statistical analysis which adjusts for such changes and differences. And logically, it is quite consistent with the postulated deterrent effect of capital punishment that there be less homicide after abolition: With retention there might have been still less.

Homicide rates do not depend exclusively on penalties any more than do other crime rates. A number of conditions which influence the propensity to crime, demographic, economic or generally social changes or differences— even such matters as changes of the divorce laws or of the cotton price— may influence the homicide rate. Therefore, variation or constancy cannot be attributed to variations or constancy of the penalties, unless we know that no other factor influencing the homicide rate has changed. Usually we don't. To believe the death penalty deterrent does not require one to believe that the death penalty, or any other, is the only, or the decisive, causal variable; this would be as absurd as the converse mistake that "social causes" are the only, or always, the decisive factor. To favor capital punishment, the efficacy of neither variable need be denied. It is enough to affirm that the severity of the penalty may influence some potential criminals, and that the added severity of the death penalty adds to deterrence, or may do so. It is quite possible that such a deterrent effect may be offset (or intensified) by nonpenal factors which affect propensity; its presence or absence therefore may be hard, and perhaps impossible to demonstrate.

Contrary to what Professor Sellin et al. seem to presume, I doubt that offenders are aware of the absence or presence of the death penalty state by state or period by period. Such unawareness argues against the assumption of a calculating murderer. However, unawareness does not argue against the death penalty if by deterrence we mean a preconscious, general response to a severe, but not necessarily specifically and explicitly apprehended, or calculated threat. A constant homicide rate, despite abolition, may occur because of unawareness and not because of lack of deterrence: People remain deterred for a lengthy interval by the severity of the penalty in the past, or by the severity of penalties used in similar circumstances nearby.

I do not argue for a version of deterrence which would require me to believe that an individual shuns murder while in North Dakota, because of the death penalty, and merrily goes to it in South Dakota since it has been abolished there; or that he will start the murderous career from which he had hitherto refrained, after abolition. I hold that the generalized threat of the death penalty may be a deterrent, and the more so, the more generally applied. Deterrence will not cease in the particular areas of abolition or at the particular times of abolition. Rather, general deterrence will be somewhat weakened, through local (partial) abolition. Even such weakening will be hard to detect owing to changes in many offsetting, or reinforcing, factors.

For all of these reasons, I doubt that the presence or absence of a deterrent effect of the death penalty is likely to be demonstrable by statistical means. The statistics presented by Professor Sellin et al. show only that there is no statistical proof for the deterrent effect of the death penalty. But they do not show that there is no deterrent effect. Not to demonstrate presence of the effect is not the same as to demonstrate its absence; certainly not when there are plausible explanations for the nondemonstrability of the effect.

It is on our uncertainty that the case for deterrence must rest.[8]

VI

If we do not know whether the death penalty will deter others, we are confronted with two uncertainties. If we impose the death penalty, and achieve no deterrent effect thereby, the life of a convicted murderer has been expended in vain (from a deterrent viewpoint). There is a net loss. If we impose the death sentence and thereby deter some future murderers, we spared the lives of some future victims (the prospective murderers gain, too; they are spared punishment because they were deterred). In this case, the death penalty has led to a net gain, unless the life of a convicted murderer is valued more highly than that of the unknown victim, or victims (and the non-imprisonment of the deterred nonmurderer).

The calculation can be turned around, of course. The absence of the death penalty may harm no one and therefore produce a gain—the life of the convicted murderer. Or it may kill future victims of murderers who could have been deterred, and thus produce a loss—their life.

To be sure, we must risk something certain—the death (or life) of the convicted man, for something uncertain—the death (or life) of the victims of murderers who may be deterred. This is in the nature of uncertainty—when we invest, or gamble, we risk the money we have for an uncertain gain. Many human actions, most commitments—including marriage and crime—share this characteristic with the deterrent purpose of any penalization, and with its rehabilitative purpose (and even with the protective).

More proof is demanded for the deterrent effect of the death penalty than is demanded for the deterrent effect of other penalties. This is not justified by the absence of other utilitarian purposes such as protection and rehabilitation; they involve no less uncertainty than deterrence.[9]

Irrevocability may support a demand for some reason to expect more deterrence than revocable penalties might produce, but not a demand for more proof of deterrence, as has been pointed out above. The reason for expecting more deterrence lies in the greater severity, the terrifying effect inherent in finality. Since it seems more important to spare victims than to spare murderers, the burden of proving that the greater severity inherent in irrevocability adds nothing to deterrence lies on those who oppose capital punishment. Proponents of the death penalty need show only that there is no more uncertainty about it than about greater severity in general.

The demand that the death penalty be proved more deterrent than alternatives cannot be satisfied any more than the demand that six years in prison be proved to be more deterrent than three. But the uncertainty which confronts us favors the death penalty as long as by imposing it we might save future victims of murder. This effect is as plausible as the general idea that penalties have deterrent effects which increase with their severity. Though we have no proof of the positive deterrence of the penalty, we also have no proof of zero, or negative effectiveness. I believe we have no right to risk additional future victims of murder for the sake of sparing convicted murderers; on the contrary, our moral obligation is to risk the possible ineffectiveness of executions. However rationalized, the opposite view appears to be motivated by the simple fact that executions are more subjected to social control than murder. However, this applies to all penalties and does not argue for the abolition of any.

NOTES

1. I am not concerned with the converse injustice, *which I regard as no less grave.*

2. Such inequity, though likely, has not been demonstrated. Note that, since there are more poor than rich, there are likely to be more guilty poor; and, if poverty contributes to crime, the proportion of the poor who are criminals also should be higher than of the rich.

3. I neglect those motivated by civil disobedience or, generally, moral or political passion. Deterring them depends less on penalties than on the moral support they receive, though penalties play a role. I also neglect those who may belong to all three groups listed, some successively, some even simultaneously, such as drug addicts. Finally, I must altogether omit the far-from-negligible role that problems of apprehension and conviction play in deterrence—beyond saying that, by reducing the government's ability to apprehend and convict, courts are able to reduce the risks of offenders.

4. I quote from the *New York Times* (November 24, 1967, p. 22). The actual psychological and other factors which bear on the disrepute—as distinguished from the rationalizations—cannot be examined here.

5. Mixed areas, incidentally, have higher crime rates than segregated ones (see, e.g., R. Ross and E. van den Haag, *The Fabric of Society* [New York: Harcourt, Brace & Co., 1957], pp. 102–104). Because slums are bad (morally) and crime is, many people seem to reason that "slums spawn crime"—which confuses some sort of moral with a causal relation.

6. Cautious revolutionaries, uncertain of final victory, might be impressed by prison sentences—but not in the acute stage, when faith in victory is high. And one can increase even the severity of a life sentence in prison. Finally, harsh punishment of rebels can intensify rebellious impulses. These points, though they qualify it, hardly impair the force of the argument.

7. Sellin considered mainly homicide statistics. His work may be found in his *Capital Punishment* (New York: Harper & Row, 1967); or, most conveniently, in H. A. Bedau, *The Death Penalty in America* (Garden City, N.Y.: Doubleday & Co., 1964), which also offers other material, mainly against the death penalty.

8. In view of the strong emotions aroused (itself an indication of effectiveness to me: Might not murderers be as upset over the death penalty as those who wish to spare them?) and because I believe penalties must reflect community feeling to be effective, I oppose mandatory death sentences and favor optional, and perhaps binding, recommendations by juries after their finding of guilt. The opposite course risks the nonconviction of guilty defendants by juries who do not want to see them executed.

9. Rehabilitation or protection are of minor importance in our actual penal system (though not in our theory). We confine many people who do not need rehabilitation and against whom we do not need protection (e.g., the exasperated husband who killed his wife); we release many unrehabilitated offenders against whom protection is needed. Certainly rehabilitation and protection are not, and deterrence is, the main actual function of legal punishment if we disregard nonutilitarian ones.

11

Casting the First Stone

Lloyd Steffen

. . . Clearly the moral passion in support of the death penalty comes not from thinking about capital punishment in abstract ways, but as a just means of retribution for individual crimes perpetrated by individual miscreants on individual victims. Nonetheless, I want to interject a caution. While individual stories certainly activate the moral imagination, dangers always exist in allowing them to govern our thinking about issues that have profound social implications. Individual stories appeal to definite moral principles even if the principles themselves are not articulated, and when we appeal to them rather than to a formal moral argument, we beg questions regarding which principles should be invoked to help us decide that one story rather than another should govern behavior and guide action. Despite these problems, I can still imagine advocates of capital punishment defending their position simply by saying "What about Theodore Bundy?"

Bundy, who died in 1989 in Florida's electric chair, is as strong an anecdotal defense of capital punishment as we could find: A mass murderer who killed innocent women in several states, Bundy appeared to be a moral incorrigible, one who killed repeatedly and without inhibition, and who provided investigators with information about many of his unsolved crimes only because it was the last card he could play to postpone his execution. Seemingly incapable of remorse, Bundy was unquestionably guilty of the crimes for which he had been convicted and many for which he hadn't. If anyone embodies the kind of moral monster who deserves the most severe punishment society can inflict, Ted Bundy did.

Reprinted, with changes, from *Christianity and Crisis* 50, no. 1 (February 5, 1990): 11–16. By permission of the author.

But if Ted Bundy's story "argues" for capital punishment, James Richardson's argues even more strongly against it.

In 1968, Richardson, a black Florida fruit picker, was tried and convicted of kiling his seven children. Richardson allegedly had taken out insurance policies the night before the murder. While this established motive sufficient to convince a jury of his guilt, neither the defense attorney nor the prosecutor pointed out that the unpaid policies were not in effect when the children died. When Richardson's three cell mates were brought in to testify that he had confessed the crime to them, no one bothered to mention that the sheriff had promised the three reduced jail time for their testimony. The one surviving witness of the three has finally admitted that Ricahrdson never made such a confession. Ricardson's lie detector results disappeared and were never disclosed, and the polygraph operator who administered another test to him in prison stated that he had "no involvement in the crime whatsoever."

Richardson's next-door neighbor actually poisoned the children while Richardson and his wife were working in the fields. Yet she was never called to testify. The authorities did not want the jury to know that her first husband had died mysteriously after eating a dinner she had prepared or that she had actually served four years in prison for killing her second husband. The woman, incidentally, after being admitted to a nursing home, confessed to staff there that she was the guilty party, but the staff, fearing loss of their jobs, did not report her confession to superiors. And the former assistant prosecutor in the town of Arcadia, where Richardson was tried, deliberately concealed over 900 pages of evidence that would have brought all of these facts to light. It took an actual theft to get these documents into the hands of *Miami Herald* reporters. Once there, the case was reopened, and after spending twenty-one years in prison for a crime he did not commit, James Richardson was released.

Richardson may not have been executed, but his is a story about capital punishment nonetheless. For he was sentenced to death, sat for four years on death row, and was even put through a harrowing "dry run" execution, complete with a shaving and a buckle-down in the chair. Richardson was not only a poor black man who received an inept defense. He was also an innocent man who was made a victim of lies, deceit, perjured testimony, false witnesses—and those who prosecuted him and knew of his innocence still demanded that he be executed. What the Richardson case points out is that the death penalty always holds the potential for interfering mightily with justice. In the Richardson case, guilt lies with the accusers, and the irrevocable nature of the death penalty would have prevented Richardson from receiving even the modicum of justice he finally did receive. Despite being the result of a legal process, his death would have constituted an unjustified killing—an actual murder.

How is justice to be exacted when a murder is committed by all of society? Is guilt to attach only to the sheriff and prosecutor in the case? Would those two be appropriate targets for the death penalty today since they violated the moral prohibition against the taking of human life and sought deliberately and with premeditation to kill an innocent man—the crime for which we wish to impose death fairly and without caprice? That these events can occur leads to a question: Is killing a Theodore Bundy so necessary that we should accept the risk capital punishment poses to a James Richardson?

Supporters of capital punishment will say justice prevailed; Richardson did not die, and the case poses no challenge. I say, however, that Richardson's case is a fundamental challenge to capital punishment, since the only good thing to come out of the situation is the simple fact that he did not die. His innocence might have come to light even if he had been killed, so it is life, not just truth, that is at stake. Only the simple fact that Richardson is alive makes possible any hope for his seeking restitution from a system that at one point forsook justice and actually conspired to kill him.

If Richardson had been executed and the truth found out, we might not even be asking whether it is morally permissible to continue a practice that by its very nature runs the risk of committing murder and depriving persons of any opportunity to redress injustice. Were Richardson dead, we would be facing social complicity in his death and probably looking for a way to justify his death in order to make it something other than murder. We would be defending ourselves with the very truths we refused to acknowledge to him: that our system of justice is fallible, that our knowledge and judgment can be swayed and distorted, that our moral certainty is neither pure nor absolute.

My religious tradition has taught me that capital punishment raises questions finally about the responsibility all of us have for each one of us. Christianity centers on a person who was condemned to death and executed by the state, a person held to be "without sin" but who, despite that religious characterization, posed a political threat to the coercive power structure of his day. By daring to propose a way of life based on compassion rather than power, he made himself more guilty of sedition than Richardson was of murder.

THE TESTIMONY OF JESUS

Twice Jesus spoke to the issue of capital punishment, and both times he challenged those who would impose death to consider their arrogation of a power that belonged to God alone. Once he intervened as an execution was about to take place. Placing himself between the executioners and the victim, he pointed to the executioners' illusion of innocence and moral purity. Speaking to the reality of moral imperfection so apparent in both the executioners and the condemned, he said, "Let him who is without sin among you be the first to throw a stone at her." The woman about to be stoned for adultery had been caught in the act. But guilty as she was, her executioners were not so innocent that they could meet the test of absolute innocence their act required. And the only one there who was innocent wanted nothing to do with killing her.

The second time Jesus addressed capital punishment was after his own execution had commenced. In a punishment our legal system has explicitly condemned as "cruel and unusual," he asked forgiveness for his executioners, saying "they know not what they do." That the punishment was brutal, oppressive, and designed to deter other enemies of the state, they knew. What the executioners did not know was that they had arrogated to themselves a power that was not theirs to assume—the power of absolute innocence, the power to destroy the life of a person who was a gift from God.

Jesus did not deserve such a death, and one meaning I take from his execution is that those who follow him ought not to inflict on others what was inflicted on him. This execution was so outrageous that nothing short of divine intervention could prevent Jesus' death from becoming the ultimate symbol of despair or the most monstrous example of what human beings can do in their mad quest to become God. Jesus' death was saved from meaninglessness because God, not the executioner, had the last word.

While the brutal instrument of Jesus' execution continues to be prominently displayed in worship settings—I have often wondered what it would be like for us to place a hangman's noose over the altar just to update things a bit—many who follow his path of faith continue to support capital punishment. This is a curious state of affairs, for the cross refutes rather than legitimates executions. It discloses the lengths human beings will go to satisfy their desire to be God, while it punctures the illusion that human beings can wield coercive power from a position of moral purity or absolute innocence. That human beings continue to assume this absolute power over the life of persons stands as evidence that God has been displaced; that indeed God is dead.

Capital punishment may well continue as accepted social policy despite the moral issues it raises for law, ethics, and theology. Regrettably, Jesus' story has failed to provoke enough people to think about the morality of the death penalty. We might be tempted to look to other stories. Should we choose James Richardson, we will find that he is a living reminder of the same justice that did away with Jesus. And he will continue to stand as an accusation against his accusers, a brutalized and injured man—one of us—pointing out the complicity in evil of all who condemned him.

What James Richardson will do now, I do not know. Perhaps he will return to obscurity to grieve for the loss of his seven children.

12

In Spite of Innocence:
Erroneous Convictions in Capital Cases

Michael L. Radelet, Hugo Adam Bedau, and Constance E. Putnam

. . . In the United States not only do countless men and women get arrested for murders they did not commit—they get convicted and often sentenced to death as well. Occasionally they are even executed, and we [have] document[ed] twenty-three such cases. . . .*

With the important exception of those twenty-three, the rest of the stories—nearly four hundred—that we . . . [have identified] in varying degrees of detail are those of the lucky defendants. They are the ones whose innocence was eventually established so convincingly that the State finally did, in one way or another, admit its errors and correct them. And 150 or so of those who were once wrongly under sentence of death did at least escape execution, their death sentences for a variety of reasons having been nullified before the ultimate tragedy occurred. Often, as we have seen, it was fickle good fortune rather than anything having to do with the rational workings of the criminal justice system that played the crucial role in sparing these innocent defendants. Yet luck was not sufficient to spare them time in prison (often many years), the agony of uncertainty over whether they would ever be vindicated and released, and blighted hopes for a decent life all too frequently destroyed by the ordeal and stigma of a murder

*See the book from which this selection is taken.

conviction. Low though the odds of convicting the innocent are, the odds of innocent prisoners—once convicted—being able to marshal the resources essential to proving their innocence are lower still.

What lessons are to be learned from these chronicles of error? What do these cases—stretching back across the twentieth century and found in every region and almost every state—have to teach us? One naturally wonders whether the errors could have been avoided and whether comparable errors can be prevented in the century ahead. If not, what are the minimal accommodations with unavoidable error and the risk of terrible tragedy that a civilized society ought to make?

Before addressing these questions, we must first make clear that the scope of the problem of erroneous conviction in homicide cases is by no means entirely before us, even now. How many other cases there may be in which good fortune, hard work, or unflagging courage was absent and the erroneous conviction was never corrected or even adequately identified (except by the prisoner and a few supporters), we cannot say. We are confident, as a result of [our] years of work . . . that there are hundreds (perhaps even thousands) of other cases in which innocent people have been convicted of homicide or sentenced to death without having been able to prove their innocence to the authorities. We also have reason to believe that there are other cases, not yet known to us, in which states have officially acknowledged, one way or another, that an innocent person was convicted of homicide. Even today, after eight years of continuous and well-publicized research into this subject, we learn of new cases at the rate of one each month. Some of these cases date back twenty or thirty years; others crop up as current news reported in the daily papers.

Since the initial publication of our research in 1987, in which 350 cases were identified, we have examined more than 100 additional cases. After careful review, we have included sixty-six of them in our Inventory of Cases. There is no reason to believe that somehow . . . we have managed to produce a complete list of all the relevant cases. As James McCloskey of Centurion Ministries noted recently, "I believe that the innocent are convicted far more frequently than the public cares to believe, and far more frequently than those who operate the system dare to believe." Despite our efforts, it is quite possible that all we have done is trace the outlines of the proverbial tip of the iceberg.

What is true of cases yet to be discovered in which an innocent person was wrongfully convicted of murder is equally true regarding the execution of the innocent. We [have reported] . . . nearly two dozen cases where we believe an innocent person was executed. We can be virtually certain there are more cases that will probably never be documented in which innocent individuals were executed before they were able to prove their innocence. As Voltaire argued in the eighteenth century and Bentham in the nineteenth, we argue in the twentieth century that the risk of executing the innocent is and will remain one of the strongest objections to capital punishment.

Defenders of the death penalty have responded to this objection in two ways. Some want to challenge our research and the adequacy of the evidence we cite in support of the twenty-three cases where we believe an innocent person was executed. Reasonable and unbiased judges, they claim, would not be persuaded by the evidence that has persuaded us. These critics remind us that no court, chief executive, or other official body has ever acknowledged that an innocent person has been executed in this century—as if that constituted evidence that it has never happened. Other critics are willing to concede, at least for the sake of argument, that some two dozen erroneous executions may have occurred, but they insist that this is a small price to pay for the benefits they claim the death penalty provides. They further argue that reasonable people would no more abolish the death penalty because of the risk of fatal error than they would outlaw truck driving because of the risk of fatal accidents.

Both these objections deserve serious thought and a considered reply. In regard to the initial objection, we would grant that more research is desirable regarding the cases of wrongful execution that we cite; we would welcome the interest of other scholars, journalists, writers, and civil rights advocates in reopening all these cases to public scrutiny. Unfortunately, much of the further research that needs to be done is likely to prove inconclusive or impossible to carry out. More often than not, the important witnesses and other participants in the case are dead, and the relevant physical evidence has long ago vanished or been destroyed. Future research efforts might very well leave us no better informed than we are now.

Our investigations lead us to believe that the small number of cases we have identified in which an innocent person was executed is an indication not of the fairness of the system but rather of its finality. Very few death penalty cases in this century have attracted the sustained interest of persons in a position to undertake the research necessary to challenge successfully a guilty verdict meted out to a defendant later executed; funds are rarely available to investigate execution of the allegedly innocent (there are not even adequate funds available to investigate thoroughly those in prison who claim to be innocent).

The 1974 Florida case of James Adams, discussed [in chapter 7 of this volume] . . . , is a perfect example. Once the defendant is dead, the best source of evidence is gone. So is the primary motive for reinvestigating the case. Further, . . . the limited resources of the defense lawyers (the ones in the best position to direct additional investigations into their deceased client's guilt or innocence) are quickly absorbed by the legal battles to save the lives of others still on death row. The result is that, as time passes, the possibility of continuing an effective investigation slowly disappears.

Neither is there now (nor has there ever been) any organization whose purpose is to gather and sift the evidence of a defendant's possible innocence after that defendant has been executed. The best-known previous investigators of wrongful convictions—Yale law professor Edwin Borchard; federal judge Jerome Frank and his attorney-daughter, Barbara; journalists Edward Radin and Eugene Block—worked essentially alone and ignored the claims to innocence of those already executed. Erle Stanley Gardner's Court of Last Resort did a remarkable job of investigating a few capital cases. . . . But we know of no instance where the Court attempted to reopen any case of allegedly erroneous execution. Moreover, that organization was in business less than two decades, and it never confined its attention to defendants under a death sentence. Centurion Ministries, founded in 1981 by James McCloskey, has helped free many innocent prisoners—including one on death row. But it understandably devotes none of its slender resources to investigating a case after a prisoner has been executed.

As if these difficulties were not enough, no matter how much evidence we might gather concerning a given case, there is simply no tribunal before which it can be placed and from which an authoritative posthumous judgment can be rendered on the innocence of an executed convict. Bluntly put, there is no forum . . . for hearing the case for innocence of someone already dead. We are necessarily confined to less formal methods and procedures, whose adequacy can always be challenged by the skeptic.

As for the fact that responsible officials have never publicly acknowledged that an innocent person has been lawfully executed, we do not think their silence ought to be taken as evidence that the system makes no fatal errors. Those involved in pressing a death penalty case from arrest to execution, whether private citizens or government officials, not surprisingly tend to close ranks and resist admission of error. More distressingly, they have been known to obstruct others even from exploring charges of erroneous execution—as every serious investigator of wrongful convictions has pointed out.

A silent witness or the real culprit is even less likely to step forward if their failure to do so earlier has already cost the life of an innocent person. . . . After sending a defendant to death—or ever death row—few are willing to admit the possibility that they were in error.

Finally, if one concedes . . . that there have been hundreds of innocent persons wrongly convicted of murder, then it seems strange and implausible to insist that the evidence is wholly insufficient to show that even one innocent person has ever been executed in the United States during this century. Are we to believe that although hundreds of demonstrably innocent persons have been erroneously imprisoned, *not even one* has been wrongfully executed? Surely there is nothing about the penalty of death and the way it is administered to make us sanguine on this point, nothing to ensure that the innocent have never been and will never be executed. On the contrary, it seems to us a virtual certainty that some, perhaps many, innocent persons—one can only speculate on the exact number—have been executed, just as hundreds have been imprisoned.

One cornerstone of this judgment is to be found in the more than two dozen cases we have identified where at the very last—days, hours, or minutes prior to execution—a reprieve or stay saved the life of a prisoner later exonerated. . . .

The second response death penalty advocates make to our claim that innocents have been executed concedes that terrible errors have occurred—and will occur again—but argues that this is a price worth paying. Our reply to this objection rests on two considerations. First, there is only the weakest possible analogy between a state-imposed system of capital punishment on the one hand and risky but lawful practices such as undersea exploration, skydiving, mining, and the ordinary operation of motor vehicles on the other. In all these activities, innocent people are occasionally killed. But although no one engaging in them behaves in an intentionally lethal manner toward anyone, the death penalty *is* deliberately—and inherently—lethal. None of the activities mentioned above coerces its participants; the death penalty most assuredly does coerce its victim. Interfering with skydiving or mining by prohibiting it under law would constitute an unreasonable interference with voluntary behavior (and on unacceptable paternalistic grounds). Abolishing the death penalty would interfere with no one's liberty.

Deciding to engage in practices that take "statistical lives" (the predictable death of innocents unidentifiable in advance in the course of risky but not intentionally lethal social practices) is justifiable only because there are otherwise unobtainable benefits to society (and given the presumed tacit consent we all give to life in a society in which such risks are created). We believe the death penalty provides no social benefits not achievable by long-term imprisonment. In any event, the costs outweigh any possible benefit by so much that a fair and reasonable cost/benefit analysis of capital punishment in our society would surely favor its abolition.

Crime control or social defense, in the form of incapacitation (*preventing* the killer from killing again) and deterrence (*discouraging* others from imitating the killer), and tax economies are the chief benefits allegedly flowing from use of the death penalty. Some want to add as further benefits such things as giving the public what it wants, vindicating the authority of the law against murder, and enhancing respect for human life. We believe, on the contrary, that these "benefits" are illusory or worse. To be sure, this is a complex matter that cannot be discussed here in the detail it deserves. Nevertheless, we believe that the existing evidence (in sources readily available in libraries throughout the nation) clearly establishes several important points:

- There is no adequate evidence that the death penalty is a better deterrent than long-term imprisonment. Such meager evidence as there is (all of it developed since the mid-1970s, relying on highly technical statistical methods, and none of it produced by criminologists) is of little or no significance when measured against the counterevidence of more numerous and more reliable investigations.

- Incapacitation can be achieved for all convicted murderers, as for persons convicted of other crimes, with existing forms of imprisonment. States such as Michigan, Wisconsin, and Minnesota—none of which has used the death penalty in this century—have amply demonstrated the feasibility of incarceration as an alternative to the death penalty.

- The public wants protection from victimization at the hands of criminals. However, survey research purporting to show overwhelming popular support for the death penalty in recent years is extremely misleading, in that it usually measures support for the death penalty against the implicit alternative of mild punishment—or no punishment whatever—for the offender. If given the choice, public opinion favors life imprisonment and compensation to the victim's family over the death penalty.

- The costs of a system of capital punishment are considerable and irreducible, unless we are prepared to sacrifice altogether the rights of due process and equal protection of the law that we all depend on—and that all who are accused and convicted deserve. A criminal justice system (like Michigan's or Canada's) that never raises the controversial question of the death penalty in a murder case is far less expensive to operate than a system (like California's or Texas's) that regularly raises the issue in every case of aggravated murder.

- Vindicating the law and showing due respect for the lives and welfare of all citizens does not require killing any prisoners already safely in custody. If anything, the nation's selective—that is, arbitrary and discriminatory—use of the death penalty constantly risks bringing the whole system of criminal justice into disrepute. "Justice" is not obtained by a punishment that is based as much on issues of race or social class or quality of attorney as it is on the heinousness of the crime.

Believing these propositions, as we do, we obviously cannot believe that the benefits of capital punishment outweigh its social and economic costs.

What, then, is to be done with a criminal justice system like ours that has been shown to be so prone to error? There seem to be only two alternatives. One is to remove the causes of error, or at least render them rare, and preserve the death penalty for very occasional use in only the gravest cases. The other is to accept the impossibility of doing much more than has already been done to reduce the risk of error, and then to eliminate the worst harm that can result from the inevitable errors by not executing (or holding under death sentence) anyone. We favor the latter alternative. Perhaps the most convincing argument for our conclusion is to be found by exploring the former alternative more fully.

Previous investigators of wrongful convictions in our system of criminal justice who brought to the subject extensive training and experience in the criminal law—notably, Edwin Borchard in 1932 and Jerome and Barbara Frank in 1957—were naturally led to propose various reforms that they believed would appreciably reduce the likelihood of miscarriages of justice. Of all such proposals, those by Borchard were the more extensive and will serve here to illustrate the futility of this approach to the problem.

Borchard advocated seven specific changes in criminal procedure: (1) prior convictions of the defendant, if any, should be introduced into evidence only in regard to sentencing, and thus only after conviction; (1a) if the preceding proposal is thought to be too restrictive, then prior convictions may be cited during trial insofar as they are for crimes like the one(s) for which the defendant is currently being tried; (2) no confession may be introduced as evidence unless it was given before a magistrate and in the presence of witnesses; (3) expert witnesses ought to be in the employ of the public and not retained solely by the defense or by the prosecution; (4) indigent defendants ought to have the services of a public defender; (5) in cases where a conviction may have been erroneous, an independent investigative body ought to be appointed to review the case; (6) appellate courts ought to be empowered to review not only the law under which the defendant was convicted but also the facts introduced into evidence against him or her; (7) no death sentence ought to issue against a defendant convicted solely on circumstantial evidence.

In the seventy years since these proposals were first introduced, no jurisdiction has seen fit to adopt them all. Except for one or another version of proposal (4)—public defenders for the poor—none has been adopted by all jurisdictions. In particular, no jurisdiction has adopted the most restrictive of Borchard's ideas, proposals (2)—limits on admissibility of confession—and (7)—no death penalty on circumstantial evidence alone. We see no likelihood that in the future these proposals, or any like them, will find favor with the American bar and bench. And without widespread support, they will continue to be merely the utopian ideas of an all-but-forgotten Ivy League law professor.

But suppose, contrary to fact, that all Borchard's proposals had been commonly part of American criminal law throughout the twentieth century. Would they have eliminated all or at least a large fraction of the cases recorded in this book? They would not. To understand why, one must remember that the erroneous convictions . . . [we have documented] rest on factors not touched by Borchard's proposed remedies and often immune to later review: mistaken eyewitness testimony, unreliable polygraph evidence, perjury by prosecution witnesses, suppression of exculpatory evidence, sloppy (not to mention corrupt) police investigation, and false confession by the accused. Most of these factors cannot be eliminated by changes in the rules of criminal procedure. Those that can (for example, not allowing the prosecution to use in court a defendant's confession) would require such drastic revision of the rules as to be impossible to enact. Hence, miscarriages of justice in capital (and noncapital) cases will continue. We deceive ourselves if we think otherwise.

Current capital punishment law already embodies several features that probably reduce the likelihood of executing the innocent. These include abolition of mandatory death penalties, bifurcation of the capital trial into two distinct phases (the first concerned solely with the guilt of the offender, and the second devoted to the issue of sentence), and the requirement of automatic appellate review of a capital conviction and sentence. All three developments have taken place within the pasty twenty years. Yet, . . . more than one hundred miscarriages of justice in homicide cases (including forty innocent defendants who were sent to death row) occurred during these same years—despite these protections. Like the procedural reforms urged by Borchard in the 1930s, the reforms actually adopted in the 1970s leave untouched the major causes of grave error. They also do not alter the fact that most of the errors caught in time are corrected not thanks to the system but in spite of the system—that is, in spite of the obstacles to reinvestigating and reopening a case, to persuading a higher court to reconsider, and to securing executive intervention to halt the march to the execution chamber.

Sixty years ago the German refugee scholar and lawyer Max Hirschberg, in his study of wrongful convictions, rightly observed, "Innocent men wrongfully convicted are countless. It is the duty of science to open our eyes to this terrible fact. It is the duty of ethics to rouse indolent and indifferent hearts." As for capital punishment, he added, "*Every* doubt, and not merely 'reasonable' doubt, should be over before a death sentence is imposed." But, as Hirschberg must have realized, it is impossible to operate a criminal justice system in which "every doubt" is resolved in favor of the accused. His demand, like Borchard's reforms, simply cannot be implemented in practice. Against the background of sixty years of studying the problem, from Borchard's day to our own, it is absurd to grope any further in the forlorn hope of eliminating the risk of executing the innocent by reforming criminal procedure.

If it is impossible, for diverse reasons, to introduce into the criminal justice system reforms that would appreciably reduce the likelihood of fatal error in capital cases, then we must live with a system essentially like the present one—and expect more errors in the decades ahead to be added to those [already] documented. . . . Many Americans seem willing to accept such errors because they believe that the really brutal killers—a multiple murderer like Gary Gilmore or a serial murderer like Ted Bundy, for example—simply *must* be executed; they believe that justice for the victims requires no less. Isn't it worth it to be able to punish cunning and remorseless killers with a richly deserved death?

There are many replies to this rhetorical question, but [our] argument . . . parries it with a counterquestion: What reason is there to believe that our criminal justice system can effectively distinguish between the Gilmores and Bundys who are guilty and arguably "deserve" to die, and the Zimmermans, Domers, and Brandleys who unarguably do not? The evidence is starkly against the capacity of police, prosecutors, witnesses, jurors, judges— the people on whom the system depends—to make this distinction with unfailing and consistent perfection, as the unimpeachable record shows.

The history of capital punishment in Western civilization might well be said to have begun with the execution of the innocent—Socrates in Athens in 399 B.C. and Jesus in Jerusalem in A.D. 30. In the centuries from those days to the present, countless others who were innocent have been put to death. Most were not famous; their names, if remembered at all, are known but to a few. Just a century ago, Illinois executed three of the Haymarket anarchists—August Spies, Adolph Fischer, and George Engel—only to have them all later exonerated by Governor Altgeld (one of the rare instances in any century that such an error has been officially admitted). What errors of the same sort in our time will historians record a century from now?

Voltaire's naive Candide, despite the endless folly and horror he encounters, stoutly maintains that his mentor, Doctor Pangloss, is right—we *do* live in "the best of all possible worlds." But Candide's beloved, the no-nonsense Cunigunde, disagrees. We side with her; we believe our world could be made significantly better by ending the death penalty for every crime, once and for all. We agree also with Voltaire's younger contemporary, the Marquis de Lafayette, who uttered these oft-quoted words: "Till the infallibility of human judgment shall have been proved to me, I shall demand the abolition of the death penalty."

13

The Morality of Anger

Walter Berns

Until recently, my business did not require me to think about the punishment of criminals in general or the legitimacy and efficacy of capital punishment in particular. In a vague way, I was aware of the disagreement among professionals concerning the purpose of punishment—whether it was intended to deter others, to rehabilitate the criminal, or to pay him back—but like most laymen I had no particular reason to decide which purpose was right or to what extent they may all have been right. I did know that retribution was held in ill repute among criminologists and jurists—to them, retribution was a fancy name for revenge, and revenge was barbaric—and, of course, I knew that capital punishment had the support only of policemen, prison guards, and some local politicians, the sort of people Arthur Koestler calls "hanghards" (Philadelphia's Mayor Rizzo comes to mind). The intellectual community denounced it as both unnecessary and immoral. It was the phenomenon of Simon Wiesenthal that allowed me to understand why the intellectuals were wrong and why the police, the politicians, and the majority of the voters were right: We punish criminals principally in order to pay them back, and we execute the worst of them out of moral necessity. Anyone who respects Wiesenthal's mission will be driven to the same conclusion.

Of course, not everyone will respect that mission. It will strike the busy man—I mean the sort of man who sees things only in the light cast by a concern for his own interests—as somewhat bizarre. Why should anyone devote his life—more than thirty years of it!—exclusively to the task of

From *For Capital Punishment: Crime and the Morality of the Death Penalty*, by Walter Berns. Copyright © 1979 by Walter Berns. Reprinted by permission of Basic Books, Inc., Publisher.

hunting down the Nazi war criminals who survived World War II and escaped punishment? Wiesenthal says his conscience forcès him "to bring the guilty ones to trial." But why punish them? What do we hope to accomplish now by punishing SS Obersturmbannführer Adolf Eichmann or SS Obersturmbannführer Franz Stangl or someday—who knows?—Reichsleiter Martin Bormann? We surely don't expect to rehabilitate them, and it would be foolish to think that by punishing them we might thereby deter others. The answer, I think, is clear: We want to punish them in order *to pay them back*. We think they must be made to pay for their crimes with their lives, and we think that we, the survivors of the world they violated, may legitimately exact that payment because we, too, are their victims. By punishing them, we demonstrate that there are laws that bind men across generations as well as across (and within) nations, that we are not simply isolated individuals, each pursuing his selfish interests and connected with others by a mere contract to live and let live. To state it simply, Wiesenthal allows us to see that it is right, morally right, to be angry with criminals and to express that anger publicly, officially, and in an appropriate manner, which may require the worst of them to be executed.

Modern civil-libertarian opponents of capital punishment do not understand this. They say that to execute a criminal is to deny his human dignity; they also say that the death penalty is not useful, that nothing useful is accomplished by executing anyone. Being utilitarians, they are essentially selfish men, distrustful of passion, who do not understand the connection between anger and justice, and between anger and human dignity.

Anger is expressed or manifested on those occasions when someone has acted in a manner that is thought to be unjust, and one of its origins is the opinion that men are responsible, and should be held responsible, for what they do. Thus, as Aristotle teaches us, anger is accompanied not only by the pain caused by the one who is the object of anger, but by the pleasure arising from the expectation of inflicting revenge on someone who is thought to deserve it. We can become angry with an inanimate object (the door we run into and then kick in return) only by foolishly attributing responsibility to it, and we cannot do that for long, which is why we do not think of returning later to revenge ourselves on the door. For the same reason, we cannot be more than momentarily angry with any one creature other than man; only a fool and worse would dream of taking revenge on a dog. And, finally, we tend to pity rather than to be angry with men who—because they are insane, for example—are not responsible for their acts. Anger, then, is a very human passion not only because only a human being can be angry, but also because anger acknowledges the humanity of its objects: it holds them accountable for what they do. And in holding particular men responsible, it pays them the respect that is due them as men. Anger recognizes that only men have the capacity to be moral beings and, in so doing, acknowledges the dignity of human beings. Anger is somehow connected with justice, and it is this that modern penology has not understood; it tends, on the whole, to regard anger as a selfish indulgence.

Anger can, of course, be that; and if someone does not become angry with an insult or an injury suffered unjustly, we tend to think he does not think much of himself. But it need not be selfish, not in the sense of being provoked only by an injury suffered by oneself. There were many angry men in America when President Kennedy was killed; one of them—Jack Ruby—took it upon himself to exact the punishment that, if indeed deserved, ought to have been exacted by the law. There were perhaps even angrier men when Martin Luther King, Jr., was killed, for King, more than anyone else at the time, embodied a people's quest for justice; the anger—more, the "black rage"—expressed on that occasion was simply a manifestation of the great change that had occurred among black men in America, a change wrought in large part by King and his associates in the civil-rights movement: the servility and fear of the past had been replaced by pride and anger, and the treatment that had formerly been accepted as a matter of course or as if it were deserved was now seen for what it was, unjust and unacceptable. King preached love, but the movement he led depended on anger as well as love, and that anger was not despicable, being neither selfish nor unjustified. On the contrary, it was a reflection of what was called solidarity and may more accurately be called a profound caring for others, black for other blacks, white for blacks, and, in the world King was trying to build, American for other Americans. If men are not saddened when someone else suffers, or angry when someone else suffers unjustly, the implication is that they do not care for anyone other than themselves or that they lack some quality that befits a man. When we criticize them for this, we acknowledge that they ought to care for others. If men are not angry when a neighbor suffers at the hands of a criminal, the implication is that their moral faculties have been corrupted, that they are not good citizens.

Criminals are properly the objects of anger, and the perpetrators of terrible crimes—for example, Lee Harvey Oswald and James Earl Ray—are properly the objects of great anger. They have done more than inflict an injury on an isolated individual; they have violated the foundations of trust and friendship, the necessary elements of a moral community, the only community worth living in. A moral community, unlike a hive of bees or a hill of ants, is one whose members are expected freely to obey the laws and, unlike those in a tyranny, are trusted to obey the laws. The criminal has violated that trust, and in so doing has injured not merely his immediate victim but the community as such. He has called into question the very possibility of that community by suggesting that men cannot be trusted to respect freely the property, the person, and the dignity of those with whom they are associated. If, then, men are not angry when someone else is robbed, raped, or murdered, the implication is that no moral community exists, because those men do not care for anyone other than themselves. Anger is an expression of that caring, and society needs men who care for one another, who share their pleasures and their pains, and do so for the sake of the others. It is the passion that can cause us to act for reasons having nothing to do with selfish or mean calculation; indeed, when educated, it can become a generous passion, the passion that protects the community or country by demanding punishment for its enemies. It is the stuff from which heroes are made.

A moral community is not possible without anger and the moral indignation that accompanies it. Thus the most powerful attack on capital punishment was written by a man, Albert Camus, who denied the legitimacy of anger and moral indignation by denying the very possibility of a moral community in our time. The anger expressed in our world, he said, is nothing but hypocrisy. His novel *L'Etranger* (variously translated as *The Stranger* or *The Outsider*) is a brilliant portrayal of what Camus insisted is our world, a world deprived of God, as he put it. It is a world we would not choose to live in and one that Camus, the hero of the French Resistance, disdained. Nevertheless, the novel is a modern masterpiece, and Meursault, its antihero (for a world without anger can have no heroes), is a murderer.

He is a murderer whose crime is excused, even as his lack of hypocrisy is praised, because the universe, we are told, is "benignly indifferent" to how we live or what we do. Of course, the law is not indifferent; the law punished Meursault and it threatens to punish us if we do as he did. But Camus the novelist teaches us that the law is simply a collection of arbitrary conceits. The people around Meursault apparently were not indifferent; they expressed dismay at his lack of attachment to his mother and disapprobation of his crime. But Camus the novelist teaches us that other people are hypocrites. They pretend not to know what Camus the opponent of capital punishment tells: namely, that "our civilization has lost the only values that, in a certain way, can justify that penalty . . . [the existence of] a truth or a principle that is superior to man." There is no basis for friendship and no moral law; therefore, no one, not even a murderer, can violate the terms of friendship or break that law; and there is no basis for the anger that we express when someone breaks that law. The only thing we share as men, the only thing that connects us one to another, is a "solidarity against death," and a judgment of capital punishment "upsets" that solidarity. The purpose of human life is to stay alive.

Like Meursault, Macbeth was a murderer, and like *L'Etranger,* Shakespeare's *Macbeth* is the story of a murder; but there the similarity ends. As Lincoln said, "Nothing equals *Macbeth.*" He was comparing it with the other Shakespearean plays he knew, the plays he had "gone over perhaps as frequently as any unprofessional reader . . . *Lear, Richard Third, Henry Eighth, Hamlet*"; but I think he meant to say more than that none of these equals *Macbeth*. I think he meant that no other literary work equals it. "It is wonderful," he said. *Macbeth* is wonderful because, to say nothing more here, it teaches us the awesomeness of the commandment "Thou shalt not kill."

What can a dramatic poet tell us about murder? More, probably, than anyone else, if he is a poet worthy of consideration, and yet nothing that does not inhere in the act itself. In *Macbeth,* Shakespeare shows us murders committed in a political world by a man so driven by ambition to rule that world that he becomes a tyrant. He shows us also the consequences, which were terrible, worse even than Macbeth feared. The cosmos rebelled, turned into chaos by his deeds. He shows a world that was not "benignly indifferent" to what we call crimes and especially to murder, a world constituted by laws divine as well as human, and Macbeth violated the most awful of those laws. Because the world was so constituted, Macbeth suffered the torments of the great and the damned, torments far beyond the "practice" of any physician. He had known glory and had deserved the respect and affection of king, countrymen, army, friends, and wife; and he lost it all. At the end he was reduced to saying that life "is a tale told by an idiot, full of sound and fury, signifying nothing"; yet, in spite of the horrors provoked in us by his acts, he excites no anger in us. We pity him; even so, we understand the anger of his countrymen and the dramatic necessity of his death. *Macbeth* is a play about ambition, murder, tyranny; about horror, anger, vengeance, and perhaps more than any other of Shakespeare's plays, justice. Because of justice, Macbeth has to die, not by his own hand—he will not "play the Roman fool, and die on [his] sword"— but at the hand of the avenging Macduff. The dramatic necessity of his death would appear to rest on its *moral* necessity. Is that right? Does this play conform to our sense of what a murder means? Lincoln thought it was "wonderful."

Surely Shakespeare's is a truer account of murder than the one provided by Camus, and by truer I mean truer to our moral sense of what a murder is and what the consequences that attend it must be. Shakespeare shows us vengeful men because there is something in the souls of men—then and now—that requires such crimes to be revenged. Can we imagine a world that does not take its revenge on the man who kills Macduff's wife and children? (Can we imagine the play in which Macbeth does not die?) Can we imagine a people that does not hate murderers? (Can we imagine a world where Meursault is an outsider only because he does not *pretend* to be outraged by murder?) Shakespeare's poetry could not have been written out of the moral sense that the death penalty's opponents insist we ought to have. Indeed, the issue of capital punishment can be said to turn on whether Shakespeare's or Camus' is the more telling account of murder.

There is a sense in which punishment may be likened to dramatic poetry. Dramatic poetry depicts men's actions because men are revealed in, or make themselves known through, their actions; and the essence of a human action, according to Aristotle, consists in its being virtuous or vicious. Only a ruler or a contender for rule can act with the freedom and on a scale that allows the virtuousness or viciousness of human deeds to be fully displayed. Macbeth was such a man, and in his fall, brought about by his own acts, and in the consequent suffering he endured, is revealed the meaning of morality. In *Macbeth* the majesty of the moral law is demonstrated to us; as I said, it teaches us the awesomeness of the commandment Thou shalt not kill. In a similar fashion, the punishments imposed by the legal order remind us of the reign of the moral order; not only do they remind us of it, but by enforcing its prescriptions, they enhance the dignity of the legal order in the eyes of moral men, in the eyes of those decent citizens who cry out "for gods who will avenge injustice." That is especially important in a self-governing community, a community that gives laws to itself.

If the laws were understood to be divinely inspired or, in the extreme case, divinely given, they would enjoy all the dignity that the opinions of men can grant and all the dignity they require to ensure their being obeyed by most of the men living under them. Like Duncan in the opinion of Macduff, the laws would be "the Lord's anointed," and would be obeyed even as Macduff obeyed the laws of the Scottish kingdom. Only a Macbeth would challenge them, and only a Meursault would ignore them. But the laws of the United States are not of this description; in fact, among the proposed amendments that became the Bill of Rights was one declaring, not that all power comes from God, but rather "that all power is originally vested in, and consequently derives from the people"; and this proposal was dropped only because it was thought to be redundant: the Constitution's preamble said essentially the same thing, and what we know as the Tenth Amendment reiterated it. So Madison proposed to make the Constitution venerable in the minds of the people, and Lincoln, in an early speech, went so far as to say that a "political religion" should be made of it. They did not doubt that the Constitution and the laws made pursuant to it would be supported by "enlightened reason," but fearing that enlightened reason would be in short supply, they sought to augment it. The laws of the United States would be obeyed by some men because they could hear and understand "the voice of enlightened reason," and by other men because they would regard the laws with that "veneration which time bestows on everything."

Supreme Court justices have occasionally complained of our habit of making "constitutionality synonymous with wisdom." But the extent to which the Constitution is venerated and its authority accepted depends on the compatibility of its rules with our moral sensibilities; despite its venerable character, the Constitution is not the only source of these moral sensibilities. There was even a period, before slavery was abolished by the Thirteenth Amendment, when the Constitution was regarded by some very moral men as an abomination: Garrison called it "a covenant with death and an agreement with Hell," and there were honorable men holding important political offices and judicial appointments who refused to enforce the Fugitive Slave Law even though its constitutionality had been affirmed. In time this opinion spread far beyond the ranks of the original abolitionists until those who held it composed a constitutional majority of the people, and slavery was abolished.

But Lincoln knew that more than amendments were required to make the Constitution once more worthy of the veneration of moral men. That is why, in the Gettysburg Address, he made the principle of the Constitution an inheritance from "our fathers." That it should be so esteemed is especially important in a self-governing nation that gives laws to itself, because it is only a short step from the principle that the laws are merely a product of one's own will to the opinion that the only consideration that informs the law is self-interest; and this opinion is only one remove from lawlessness. A nation of simple self-interested men will soon enough perish from the earth.

It was not an accident that Lincoln spoke as he did at Gettysburg or that he chose as the occasion for his words the dedication of a cemetery built on a portion of the most significant battlefield of the Civil War. Two and a half years earlier, in his First Inaugural Address, he had said that Americans, north and south, were not and must not be enemies, but friends. Passion had strained but must not be allowed to break the bonds of affection that tied them one to another. He closed by saying this: "The mystic chords of memory, stretching from every battlefield, and patriot grave, to every living heart and hearthstone, all over this broad land, will yet swell the chorus of the Union, when again touched, as surely they will be, by the better angels of our nature." The chords of memory that would swell the chorus of the Union could be touched, even by a man of Lincoln's stature, only on the most solemn occasions, and in the life of a nation no occasion is more solemn than the burial of the patriots who have died defending it on the field of battle. War is surely an evil, but as Hegel said, it is not an "absolute evil." It exacts the supreme sacrifice, but precisely because of that it can call forth such sublime rhetoric as Lincoln's. His words at Gettysburg serve to remind Americans in particular of what Hegel said people in general needed to know, and could be made to know by means of war and the sacrifices demanded of them in wars: namely, that their country is something more than a "civil society" the purpose of which is simply the protection of individual and selfish interests.

Capital punishment, like Shakespeare's dramatic and Lincoln's political poetry (and it is surely that, and was understood by him to be that), serves to remind us of the majesty of the moral order that is embodied in our law, and of the terrible consequences of its breach. The law must not be understood to be merely a statute that we enact or repeal at our will, and obey or disobey at our convenience—especially not the criminal law. Wherever law is regarded as merely statutory, men will soon enough disobey it, and will learn how to do so without any inconvenience to themselves. The criminal law must possess a dignity far beyond that possessed by mere statutory enactment or utilitarian and self-interested calculations. The most powerful means we have to give it that dignity is to authorize it to impose the ultimate penalty. The criminal law must be made awful, by which I mean inspiring, or commanding "profound respect or reverential fear." It must remind us of the moral order by which alone we can live as *human* beings, and in America, now that the Supreme Court has outlawed banishment, the only punishment that can do this is capital punishment.

The founder of modern criminology, the eighteenth-century Italian Cesare Beccaria, opposed both banishment and capital punishment because he understood that both were inconsistent with the principle of self-interest, and self-interest was the basis of the political order he favored. If a man's first or only duty is to himself, of course he will prefer his money to his country; he will also prefer his money to his brother. In fact, he will prefer his brother's money to his brother, and a people of this description, or a country that understands itself in this Beccarian manner, can put the mark of Cain on no one. For the same reason, such a country can have no legitimate reason to execute its criminals, or, indeed, to punish them in any manner. What would be accomplished by punishment in such a place? Punishment arises out of the demand for justice, and justice is demanded by angry, morally indignant men; its purpose is to satisfy that moral indignation and thereby promote the law-abidingness that, it is assumed, accompanies it. But the principle of self-interest denies the moral basis of that indignation.

Not only will a country based solely on self-interest have no legitimate reason to punish; it may have no need to punish. It may be able to solve what we call the crime problem by substituting a law of contracts for a law of crimes. According to Beccaria's social contract, men agree to yield their natural freedom to the "sovereign" in exchange for his promise to keep the peace. As it becomes more difficult for the sovereign to fulfill his part of the contract, there is a demand that he be made to pay for his nonperformance. From this comes compensation or insurance schemes embodied in statutes whereby the sovereign (or state), being unable to keep the peace by punishing criminals, agrees to compensate its contractual partners for injuries suffered at the hands of criminals, injuries the police are unable to prevent. The insurance policy takes the place of law enforcement and the *posse comitatus,* and John Wayne and Gary Cooper give way to Mutual of Omaha. There is no anger in this kind of law, and none (or no reason for any) in the society. The principle can be carried further still. If we ignore the victim (and nothing we do can restore his life anyway), there would appear to be no reason why—the worth of a man being his price, as Beccaria's teacher, Thomas Hobbes, put it—coverage should not be extended to the losses incurred in a murder. If we ignore the victim's sensibilities (and what are they but absurd vanities?), there would appear to be no reason why—the worth of a woman being *her* price—coverage should not be extended to the losses incurred in a rape. Other examples will no doubt suggest themselves.

This might appear to be an almost perfect solution to what we persist in calling the crime problem, achieved without risking the terrible things sometimes done by an angry people. A people that is not angry with criminals will not be able to deter crime, but a people fully covered by insurance has no need to deter crime: they will be insured against all the losses they can, in principle, suffer. What is now called crime can be expected to increase in volume, of course, and this will cause an increase in the premiums paid, directly or in the form of taxes. But it will no longer be necessary to apprehend, try, and punish criminals, which now costs Americans more than $1.5 billion a month (and is increasing at an annual rate of about 15 percent), and one can buy a lot of insurance for $1.5 billion. There is this difficulty, as Rousseau put it: To exclude anger from the human community is to concentrate all the passions in a "self-interest of the meanest sort," and such a place would not be fit for human habitation.

When, in 1976, the Supreme Court declared death to be a constitutional penalty, it decided that the United States was not that sort of country; most of us, I think, can appreciate that judgment. We want to live among people who do not value their possessions more than their citizenship, who do not think exclusively or even primarily of their own rights, people whom we can depend on even as they exercise their rights, and whom we can trust, which is to say, people who, even in the absence of a policeman, will not assault our bodies or steal our possessions, and might even come to our assistance when we need it, and who stand ready, when the occasion demands it, to risk their lives in defense of their country. If we are of the opinion that the United States may rightly ask of its citizens this awful sacrifice, then we are also of the opinion that it may rightly impose the most awful penalty; if it may rightly honor its heroes, it may rightly execute the worst of its criminals. By doing so, it will remind its citizens that it is a country worthy of heroes.

14

Does It Matter If the Death Penalty Is Arbitrarily Administered?

Stephen Nathanson

I

In this article, I will examine the argument that capital punishment ought to be abolished because it has been and will continue to be imposed in an arbitrary manner.

This argument has been central to discussions of capital punishment since the Supreme Court ruling in the 1972 case *Furman* v. *Georgia*. In a 5–4 decision, the Court ruled that capital punishment as then administered was unconstitutional. Although the Court issued several opinions, the problem of arbitrariness is widely seen as having played a central role in the Court's thinking. As Charles Black, Jr., has put it,

> . . . The decisive ground of the 1972 Furman case anti-capital punishment ruling—the ground persuasive to the marginal justices needed for a majority—was that, out of a large number of persons "eligible" in law for the punishment of death, a few were selected as if at random, by no stated (or perhaps statable) criteria, while all the rest suffered the lesser penalty of imprisonment.[1]

Among those justices moved by the arbitrariness issue, some stressed the discriminatory aspects of capital punishment, the tendency of legally irrelevant factors like race and economic status to determine the severity

From *Philosophy & Public Affairs* 14, no. 2 (Spring 1985). Copyright © 1985 by Princeton University Press. Reprinted with permission of Princeton University Press.

of sentence, while others emphasized the "freakish" nature of the punishment, the fact that it is imposed on a miniscule percentage of murderers who are not obviously more deserving of death than others.

Although the Supreme Court approved new death penalty laws in *Gregg* v. *Georgia* (1976), the reasoning of *Furman* was not rejected. Rather, a majority of the Court determined that Georgia's new laws would make arbitrary imposition of the death penalty much less likely. By amending procedures and adding criteria which specify aggravating and mitigating circumstances, Georgia had succeeded in creating a system of "guided discretion," which the Court accepted in the belief that it was not likely to yield arbitrary results.

The *Gregg* decision has prompted death penalty opponents to attempt to show that "guided discretion" is an illusion. This charge has been supported in various ways. Charles Black has supported it by analyzing both the legal process of decision making in capital cases and the legal criteria for determining who is to be executed. He has argued that, appearances to the contrary, there are no meaningful standards operating in the system. Attacking from an empirical angle, William Bowers and Glenn Pierce have tried to show that even after *Furman* and under new laws, factors like race and geographic location of the trial continue to play a large role and that the criteria which are supposed to guide judgment do not separate those sentenced into meaningfully distinct groups. Perhaps the most shocking conclusion of Bowers and Pierce concerns the large role played by the race of the killer and the victims, as the chances of execution are by far the greatest when blacks kill whites and least when whites kill blacks.[2]

The upshot of both these approaches is that "guided discretion" is not working and, perhaps, cannot work. If this is correct and if the argument from arbitrariness is accepted, then it would appear that a return from *Gregg* to *Furman* is required. That is, the Court should once again condemn capital punishment as unconstitutional.

I have posed these issues in terms of the Supreme Court's deliberations. Nonetheless, for opponents of the death penalty, the freakishness of its imposition and the large role played by race and other irrelevant factors are a moral as well as a legal outrage. For them, there is a fundamental moral injustice in the practice of capital punishment and not just a departure from the highest legal and constitutional standards.

II

The argument from arbitrariness has not, however, been universally accepted, either as a moral or a constitutional argument. Ernest van den Haag, an articulate and long-time defender of the death penalty, has claimed that the Supreme Court was wrong to accept this argument in the first place and thus that the evidence of arbitrariness presented by Black, Bowers and Pierce and others is beside the point. In his words:

> . . . the abolitionist argument from capriciousness, or discretion, or discrimination, would be more persuasive if it were alleged that those selectively executed are not guilty. But the argument merely maintains that some other guilty but more favored persons, or groups, escape the death penalty. This is hardly sufficient for letting anyone else found guilty escape the penalty. On the contrary, that some guilty persons or groups elude it argues for extending the death penalty to them.[3]

Having attacked the appeal to arbitrariness, van den Haag goes on to spell out his own conception of the requirements of justice. He writes:

> Justice requires punishing the guilty—as many of the guilty as possible, even if only some can be punished—and sparing the innocent—as many of the innocent as possible, even if not all are spared. It would surely be wrong to treat everybody with equal injustice in preference to meting out justice at least to some. . . . [I]f the death penalty is morally just, *however discriminatorily applied to only some of the guilty,* it does remain just *in each case* in which it is applied. (emphasis added)[4]

Distinguishing sharply between the demands of justice and the demands of equality, van den Haag claims that the justice of individual punishments depends on individual guilt alone and not on whether punishments are equally distributed among the class of guilty persons.

Van den Haag's distinction between the demands of justice and the demands of equality parallels the distinction drawn by Joel Feinberg between "noncomparative" and "comparative" justice.[5] Using Feinberg's terminology, we can express van den Haag's view by saying that he believes that the justice of a particular punishment is a *noncomparative* matter. It depends solely on what a person deserves and not on how others are treated. For van den Haag, then, evidence of arbitrariness and discrimination is irrelevant, so long as those who are executed are indeed guilty and deserve their punishment.

There is no denying the plausibility of van den Haag's case. In many instances, we believe it is legitimate to punish or reward deserving individuals, even though we know that equally deserving persons are unpunished or unrewarded. Consider two cases:

A. A driver is caught speeding, ticketed, and required to pay a fine. We know that the percentage of speeders who are actually punished is extremely small, yet we would probably regard it as a joke if the driver protested that he was being treated unjustly or if someone argued that no one should be fined for speeding unless all speeders were fined.

B. A person performs a heroic act and receives a substantial reward, in addition to the respect and admiration of his fellow citizens. Because he deserves the reward, we think it just that he receive it, even though many equally heroic persons are not treated similarly. That most heroes are unsung is no reason to avoid rewarding this particular heroic individual.

Both of these instances appear to support van den Haag's claim that we should do justice whenever we can in individual cases and that failure to do justice in all cases is no reason to withhold punishment or reward from individuals.

III

Is the argument from arbitrariness completely unfounded then? Should we accept van den Haag's claim that "unequal justice is justice still"?

In response to these questions, I shall argue that van den Haag's case is not as strong as it looks and that the argument from arbitrariness can be vindicated.

As a first step in achieving this, I would like to point out that there are in fact several different arguments from arbitrariness. While some of these arguments appeal to the random and freakish nature of the death penalty, others highlight the discriminatory effects of legally irrelevant factors. Each of these kinds of arbitrariness raises different sorts of moral and legal issues.

For example, though we may acknowledge the impossibility of ticketing all speeding drivers and still favor ticketing some, we will not find every way of determining which speeders are ticketed equally just. Consider the policy of ticketing only those who travel at extremely high speeds, as opposed to that of ticketing every tenth car. Compare these with the policy of giving tickets only to speeders with beards and long hair or to speeders whose cars bear bumper stickers expressing unpopular political views. While I shall not pursue this point in detail, I take it to be obvious that these different selection policies are not all equally just or acceptable.

A second difference between versions of the argument from arbitrariness depends on whether or not it is granted that we can accurately distinguish those who deserve to die from those who do not. As van den Haag presents the argument, it assumes that we are able to make this distinction. Then, the claim is made that from this class of people who deserve to die, only some are selected for execution. The choice of those specific persons from the general class of persons who deserve to die is held to be arbitrary.

Van den Haag neglects a related argument which has been forcefully defended by Charles Black. Black's argument is that the determination of *who* deserves to die—the first step—is itself arbitrary. So his claim is not merely that arbitrary factors determine who among the deserving will be executed. His point is that the determination of who deserves to die is arbitrary. His main argument is that

> the official choices—by prosecutors, judges, juries, and governors—that divide those who are to die from those who are to live are on the whole not made, and cannot be made, under standards that are consistently meaningful and clear, but that they are often made, and in the foreseeable future will continue often to be made, under no standards at all or under pseudostandards without discoverable meaning.[6]

According to Black, even the most conscientious officials could not make principled judgments about desert in these instances, because our laws do not contain clear principles for differentiating those who deserve to die from those who do not. While I shall not try to summarize Black's analysis of the failures of post-*Furman* capital punishment statutes, it is clear that if van den Haag were to meet this argument, he would have to provide his own analysis of these laws in order to show that they do provide clear and meaningful standards. Or, he would have to examine the actual disposition of cases under these laws to show that the results have not been arbitrary. Van den Haag does not attempt to do either of these things. This seems to result from a failure to distinguish (a) the claim that judgments concerning *who deserves to die* are arbitrarily made, from (b) the claim that judgments concerning *who among the deserving shall be executed* are arbitrarily made.

Van den Haag may simply assume that the system does a decent job of distinguishing those who deserve to die from those who do not, and his assumption gains a surface plausibility because of his tendency to over-simplify the nature of the judgments which need to be made. In contrast to Black, who stresses the complexity of the legal process and the complexity of the judgments facing participants in that process, van den Haag is content to say simply that "justice requires punishing the guilty . . . and sparing the innocent." This maxim makes it look as if officials and jurors need only divide people into two neat categories, and if we think of guilt and innocence as *factual* categories, it makes it look as if the only judgment necessary is whether a person did or did not kill another human being.

In fact, the problems are much more complicated than this. Not every person who kills another human being is guilty of the same crime. Some may have committed no crime at all, if their act is judged to be justifiable homicide. Among others, they may have committed first-degree murder, second-degree murder, or some form of manslaughter. Furthermore, even if we limit our attention to those who are convicted of first-degree murder, juries must consider aggravating and mitigating circumstances in order to judge whether someone is guilty enough to deserve the death penalty. It is clear, then, that simply knowing that someone is factually guilty of killing another person is far from sufficient for determining that he deserves to die, and if prosecutors, juries, and judges do not have criteria which enable them to classify those who are guilty in a just and rational way, then their judgments about who deserves to die will necessarily be arbitrary and unprincipled.

Once we appreciate the difficulty and complexity of the judgments which must be made about guilt and desert, it is easier to see how they might be influenced by racial characteristics and other irrelevant factors. The statistics compiled by Bowers and Pierce show that blacks killing whites have the greatest chance of being executed, while whites killing blacks have the least chance of execution. What these findings strongly suggest is that officials and jurors think that the killing of a white by a black is a more serious crime than the killing of a black by a white. Hence, they judge that blacks killing whites *deserve* a more serious punishment than whites killing blacks. Given the bluntness of our ordinary judgments about desert and the complexity of the choices facing jurors and officials, it may not be surprising either that people find it difficult to make the fine discriminations required by law or that such judgments are influenced by deep-seated racial or social attitudes.

Both legal analysis and empirical studies should undermine our confidence that the legal system sorts out those who deserve to die from those who do not in a nonarbitrary manner. If we cannot be confident that those who are executed in fact deserve to die, then we ought not to allow executions to take place at all.

Because van den Haag does not distinguish this argument from other versions of the argument from arbitrariness, he simply neglects it. His omission is serious because this argument is an independent, substantial argument against the death penalty. It can stand even if other versions of the argument from arbitrariness fall.

IV

I would like now to turn to the form of the argument which van den Haag explicitly deals with and to consider whether it is vulnerable to his criticisms. Let us assume that there is a class of people whom we know to be deserving of death. Let us further assume that only some of these people are executed and that the executions are arbitrary in the sense that those executed have not committed worse crimes than those not executed. This is the situation which Justice Stewart described in *Furman*. He wrote:

> These death sentences are cruel and unusual in the same way that being struck by lightning is cruel and unusual. For of all the people convicted

of rapes and murders in 1967 and 1968, *many just as reprehensible as these,* the petitioners are among *a capriciously selected random handful* upon whom the sentence of death has in fact been imposed. (emphasis added)[7]

What is crucial here (and different from the argument previously discussed) is the assumption that we can judge the reprehensibility of both the petitioners and others convicted of similar crimes. Stewart does not deny that the petitioners deserve to die, but because other equally deserving people escape the death penalty for no legally respectable reasons, the executions of the petitioners, Stewart thought, would violate the Eighth and Fourteenth Amendments.

This is precisely the argument van den Haag rejected. We can sum up his reasons in the following rhetorical questions: How can it possibly be unjust to punish someone if he deserves the punishment? Why should it matter whether or not others equally deserving are punished?

I have already acknowledged the plausibility of van den Haag's case and offered the examples of the ticketed speeder and the rewarded hero as instances which seem to confirm his view. Nonetheless, I think that van den Haag is profoundly mistaken in thinking that the justice of a reward or punishment depends solely on whether the recipient deserves it.

Consider the following two cases which are structurally similar to A and B (given above) but which elicit different reactions:

C. I tell my class that anyone who plagiarizes will fail the course. Three students plagiarize papers, but only one receives a failing grade. The other two, in describing their motivation, win my sympathy, and I give them passing grades.

D. At my child's birthday party, I offer a prize to the child who can solve a particular puzzle. Three children, including my own, solve the puzzle. I cannot reward them all, so I give the prize to my own child.

In both cases, as in van den Haag's, only some of those deserving a reward or punishment receive it. Unlike cases A and B, however, C and D do not appear to be just, in spite of the fact that the persons rewarded or punished deserve what they get. In these cases, the justice of giving them what they deserve appears to be affected by the treatment of others.

About these cases I am inclined to say the following. The people involved have not been treated justly. It was unjust to fail the single plagiarizer and unjust to reward my child. It would have been better—because more just— to have failed no one than to have failed the single student. I would have been better to have given a prize to no one than to give the prize to my child alone.

The unfairness in both cases appears to result from the fact that the reasons for picking out those rewarded or punished are irrelevant and hence that the choice is arbitrary. If I have a stated policy of failing students who plagiarize, then it is unjust for me to pass students with whom I sympathize. Whether I am sympathetic or not is irrelevant, and I am treating the student whom I do fail unjustly because I am not acting simply on the basis of desert. Rather, I am acting on the basis of desert plus degree of sympathy. Likewise, in the case of the prize, it appears that I am preferring my own child in giving out the reward, even though I announced that receipt of the award would depend only on success in solving the puzzle.

This may be made clearer by varying the plagiarism example. Suppose that in spite of my stated policy of failing anyone who plagiarizes, I am regularly lenient toward students who seem sufficiently repentant. Suppose further that I am regularly more lenient with attractive female students than with others. Or suppose that it is only redheads or wealthy students whom I fail. If such patterns develop, we can see that whether a student fails or not does not depend simply on being caught plagiarizing. Rather, part of the explanation of a particular student's being punished is that he or she is (or is not) an attractive female, redheaded or wealthy. In these instances, I think the plagiarizers who are punished have grounds for complaint, even though they were, by the announced standards, clearly guilty and deserving of punishment.

If this conclusion is correct, then doing justice is more complicated than van den Haag realizes. He asserts that it would be "wrong to treat everybody with equal injustice in preference to meting out justice at least to some." If my assessment of cases C and D is correct, however, it is better that everyone in those instances be treated "unjustly" than that only some get what they deserve. Whether one is treated justly or not depends on how others are treated and not solely on what one deserves.[8]

In fact, van den Haag implicitly concedes this point in an interesting footnote to his essay. In considering the question of whether capital punishment is a superior deterrent, van den Haag mentions that one could test the deterrent power of the death penalty by allowing executions for murders committed on Monday, Wednesday, and Friday, while setting life imprisonment as the maximum penalty for murders committed on other days. In noting the obstacles facing such an experiment, he writes:

> . . . it is not acceptable to our sense of justice that *people guilty of the same crime would get different punishments* and that the difference would be made to depend deliberately on *a factor irrelevant to the nature of the crime* or of the criminal. (emphasis added)[9]

Given his earlier remarks about the argument from arbitrariness, this is a rather extraordinary comment, for van den Haag concedes that the justice of a punishment is not solely determined by what an individual deserves but is also a function of how equally deserving persons are treated in general.

In his case, what he finds offensive is that there is no difference between what the Monday, Wednesday, Friday murderers deserve and what the Tuesday, Thursday, Saturday, and Sunday murderers deserve. Yet the morally irrelevant factor of date is decisive in determining the severity of the punishment. Van den Haag (quite rightly) cannot swallow this.

Yet van den Haag's example is exactly parallel to the situation described by opponents of the death penalty. For, surely, the race of the criminal or victim, the economic or social status of the criminal or victim, the location of the crime or trial and other such factors are as irrelevant to the gravity of the crime and the appropriate severity of the punishment as is the day of the week on which the crime is committed. It would be as outrageous for the severity of the punishment to depend on these factors as it would be for it to depend on the day of the week on which the crime was committed.

In fact, it is more outrageous that death sentences depend on the former factors because a person can control the day of the week on which he murders in a way in which he cannot control his race or status. Moreover, we are committed to banishing the disabling effects of race and economic status from the law. Using the day of the week as a critical factor is at least not invidiously discriminatory, as it neither favors nor disfavors previously identifiable or disadvantaged groups.

In reply, one might contend that I have overlooked an important feature of van den Haag's example. He rejected the deterrence experiment not merely because the severity of punishment depended on irrelevant factors but also because the irrelevant factors were *deliberately* chosen as the basis of punishment. Perhaps it is the fact that irrelevant factors are deliberately chosen which makes van den Haag condemn the proposed experiment.

This is an important point. It certainly makes matters worse to decide deliberately to base life and death choices on irrelevant considerations. However, even if the decision is not deliberate, it remains a serious injustice if irrelevant considerations play this crucial role. Individuals might not even be aware of the influence of these factors. They might genuinely believe that their judgments are based entirely on relevant considerations. It might require painstaking research to discover the patterns underlying sentencing, but once they are known, citizens and policymakers must take them into consideration. Either the influence of irrelevant factors must be eradicated or, if we determine that this is impossible, we may have to alter our practices more radically.

This reasoning, of course, is just the reasoning identified with the *Furman* case. As Justice Douglas wrote:

A law that stated that anyone making more than $50,000 would be exempt from the death penalty would plainly fall, as would a law that in terms said that blacks, those who never went beyond the fifth grade in school, those who make less than $3,000 a year, or those who were unpopular or unstable should be the only people executed. A law which in the overall view reaches the same result in practice has no more sanctity than a law which in terms provides the same.[10]

The problem, in Douglas's view, was that the system left life and death decisions to the "uncontrolled discretion of judges or juries," leading to the unintended but nonetheless real result that death sentences were based on factors which had nothing to do with the nature of the crime.

What I want to stress here is that the arbitrariness and discrimination need not be purposeful or deliberate. We might discover, as critics allege, that racial prejudice is so deeply rooted in our society that prosecutors, juries, and judges cannot free themselves from prejudice when determining how severe a punishment for a crime should be. Furthermore, we might conclude that these tendencies cannot be eradicated, especially when juries are called upon to make subtle and complex assessments of cases in the light of confusing, semi-technical criteria. Hence, although no one *decides* that race will be a factor, we may *predict* that it will be a factor, and this knowledge must be considered in evaluating policies and institutions.

If factors *as irrelevant as* the day of the crime determine whether people shall live or die and if the influence of these factors is ineradicable, then we must conclude that we cannot provide a just system of punishment and even those who are guilty and deserving of the most severe punishments (like the Monday killers in van den Haag's experiment) will have a legitimate complaint that they have been treated unjustly.

I conclude, then, that the treatment of *classes* of people is relevant to determining the justice of punishments for *individuals* and van den Haag is wrong to dismiss the second form of the argument from arbitrariness. That argument succeeds in showing that capital punishment is unjust and thus provides a powerful reason for abolishing it.

V

Supporters of the death penalty might concede that serious questions of justice are raised by the influence of arbitrary factors and still deny that this shows that capital punishment ought to be abolished. They could argue that some degree of arbitrariness is present throughout the system of legal punishment, that it is unreasonable to expect our institutions to be perfect, and that acceptance of the argument from arbitrariness would commit us to abolishing all punishment.

In fact, van den Haag makes just these points in his essay. He writes:

> The Constitution, though it enjoins us to minimize capriciousness, does not enjoin a standard of unattainable perfection or exclude penalties because that standard has not been attained. . . . I see no more merit in the attempt to persuade the courts to let all capital-crime defendants go free of capital punishment because some have wrongly escaped it than I see in an attempt to persuade the courts to let all burglars go because some have wrongly escaped imprisonment.[11]

It is an important feature of this objection that it could be made even by one who conceded the injustice of arbitrarily administered death sentences. Rather than agreeing that capital punishment should be abolished, however, this objection moves from the premise that the flaws revealed in capital punishment are shared by *all* punishments to the conclusion that we must either (a) reject all punishments (because of the influence of arbitrary factors on them) or (b) reject the idea that arbitrariness provides a sufficient ground for abolishing the death penalty.

Is there a way out of this dilemma for death penalty opponents?

I believe that there is. Opponents of the death penalty may continue to support other punishments, even though their administration also involves arbitrariness. This is not to suggest, of course, that we should be content with arbitrariness or discrimination in the imposition of any punishment.[12] Rather the point is to emphasize that the argument from arbitrariness counts against the death penalty with special force. There are two reasons for this.

First, death is a much more severe punishment than imprisonment. This is universally acknowledged by advocates and opponents of the death penalty alike. It is recognized in the law by the existence of special procedures for capital cases. Death obliterates the person, depriving him or her of life and thereby, among other things, depriving him or her of any further rights of legal appeal, should new facts be discovered or new understandings of the law be reached. In this connection, it is worth recalling that many people were executed and are now dead because they were tried and sentenced under the pre-*Furman* laws which allowed the "uncontrolled discretion of judges and juries."

Second, though death is the most severe punishment in our legal system, it appears to be unnecessary for protecting citizens, while punishments generally are thought to promote our safety and well-being. The contrast between death and other punishments can be brought out by asking two questions. What would happen if we abolished all punishments? And, what would happen if we abolished the death penalty?

Most of us believe that if all punishments were abolished, there would be social chaos, a Hobbesian war of all against all. To do away with punishment entirely would be to do away with the criminal law and the system of constraints which it supports. Hence, even though the system is not a just one, we believe that we must live with it and strive to make it as fair as possible. On the other hand, if we abolish capital punishment, there is reason to believe that nothing will happen. There is simply no compelling evidence that capital punishment prevents murders better than long-term prison sentences. Indeed, some evidence even suggests that capital punishment increases the number of murders. While I cannot review the various empirical studies of these questions here, I think it can plausibly be asserted that the results of abolishing punishment generally would be disastrous, while the results of abolishing capital punishment are likely to be insignificant.[13]

I conclude then that the argument from arbitrariness has special force against the death penalty because of its extreme severity and its likely uselessness. The arbitrariness of other punishments may be outweighed by their necessity, but the same cannot be said for capital punishment.

VI

In closing, I would like to comment briefly on one other charge made by van den Haag, the charge that the argument from arbitrariness is a "sham" argument because it is not the real reason why people oppose the death penalty. Those who use this argument, van den Haag claims, would oppose capital punishment even if it were not arbitrarily imposed.

At one level, this charge is doubly fallacious. The suggestion of dishonesty introduced by the word "sham" makes the argument into an *ad hominem*. In addition, the charge suggests that there cannot be more than one reason in support of a view. There are many situations in which we offer arguments and yet would not change our view if the argument were refuted, not because the argument is a sham, but because we have additional grounds for what we believe.

Nonetheless, van den Haag's charge may indicate a special difficulty for the argument from arbitrariness, for the argument may well strike people as artificial and legalistic. Somehow, one may feel that it does not deal with the real issues—the wrongness of killing, deterrence, and whether murderers deserve to die.

Part of the problem, I think, is that our ordinary moral thinking involves specific forms of conduct or general rules of personal behavior. The argument from arbitrariness deals with a feature of an *institution,* and thinking about institutions seems to raise difficulties for many people. Believing that an individual murderer deserves to die for a terrible crime, they infer that there ought to be capital punishment, without attending to all of the implications for other individuals which will follow from setting up this practice.

The problem is similar to one that John Stuart Mill highlighted in

On Liberty. For many people, the fact that an act is wrong is taken to be sufficient ground for its being made illegal. Mill argued against the institutionalization of all moral judgments, and his argument still strikes many people as odd. If the act is wrong, they ask, shouldn't we do everything in our power to stop it? What they fail to appreciate, however, are all of the implications of institutionalizing such judgments.

Likewise, people ask, If so and so deserves to die, shouldn't we empower the state to execute him? The problem, however—or one of many problems—is that institutionalizing this judgment about desert yields a system which makes neither moral nor legal sense. Moreover, it perpetuates and exacerbates the liabilities and disadvantages which unjustly befall many of our fellow citizens. These are genuine and serious problems, and those who have raised them in the context of the capital punishment debate have both exposed troubling facts about the actual workings of the criminal law and illuminated the difficulties of acting justly. Most importantly, they have produced a powerful argument against authorizing the state to use death as a punishment for crime.

NOTES

1. *Capital Punishment: The Inevitability of Caprice and Mistake,* 2d ed. (New York: W. W. Norton & Co., 1981), p. 20.

2. Ibid., *passim;* W. Bowers and G. Pierce, "Arbitrariness and Discrimination under Post-*Furman* Capital Statutes," *Crime & Delinquency* 26 (1980): 563–635. Reprinted in *The Death Penalty in America,* 3d ed., ed. Hugo Bedau (New York: Oxford University Press, 1982), pp. 206–24.

3. "The Collapse of the Case against Capital Punishment," *National Review,* March 31, 1978, p. 397. A briefer version of this paper appeared in the *Criminal Law Bulletin* 14 (1978): 51–68, and is reprinted in Bedau, *The Death Penalty in America,* pp. 323–33.

4. Ibid.

5. "Noncomparative Justice," in *Rights, Justice, and the Bounds of Liberty: Essays in Social Philosophy* (Princeton, N.J.: Princeton University Press, 1980); originally published in the *Philosophical Review* 83 (1974): 297–338.

6. Black, *Capital Punishment,* p. 29.

7. Reprinted in Bedau, *The Death Penalty in America,* pp. 263–64.

8. Using Feinberg's terminology, these can be described as cases in which the criteria of comparative and noncomparative justice conflict with one another. I am arguing that in these instances, the criteria of comparative justice take precedence. Although Feinberg does discuss such conflicts, it is unclear to me from his essay whether he would agree with this claim.

9. Van den Haag, "The Collapse of the Case against Capital Punishment," p. 403, n. 14. (This important footnote does not appear in the shorter version of the paper.)

10. Reprinted in Bedau, *The Death Penalty in America,* pp. 255–56.

11. Van den Haag, "The Collapse of the Case against Capital Punishment," p. 397.

12. For a discussion of the role of discrimination throughout the criminal justice system and recommendations for reform, see American Friends Service Committee, *Struggle for Justice* (New York: Hill and Wang, 1971).

13. In support of the superior deterrent power of the death penalty, van den Haag cites I. Ehrlich, "The Deterrent Effect of Capital Punishment: A Question of Life and Death," *American Economic Review* 65 (1975): 397-417. Two reviews of the evidence on deterrence, both of which criticize Ehrlich at length, are Hans Zeisel, "The Deterrent Effect of the Death Penalty: Facts v. Faith," and Lawrence Klein et al., "The Deterrent Effect of Capital Punishment: An Assessment of the Evidence." (Both these articles appear in Bedau, *The Death Penalty in America*.) The thesis that executions increase the number of homicides is defended by W. Bowers and G. Pierce in "Deterrence or Brutalization: What Is the Effect of Executions?" *Crime & Delinquency* 26 (1980): 453-84.

My thanks are due to Hugo Bedau, William Bowers, Richard Daynard, and Ernest van den Haag for reactions to my thinking about the death penalty. I would especially like to thank Ursula Bentele for helpful discussions and access to unpublished research; Nelson Lande for spirited comments (both philosophical and grammatical); and John Troyer, whose keen and persistent criticisms of my views forced me to write this article.

15

Justice, Civilization, and the Death Penalty: Answering van den Haag

Jeffrey H. Reiman

On the issue of capital punishment, there is as clear a clash of moral intuitions as we are likely to see. Some (now a majority of Americans) feel deeply that justice requires payment in kind and thus that murderers should die; and others (once, but no longer, nearly a majority of Americans) feel deeply that the state ought not be in the business of putting people to death.[1] Arguments for either side that do not do justice to the intuitions of the other are unlikely to persuade anyone not already convinced. And, since, as I shall suggest, there is truth on both sides, such arguments are easily refutable, leaving us with nothing but conflicting intuitions and no guidance from reason in distinguishing the better from the worse. In this context, I shall try to make an argument for the abolition of the death penalty that does justice to the intuitions on both sides. I shall sketch out a conception of retributive justice that accounts for the justice of executing murderers, and then I shall argue that *though the death penalty is a just punishment for murder,* abolition of the death penalty is part of the civilizing mission of modern states. Before getting to this, let us briefly consider the challenges confronting those who would argue against the death penalty. In my view, these challenges have been most forcefully put by Ernest van den Haag.

From *Philosophy & Public Affairs* 14, no. 2 (Spring 1985). Copyright © 1985 by Princeton University Press. Reprinted with permission of Princeton University Press.

I. THE CHALLENGE TO THE ABOLITIONIST

The recent book, *The Death Penalty: A Debate,* in which van den Haag argues for the death penalty and John P. Conrad argues against, proves how difficult it is to mount a telling argument against capital punishment.[2] Conrad contends, for example, that "To kill the offender [who has committed murder in the first degree] is to respond to his wrong by doing the same wrong to him" (p. 60). But this popular argument is easily refuted.[3] Since we regard killing in self-defense or in war as morally permissible, it cannot be that we regard killing per se as wrong. It follows that the wrong in murder cannot be that it is killing per se, but that it is (among other things) the killing of an innocent person. Consequently, if the state kills a murderer, though it does the same physical act that he did, it does not do the wrong that he did, since the state is not killing an innocent person (see p. 62). Moreover, unless this distinction is allowed, all punishments are wrong, since everything that the state does as punishment is an act which is physically the same as an act normally thought wrong. For example, if you lock an innocent person in a cage, that is kidnapping. If the state responds by locking you in prison, it can hardly be said to be responding to your wrong by doing you a wrong in return. Indeed, it will be said that it is precisely because what you did was wrong that locking you up, which would otherwise be wrong, is right.[4]

Conrad also makes the familiar appeal to the possibility of executing an innocent person and the impossibility of correcting this tragic mistake. "An act by the state of such monstrous proportions as the execution of a man who is not guilty of the crime for which he was convicted should be avoided at all costs. . . . The abolition of capital punishment is the certain means of preventing the worst injustice" (p. 60). This argument, while not so easily disposed of as the previous one, is, like all claims about what "should be avoided at all costs," neither very persuasive. There is invariably some cost that is prohibitive such that if, for example, capital punishment were necessary to save the lives of potential murder victims, there must be a point at which the number of saved victims would be large enough to justify the risk of executing an innocent—particularly where trial and appellate proceedings are designed to reduce this risk to a minimum by giving the accused every benefit of the doubt.[5] Since we tolerate the death of innocents, in mines or on highways, as a cost of progress, and, in wars, as an inevitable accompaniment to aerial bombardment and the like, it cannot convincingly be contended that, kept to a minimum, the risk of executing an innocent is still so great an evil as to outweigh all other considerations (see pp. 230–31).

Nor will it do to suggest, as Conrad does, that execution implies that offenders are incapable of change and thus presumes the offenders' "total identification with evil," a presumption reserved only to God or, in any case, beyond the province of (mere) men (p. 27; also, pp. 42–43). This is not convincing since no punishment, whether on retributive or deterrent grounds, need imply belief in the total evilness of the punishee—all that need be believed (for retribution) is that what the offender has done is as evil as the punishment is awful, or (for deterrence) that what he has done is awful enough to warrant whatever punishment will discourage others from doing it. "Execution," writes van den Haag, "merely presumes an identification [with evil] sufficient to disregard what good qualities the convict has (he may be nice to animals and love his mother).

No total identification with evil—whatever that means—is required; only a "sufficiently wicked crime" (p. 35).

Thus far I have tried to indicate how difficult it is to make an argument for the abolition of the death penalty against which the death penalty advocate cannot successfully defend himself. But van den Haag's argument is not merely defensive—he poses a positive challenge to anyone who would take up the abolitionist cause. For van den Haag, in order to argue convincingly for abolition, one must prove either that "no [criminal] act, however horrible, justifies [that is, deserves] the death penalty," or that, if capital punishment were found to deter murder more effectively than life imprisonment, we should still "prefer to preserve the life of a convicted murderer rather than the lives of innocent victims, even if it were certain that these victims would be spared if the murderer were executed" (p. 275).

If van den Haag is right and the abolitionist cause depends on proving either or both of these assertions, then it is a lost cause, since I believe they cannot be proven for reasons of the following sort: If people ever deserve anything for their acts, then it seems that what they deserve is something commensurate in cost or in benefit to what they have done. However horrible executions are, there are surely some acts to which they are commensurate in cost. If, as Camus says, the condemned man dies two deaths, one on the scaffold and one anticipating it, then isn't execution justified for one who has murdered two people? if not two, then ten?[6] As for the second assertion, since we take as justified the killing of innocent people (say, homicidal maniacs) in self-defense (that is, when necessary to preserve the lives of their innocent victims), then it seems that we must take as justified the killing of *guilty* people if it is necessary to preserve the lives of innocent victims. Indeed, though punishment is not the same as self-defense, it is, when practiced to deter crimes, arguably a form of social defense—and parity of reason would seem to dictate that if killing is justified when necessary for self-defense, then it is justified when necessary for social defense.

It might be thought that injuring or killing others in self-defense is justifiable in that it aims to stop the threatening individual himself but that punishing people (even guilty people) to deter others is a violation of the Kantian prohibition against using people merely as means to the well-being of others.[7] It seems to me that this objection is premised on the belief that what deters potential criminals are the individual acts of punishment. In that case, each person punished is truly being used for the benefit of others. If, however, what deters potential criminals is the existence of a functioning punishment system, then everyone is benefited by that system, including those who end up being punished by it, since they too have received the benefit of enhanced security due to the deterring of some potential criminals. Even criminals benefit from what deters other criminals from preying on them. Then, each act of punishment is done as a necessary condition of the existence of a system that benefits all; and no one is used or sacrificed *merely* for the benefit or others.

If I am correct in believing that the assertions that van den Haag challenges the abolitionist to prove cannot be proven, then the case for the abolition of the death penalty must be made while accepting that some crimes deserve capital punishment, and that evidence that capital punishment was a substantially better deterrent to murder than life imprisonment would justify imposing it. This is what I shall attempt to do. Indeed, I shall begin the case for the abolition of the death penalty by defending the justice of the death penalty as a punishment for murder.

II. JUST DESERTS AND JUST PUNISHMENTS

In my view, the death penalty is a just punishment for murder because the *lex talionis,* an eye for an eye, and so on, is just, although, as I shall suggest at the end of this section, it can only be rightly applied when its implied preconditions are satisfied. The *lex talionis* is a version of retributivism. Retributivism—as the word itself suggests—is the doctrine that the offender should be *paid back* with suffering he deserves because of the evil he has done, and the *lex talionis* asserts that injury equivalent to that he imposed is what the offender deserves.[8] But the *lex talionis* is not the only version of retributivism. Another, which I shall call "proportional retributivism," holds that what retribution requires is not equality of injury between crimes and punishments, but "fit" or proportionality, such that the worst crime is punished with the society's worst penalty, and so on, though the society's worst punishment need not duplicate the injury of the worst crime.[9] Later, I shall try to show how a form of proportional retributivism is compatible with acknowledging the justice of the *lex talionis.* Indeed, since I shall defend the justice of the *lex talionis,* I take such compatibility as a necessary condition of the validity of any form of retributivism.[10]

There is nothing self-evident about the justice of the *lex talionis* nor, for that matter, of retributivism.[11] The standard problem confronting those who would justify retributivism is that of overcoming the suspicion that it does no more than sanctify the victim's desire to hurt the offender back. Since serving that desire amounts to hurting the offender simply for the satisfaction that the victim derives from seeing the offender suffer, and since deriving satisfaction from the suffering of others seems primitive, the policy of imposing suffering on the offender for no other purpose than giving satisfaction to his victim seems primitive as well. Consequently, defending retributivism requires showing that the suffering imposed on the wrongdoer has some worthy point beyond the satisfaction of victims. In what follows, I shall try to identify a proposition—which I call the *retributivist principle*— that I take to be the nerve of retributivism. I think this principle accounts for the justice of the *lex talionis* and indicates the point of the suffering demanded by retributivism. Not to do too much of the work of the death penalty advocate, I shall make no extended argument for this principle beyond suggesting the considerations that make it plausible. I shall identify these considerations by drawing, with considerable license, on Hegel and Kant.

I think that we can see the justice of the *lex talionis* by focusing on the striking affinity between it and the *golden rule*. The *golden rule* mandates "Do unto others as you would have others do unto you," while the *lex talionis* counsels "Do unto others as they have done unto you." It would not be too far-fetched to say that the *lex talionis* is the law enforcement arm of the golden rule, at least in the sense that if people were actually treated as they treated others, then everyone would necessarily follow the golden rule because then people could only willingly act toward others as they were willing to have others act toward them. This is not to suggest that the *lex talionis* follows from the golden rule, but rather that the two share a common moral inspiration: the equality of persons. Treating others as you *would* have them treat you means treating others as equal to you, because adopting the golden rule as one's guiding principle implies that one counts the suffering of others to be as great a calamity as one's own suffering, that one counts one's right to impose suffering on others as no greater than their right to impose suffering on one, and so on. This leads to the *lex talionis* by two approaches that start from different points and converge.

I call the first approach "Hegelian" because Hegel held (roughly) that crime upsets the equality between persons and retributive punishment restores that equality by "annulling" the crime.[12] As we have seen, acting according to the golden rule implies treating others as your equals. Conversely, violating the golden rule implies the reverse: Doing to another what you would *not* have that other do to you violates the equality of persons by asserting a right toward the other that the other does not possess toward you. Doing back to you what you did "annuls" your violation by reasserting that the other has the same right toward you that you assert toward him. Punishment according to the *lex talionis* cannot heal the injury that the other has suffered at your hands, rather it rectifies the indignity he has suffered, by restoring him to equality with you.

"Equality of persons" here does not mean equality of concern for their happiness, as it might for a utilitarian. On such a (roughly) utilitarian understanding of equality, imposing suffering on the wrongdoer equivalent to the suffering he has imposed would have little point. Rather, equality of concern for people's happiness would lead us to impose as little suffering on the wrongdoer as was compatible with maintaining the happiness of others. This is enough to show that retributivism (at least in this "Hegelian" form) reflects a conception of morality quite different from that envisioned by utilitarianism. Instead of seeing morality as administering doses of happiness to individual recipients, the retributivist envisions morality as maintaining the relations appropriate to equally sovereign individuals. A crime, rather than representing a unit of suffering added to the already considerable suffering in the world, is an assault on the sovereignty of an individual that temporarily places one person (the criminal) in a position of illegitimate sovereignty over another (the victim). The victim (or his representative, the state) then has the right to rectify this loss of standing relative to the criminal by meting out a punishment that reduces the criminal's sovereignty in the degree to which he vaunted it above his victim's. It might be thought that this is a duty, not just a right, but that is surely too much. The victim has the right to forgive the violator without punishment, which suggests that it is by virtue of having the right to punish the violator (rather than the duty) that the victim's equality with the violator is restored.

I call the second approach "Kantian" since Kant held (roughly) that, since reason (like justice) is no respecter of the sheer difference between individuals, when a rational being decides to act in a certain way toward his fellows, he implicitly authorizes similar action by his fellows toward him.[13] A version of the golden rule, then, is a requirement of reason: acting rationally, one always acts as he would have others act toward him. Consequently, to act toward a person as he has acted toward others is to treat him as a rational being, that is, as if his act were the product of a rational decision. From this, it may be concluded that we have a duty to do to offenders what they have done, since this amounts to according them the respect due rational beings.[14] Here too, however, the assertion of a duty to punish seems excessive, since, if this duty arises because doing to people what they have done to others is necessary to accord them the respect due rational beings, then we would have a duty to do to all rational persons *everything*— good, bad, or indifferent—that they do to others. The point rather is that, by his acts, a rational being *authorizes* others to do the same to him, he doesn't *compel* them to. Here too, then, the argument leads to a right, rather than a duty, to exact the *lex talionis*. And this is supported by the fact that we can conclude from Kant's argument that a rational being cannot validly complain of being treated in the way he has treated others, and where there is no valid complaint, there is no injustice, and where there is no injustice, others have acted within their rights.[15] It should be clear that the Kantian argument also rests on the equality of persons, because a rational agent only implicitly authorizes having done to him action similar to what he has done to another, if he and the other are similar in the relevant ways.

The "Hegelian" and "Kantian" approaches arrive at the same destination from opposite sides. The "Hegelian" approach starts from the victim's equality with the criminal, and infers from it the victim's right to do to the criminal what the criminal has done to the victim. The "Kantian" approach starts from the criminal's rationality, and infers from it the criminal's authorization of the victim's right to do to the criminal what the criminal has done to the victim. Taken together, these approaches support the following proposition: The equality and rationality of persons implies that an offender deserves and his victim has the right to impose suffering on the offender equal to that which he imposed on the victim. This is the proposition I call the *retributivist principle,* and I shall assume henceforth that it is true. This principle provides that the *lex talionis* is the criminal's just desert and the victim's (or as his representative, the state's) right. Moreover, the principle also indicates the point of retributive punishment, namely, it affirms the equality and rationality of persons, victims and offenders alike.[16] And the point of this affirmation is, like any moral affirmation, to make a statement, to the criminal, to impress upon him his equality with his victim (which earns him a like fate) and his rationality (by which his actions are held to authorize his fate), and to the society, so that recognition of the equality and rationality of persons becomes a visible part of our shared moral environment that none can ignore in justifying their actions to one another.

When I say that with respect to the criminal, the point of retributive punishment is to impress upon him his equality with his victim, I mean to be understood quite literally. If the sentence is just and the criminal rational, then the punishment should normally *force* upon him recognition of his equality with his victim, recognition of their shared vulnerability to suffering and their shared desire to avoid it, as well as recognition of the fact that he counts for no more than his victim in the eyes of their fellows. For this reason, the retributivist requires that the offender be sane, not only at the moment of his crime, but also at the moment of his punishment— while this latter requirement would seem largely pointless (if not downright malevolent) to a utilitarian. Incidentally, it is, I believe, the desire that the offender be forced by suffering punishment to recognize his equality with his victim, rather than the desire for that suffering itself, that constitutes what is rational in the desire for revenge.

The retributivist principle represents a conception of moral desert whose complete elaboration would take us far beyond the scope of the present essay. In its defense, however, it is worth noting that our common notion of moral desert seems to include (at least) two elements: (1) a conception of individual responsibility for actions that is "contagious," that is, one which confers moral justification on the punishing (or rewarding) reactions of others; and (2) a measure of the relevant worth of actions that determines the legitimate magnitude of justified reactions. Broadly speaking, the "Kantian" notion of authorization implicit in rational action supplies the first element, and the "Hegelian" notion of upsetting and restoring equality of standing supplies the second. It seems, then, reasonable to take the equality and rationality of persons as implying moral desert in the way asserted in the retributivist principle. I shall assume henceforth that the retributivist principle is true.

The truth of the retributivist principle establishes the justice of the *lex talionis*, but, since it establishes this as a right of the victim rather than a duty, it does not settle the question of whether or to what extent the victim or the state should exercise this right and exact the *lex talionis*. This is a separate moral question because strict adherence to the *lex talionis* amounts to allowing criminals, even the most barbaric of them, to dictate our punishing behavior. It seems certain that there are at least some crimes, such as rape or torture, that we ought not try to match. And this is not merely a matter of imposing an alternative punishment that produces an equivalent amount of suffering, as, say, some number of years in prison that might "add up" to the harm caused by a rapist or a torturer. Even if no amount of time in prison would add up to the harm caused by a torturer, it still seems that we ought not torture him even if this were the only way of making him suffer as much as he has made his victim suffer. Or, consider someone who has committed several murders in cold blood. On the *lex talionis*, it would seem that such a criminal might justly be brought to within an inch of death and then revived (or to within a moment of execution and then reprieved) as many times as he has killed (minus one), and then finally executed. But surely this is a degree of cruelty that would be monstrous.[17]

Since the retributivist principle establishes the *lex talionis* as the victim's right, it might seem that the question of how far this right should be exercised is "up to the victim." And indeed, this would be the case in the state of nature. But once, for all the good reasons familiar to readers of John Locke, the state comes into existence, public punishment replaces private, and the victim's right to punish reposes in the state. With this, the decision as to how far to exercise this right goes to the state as well. To be sure, since (at least with respect to retributive punishment) the victim's right is the source of the state's right to punish, the state must exercise its right in ways that are faithful to the victim's right. Later, when I try to spell out the upper and lower limits of just punishment, these may be taken as indicating the range within which the state can punish and remain faithful to the victim's right.

I suspect that it will be widely agreed that the state ought not administer punishments of the sort described above even if required by the letter of the *lex talionis*, and thus, even granting the justice of *lex talionis*, there are occasions on which it is morally appropriate to diverge from its requirements. We must, of course, distinguish such morally based divergence from that which is based on practicality. Like any moral principle, the *lex talionis* is subject to "ought implies can." It will usually be impossible to do to an offender exactly what he has done—for example, his offense will normally have had an element of surprise that is not possible for a judicially imposed punishment, but this fact can hardly free him from having to bear the suffering he has imposed on another. Thus, for reasons of practicality, the *lex talionis* must necessarily be qualified to call for doing to the offender *as nearly as possible* what he has done to his victim. When, however, we refrain from raping rapists or torturing torturers, we do so for reasons of morality, not of practicality. And, given the justice of the *lex talionis*, these moral reasons cannot amount to claiming that it would be *unjust* to rape rapists or torture torturers. Rather the claim must be that, even though it would be just to rape rapists and torture torturers, other moral considerations weigh against doing so.

On the other hand, when, for moral reasons, we refrain from exacting the *lex talionis*, and impose a less harsh alternative punishment, it may be said that we are not doing full justice to the criminal, but it cannot automatically be the case that we are doing an *injustice* to his victim. Otherwise we would have to say it was unjust to imprison our torturer rather than torturing him or to simply execute our multiple murderer rather than multiply "executing" him. Surely it is counterintuitive (and irrational to boot) to set the demands of justice so high that a society would have to choose between being barbaric or being unjust. This would effectively price justice out of the moral market.

The implication of this is that there is a range of just punishments that includes some that are just though they exact less than the full measure of the *lex talionis*. What are the top and bottom ends of this range? I think that both are indicated by the *retributivist principle*. The principle identifies the *lex talionis* as the offender's desert and since, on retributive grounds, punishment beyond what one deserves is unjust for the same reasons that make punishment of the innocent unjust, the *lex talionis* is the upper limit of the range of just punishments. On the other hand, if the retributivist principle is true, then denying that the offender deserves suffering equal to that which he imposed amounts to denying the equality and rationality of persons. From this it follows that we fall below the bottom end of the range of just punishments when we act in ways that are incompatible with the *lex talionis* at the top end. That is, we fall below the bottom end and commit an injustice to the victim when we treat the offender in a way that is no longer compatible with sincerely believing that he deserves to have done to him what he has done to his victim. Thus, the upper limit of the range of just punishments is the point after which more punishment is unjust to the offender, and the lower limit is the point after which less punishment is unjust to the victim. In this way, the range of just punishments remains faithful to the victim's right which is their source.

This way of understanding just punishment enables us to formulate proportional retributivism so that it is compatible with acknowledging the justice of the *lex talionis:* If we take the *lex talionis* as spelling out the offender's just deserts, and if other moral considerations require us to refrain from matching the injury caused by the offender while still allowing us to punish justly, then surely we impose just punishment if we impose the closest morally acceptable approximation to the *lex talionis.* Proportional retributivism, then, in requiring that the worst crime be punished by the society's worst punishment and so on, could be understood as translating the offender's just desert into its nearest equivalent in the society's table of morally acceptable punishments. Then the two versions of retributivism (*lex talionis* and proportional) are related in that the first states what just punishment would be if nothing but the offender's just desert mattered, and the second locates just punishment at the meeting point of the offender's just deserts and the society's moral scruples. And since this second version only modifies the requirements of the *lex talionis* in light of other moral considerations, it is compatible with believing that the *lex talionis* spells out the offender's just deserts, much in the way that modifying the obligations of promisers in light of other moral considerations is compatible with believing in the binding nature of promises.

Proportional retributivism so formulated preserves the point of retributivism and remains faithful to the victim's right which is its source. Since it punishes with the closest morally acceptable approximation to the *lex talionis,* it effectively says to the offender, you deserve the equivalent of what you did to your victim and you are getting less only to the degree that *our* moral scruples limit us from duplicating what you have done. Such punishment, then, affirms the equality of persons by respecting *as far as is morally permissible* the victim's right to impose suffering on the offender equal to what he received, and it affirms the rationality of the offender by treating him as authorizing others to do to him what he has done though they take him up on it only *as far as is morally permissible.* Needless to say, the alternative punishments must in some convincing ways be comparable in gravity to the crimes which they punish, or else they will trivialize the harms those crimes caused and be no longer compatible with sincerely believing that the offender deserves to have done to him what he has done to his victim and no longer capable of impressing upon the criminal his equality with the victim. If we punish rapists with a small fine or a brief prison term, we do an injustice to their victims, because this trivializes the suffering rapists have caused and thus is incompatible with believing that they deserve to have done to them something comparable to what they have done to their victims. If, on the other hand, instead of raping rapists we impose on them some grave penalty, say a substantial term of imprisonment, then we do no injustice even though we refrain from exacting the *lex talionis*.

To sum up, I take the *lex talionis* to be the top end of the range of just punishments. When, because we are simply unable to duplicate the criminal's offense, we modify the *lex talionis* subject to call for imposing on the offender as nearly as possible what he has done, we are still at this top end, applying the *lex talionis* subject to "ought implies can." When we do less than this, we still act justly as long as we punish in a way that is compatible with sincerely believing that the offender deserves the full measure of the *lex talionis,* but receives less for reasons that do not undermine this belief. If this is true, then it is not unjust to spare murderers as long as they can be punished in some other suitably grave way. I leave open the question of what such an alternative punishment might be, except to say that it need not be limited to such penalties as are currently imposed. For example, though rarely carried out in practice, a life sentence with no chance of parole might be a civilized equivalent of the death penalty—after all, people sentenced to life imprisonment have traditionally been regarded as "civilly dead."[18]

It might be objected that no punishment short of death will serve the point of retributivism with respect to murderers because no punishment short of death is commensurate with the crime of murder since, while some number of years of imprisonment may add up to the amount of harm done by rapists or assaulters or torturers, no number of years will add up to the harm done to the victim of murder. But justified divergence from the *lex talionis* is not limited only to changing the form of punishment while maintaining equivalent severity. Otherwise, we would have to torture torturers rather than imprison them if they tortured more than could be made up for by years in prison (or by the years available to them to spend in prison, which might be few for elderly torturers), and we would have to subject multiple murderers to multiple "executions." If justice allows us to refrain from these penalties, then justice allows punishments that are not equal in suffering to their crimes. It seems to me that if the objector grants this much, then he must show that a punishment less than death is not merely incommensurate to the harm caused by murder, but so far out of proportion to that harm that it trivializes it and thus effectively denies the equality and rationality of persons. Now, I am vulnerable to the claim that a sentence of life in prison that allows parole after eight or ten years does indeed trivialize the harm of (premeditated, coldblooded) murder. But I cannot see how a sentence that would require a murderer to spend his full natural life in prison, or even the lion's share of his adult life (say, the thirty years between age twenty and age fifty), can be regarded as anything less than extremely severe and thus no trivialization of the harm he has caused.

I take it then that the justice of the *lex talionis* implies that it is just to execute murderers, but not that it is unjust to spare them as long as they are systematically punished in some other suitably grave way. Before developing the implications of this claim, a word about the implied preconditions of applying the *lex talionis* is in order.

Since this principle calls for imposing on offenders the harms they are responsible for imposing on others, the implied preconditions of applying it to any particular harm include the requirement that the harm be one that the offender is fully responsible for, where responsibility is both psychological, the capacity to tell the difference between right and wrong and control one's actions, and social. If people are subjected to remediable unjust social circumstances beyond their control, and if harmful actions are a predictable response to those conditions, then those who benefit from the unjust conditions and refuse to remedy them share responsibility for the harmful acts—and thus neither their doing nor their cost can be assigned fully to the offenders alone. For example, if a slave kills an innocent person while making his escape, at least part of the blame for the killing must fall on those who have enslaved him. And this is because slavery is unjust, not merely because the desire to escape from slavery is understandable. The desire to escape from prison is understandable as well, but if the imprisonment were a just sentence, then we would hold the prisoner, and not his keepers, responsible if he killed someone while escaping.

Since I believe that the vast majority of murders in America are a predictable response to the frustrations and disabilities of impoverished social circumstances,[19] and since I believe that that impoverishment is a remediable injustice from which others in America benefit, I believe that we have no right to exact the full cost of murders from our murderers until we have done everything possible to rectify the conditions that produce their crimes.[20] But these are the "Reagan years," and not many—who are not already susceptible—will be persuaded by this sort of argument.[21] This does not, in my view, shake its validity; but I want to make an argument whose appeal is not limited to those who think that crime is the result of social injustice.[22] I shall proceed then, granting not only the justice of the death penalty, but also, at least temporarily, the assumption that our murderers are wholly deserving of dying for their crimes. If I can show that it would still be wrong to execute murderers, I believe I shall have made the strongest case for abolishing the death penalty.

III. CIVILIZATION, PAIN, AND JUSTICE

As I have already suggested, from the fact that something is justly deserved, it does not automatically follow that it should be done, since there may be other moral reasons for not doing it such that, all told, the weight of moral reasons swings the balance against proceeding. The same argument that I have given for the justice of the death penalty for murderers proves the justice of beating assaulters, raping rapists, and torturing torturers. Nonetheless, I believe, and suspect that most would agree, that it would not be right for us to beat assaulters, rape rapists, or torture torturers, *even though it were their just deserts*—and even if this were the only way to make them suffer as much as they had made their victims suffer. Calling for the abolition of the death penalty, though it be just, then, amounts to urging that as a society we place execution in the same category of sanction as beating, raping, and torturing, and treat it as something it would also not be right for us to do to offenders, *even if it were their just deserts.*

To argue for placing execution in this category, I must show what would be gained therefrom; and to show that, I shall indicate what we gain from placing torture in this category and argue that a similar gain is to be had from doing the same with execution. I select torture because I think the reasons for placing it in this category are, due to the extremity of torture, most easily seen—but what I say here applies with appropriate modification to other severe physical punishments, such as beating and raping. First, and most evidently, placing torture in this category broadcasts the message that we as a society judge torturing so horrible a thing to do to a person that we refuse to do it even when it is deserved. Note that such a judgment does not commit us to an absolute prohibition on torturing. No matter how horrible we judge something to be, we may still be justified in doing it if it is necessary to prevent something even worse. Leaving this aside for the moment, what is gained by broadcasting the public judgment that torture is too horrible to inflict even if deserved?

I think the answer to this lies in what we understand as civilization. In *The Genealogy of Morals,* Nietzsche says that in early times "pain did not hurt as much as it does today."[23] The truth in this puzzling remark is that progress in civilization is characterized by a lower tolerance for one's own pain and that suffered by others. And this is appropriate, since, via growth in knowledge, civilization brings increased power to prevent or reduce pain and, via growth in the ability to communicate and interact with more and more people, civilization extends the circle of people with whom we empathize.[24] If civilization is characterized by lower tolerance for our own pain and that of others, then publicly refusing to do horrible things to our fellows both signals the level of our civilization *and, by our example, continues the work of civilizing.* And this gesture is all the more powerful if we refuse to do horrible things to those who deserve them. I contend then that the more things we are able to include in this category, the more civilized we are and the more civili*zing*. Thus we gain from including torture in this category, and if execution is especially horrible, we gain still more by including it.

Needless to say, the content, direction, and even the worth of civilization are hotly contested issues, and I shall not be able to win those contests in this brief space. At a minimum, however, I shall assume that civilization involves the taming of the natural environment and of the human animals in it, and that the overall trend in human history is toward increasing this taming, though the trend is by no means unbroken or without reverses. On these grounds, we can say that growth in civilization generally marks human history, that a reduction in the horrible things we tolerate doing to our fellows (even when they deserve them) is part of this growth, and that once the work of civilization is taken on consciously, it includes carrying forward and expanding this reduction.

This claim broadly corresponds to what Emile Durkheim identified, nearly a century ago, as "two laws which seem . . . to prevail in the evolution of the apparatus of punishment." The first, the law of quantitative change, Durkheim formulates as:

> *The intensity of punishment is the greater the more closely societies approximate to a less developed type—and the more the central power assumes an absolute character.*

And the second, which Durkheim refers to as the law of qualitative change, is:

> *Deprivations of liberty, and of liberty alone, varying in time according to the seriousness of the crime, tend to become more and more the normal means of social control.*[25]

Several things should be noted about these laws. First of all, they are not two separate laws. As Durkheim understands them, the second exemplifies the trend toward moderation of punishment referred to in the first.[26] Second, the first law really refers to two distinct trends, which usually coincide but do not always. That is, moderation of punishment accompanies *both* the movement from less to more advanced types of society *and* the movement from more to less absolute rule. Normally these go hand in hand, but where they do not, the effect of one trend may offset the effect of the other. Thus, a primitive society without absolute rule may have milder punishments than an equally primitive but more absolutist society.[27] This complication need not trouble us, since the claim I am making refers to the first trend, namely, that punishments tend to become milder as societies become more advanced;

and that this is a trend in history is not refuted by the fact that it is accompanied by other trends and even occasionally offset by them. Moreover, I shall close this article with a suggestion about the relation between the intensity of punishment and the justice of society, which might broadly be thought of as corresponding to the second trend in Durkheim's first law. Finally, and most important for our purposes, is the fact that Durkheim's claim that punishment becomes less intense as societies become more advanced is a generalization that he supports with an impressive array of evidence from historical societies from pre-Christian times to the time in which he wrote—and this in turn supports my claim that the reduction in the horrible things we do to our fellows is in fact part of the advance of civilization.[28]

Against this it might be argued that many things grow in history, some good, some bad, and some mixed, and thus the fact that there is some historical trend is not a sufficient reason to continue it. Thus, for example, history also brings growth in population, but we are not for that reason called upon to continue the work of civilization by continually increasing our population. What this suggests is that in order to identify something as part of the work of civilizing, we must show not only that it generally grows in history, but that its growth is, on some independent grounds, clearly an advance for the human species—that is, either an unmitigated gain or at least consistently a net gain. And this implies that even trends which we might generally regard as advances may in some cases bring losses with them, such that when they did it would not be appropriate for us to lend our efforts to continuing them. Of such trends we can say that they are advances in civilization except when their gains are outweighed by the losses they bring—and that we are only called upon to further these trends when their gains are *not* outweighed in this way. It is clear in this light that increasing population is a mixed blessing at best, bringing both gains and losses. Consequently, it is not always an advance in civilization that we should further, though at times it may be.

What can be said of reducing the horrible things that we do to our fellows even when deserved? First of all, given our vulnerability to pain, it seems clearly a gain. Is it however an unmitigated gain? That is, would such a reduction ever amount to a loss? It seems to me that there are two conditions under which it would be a loss, namely, if the reduction made our lives more dangerous, or if not doing what is justly deserved were a loss in itself. Let us leave aside the former, since, as I have already suggested and as I will soon indicate in greater detail, I accept that if some horrible punishment is necessary to deter equally or more horrible acts, then we may have to impose the punishment. Thus my claim is that reduction in the horrible things we do to our fellows is an advance in civilization *as long as our lives are not thereby made more dangerous,* and that it is only then that we are called upon to extend that reduction as part of the work of civilization. Assuming then, for the moment, that we suffer no increased danger by refraining from doing horrible things to our fellows when they justly deserve them, does such refraining to do what is justly deserved amount to a loss?

It seems to me that the answer to this must be that refraining to do what is justly deserved is only a loss where it amounts to doing an injustice. But such refraining to do what is just is not doing what is unjust, unless what we do instead falls below the bottom end of the range of just punishments. Otherwise, it would be unjust to refrain from torturing torturers, raping rapists, or beating assaulters. In short, I take it that if there is no injustice in refraining from torturing torturers, then there is no injustice in refraining to do horrible things to our fellows generally, when they deserve them, as long as what we do instead is compatible with believing that they do deserve them. And thus that if such refraining does not make our lives more dangerous, then it is no loss, and given our vulnerability to pain, it is a gain. Consequently, reduction in the horrible things we do to our fellows, when not necessary to our protection, is an advance in civilization that we are called upon to continue once we consciously take upon ourselves the work of civilization.

To complete the argument, however, I must show that execution is horrible enough to warrant its inclusion alongside torture. Against this it will be said that execution is not especially horrible since it only hastens a fate that is inevitable for us.[29] I think that this view overlooks important differences in the manner in which people reach their inevitable ends. I contend that execution is especially horrible, and it is so in a way similar to (though not identical with) the way in which torture is especially horrible. I believe we view torture as especially awful because of two of its features, which also characterize execution: intense pain and the spectacle of one human being completely subject to the power of another. This latter is separate from the issue of pain since it is something that offends us about unpainful things, such as slavery (even voluntarily entered) and prostitution (even voluntarily chosen as an occupation).[30] Execution shares this separate feature, since killing a bound and defenseless human being enacts the total subjugation of that person to his fellows. I think, incidentally, that this accounts for the general uneasiness with which execution by lethal injection has been greeted. Rather than humanizing the event, it seems only to have purchased a possible reduction in physical pain at the price of increasing the spectacle of subjugation—with no net gain in the attractiveness of the death penalty. Indeed, its net effect may have been the reverse.

In addition to the spectacle of subjugation, execution, even by physically painless means, is also characterized by a special and intense psychological pain that distinguishes it from the loss of life that awaits us all. Interesting in this regard is the fact that although we are not terribly squeamish about the loss of life itself, allowing it in war, self-defense, as a necessary cost of progress, and so on, we are, as the extraordinary hesitance of our courts testifies, quite reluctant to execute. I think this is because execution involves the most psychologically painful features of deaths. We normally regard death from human causes as worse than death from natural causes, since a humanly caused shortening of life lacks the consolation of unavoidability. And we normally regard death whose coming is foreseen by its victim as worse than sudden death, because a foreseen death adds to the loss of life the terrible consciousness of that impending loss.[31] As a humanly caused death whose advent is foreseen by its victim, an execution combines the worst of both.

Thus far, by analogy with torture, I have argued that execution should be avoided because of how horrible it is to the one executed. But there are reasons of another sort that follow from the analogy with torture. Torture is to be avoided not only because of what it says about *what* we are willing to do to our fellows, but also because of what it says about *us* who are willing to do it. To torture someone is an awful spectacle not only because of the intensity of pain imposed, but because of what is required to be able to impose such pain on one's fellows. The tortured body cringes, using its full exertion to escape the pain imposed upon it—it literally begs for relief with its muscles as it does with its cries. To torture someone is to demonstrate a capacity to resist this begging, and that in turn demonstrates a kind of hardheartedness that a society ought not parade.

And this is true not only of torture, but of all severe corporal punishment. Indeed, I think this constitutes part of the answer to the puzzling question of why we refrain from punishments like whipping, even when the alternative (some months in jail versus some lashes) seems more costly to the offender. Imprisonment is painful to be sure, but it is a reflective pain, one that comes with comparing what is to what might have been, and that can be temporarily ignored by thinking about other things. But physical pain has an urgency that holds body and mind in a fierce grip. Of physical pain, as Orwell's Winston Smith recognized, "you could only wish one thing: that it should stop."[32] Refraining from torture in particular and corporal punishment in general, we both refuse to put a fellow human being in this grip *and* refuse to show our ability to resist this wish. The death penalty is the last corporal punishment used officially in the modern world. And it is corporal not only because administered via the body, but because the pain of foreseen, humanly administered death strikes us with the urgency that characterizes intense physical pain, causing grown men to cry, faint, and lose control of their bodily functions. There is something to be gained by refusing to endorse the hardness of heart necessary to impose such a fate.

By placing execution alongside torture in the category of things we will not do to our fellow human beings even when they deserve them, we broadcast the message that totally subjugating a person to the power of others *and* confronting him with the advent of his own humanly administered demise is too horrible to be done by civilized human beings to their fellows even when they have earned it: too horrible to do, and too horrible to be capable of doing. And I contend that broadcasting this message loud and clear would in the long run contribute to the general detestation of murder and be, to the extent to which it worked itself into the hearts and minds of the populace, a deterrent. In short, refusing to execute murderers though they deserve it both reflects and continues the taming of the human species that we call civilization. Thus, I take it that the abolition of the death penalty, though it is a just punishment for murder, is part of the civilizing mission of modern states.

IV. CIVILIZATION, SAFETY, AND DETERRENCE

Earlier I said that judging a practice too horrible to do even to those who deserve it does not exclude the possibility that it could be justified if necessary to avoid even worse consequences. Thus, were the death penalty clearly proven a better deterrent to the murder of innocent people than life in prison, we might have to admit that we had not yet reached a level of civilization at which we could protect ourselves without imposing this horrible fate on murderers, and thus we might have to grant the necessity of instituting the death penalty.[33] But this is far from proven. The available research by no means clearly indicates that the death penalty reduces the incidence of homicide more than life imprisonment does. Even the econometric studies of Isaac Ehrlich, which purport to show that each execution saves seven or eight potential murder victims, have not changed this fact, as is testified to by the controversy and objections from equally respected statisticians that Ehrlich's work has provoked.[34]

Conceding that it has not been proven that the death penalty deters more murders than life imprisonment, van den Haag has argued that neither has it been proven that the death penalty does *not* deter more murders,[35] and thus we must follow common sense which teaches that the higher the cost of something, the fewer people will choose it, and therefore at least some potential murderers who would not be deterred by life imprisonment will be deterred by the death penalty. Van den Haag writes:

> . . . our experience shows that the greater the threatened penalty, the more it deters.
> . . . Life in prison is still life, however unpleasant. In contrast, the death penalty does not just threaten to make life unpleasant—it threatens to take life altogether. This difference is perceived by those affected. We find that when they have the choice between life in prison and execution, 99 percent of all prisoners under sentence of death prefer life in prison. . . .

> From this unquestioned fact a reasonable conclusion can be drawn in favor of the superior deterrent effect of the death penalty. Those who have the choice in practice . . . fear death more than they fear life in prison. . . . If they do, it follows that the threat of the death penalty, all other things equal, is likely to deter more than the threat of life in prison. One is most deterred by what one fears most. From which it follows that whatever statistics fail, or do not fail, to show, the death penalty is likely to be more deterrent than any other. (pp. 68–69)[36]

Those of us who recognize how commonsensical it was, and still is, to believe that the sun moves around the earth, will be less willing than Professor van den Haag to follow common sense here, especially when it comes to doing something awful to our fellows. Moreover, there are good reasons for doubting common sense on this matter. Here are four:

1. From the fact that one penalty is more feared than another, it does not follow that the more feared penalty will deter more than the less feared, unless we know that the less feared penalty is not fearful enough to deter everyone who can be deterred—and this is just what we don't know with regard to the death penalty. Though I fear the death penalty more than life in prison, I can't think of any act that the death penalty would deter me from that an equal likelihood of spending my life in prison wouldn't deter me from as well.[37] Since it seems to me that whoever would be deterred by a given likelihood of death would be deterred by an *equal* likelihood of life behind bars, I suspect that the commonsense argument only seems plausible because we evaluate it unconsciously assuming that potential criminals will face larger likelihoods of death sentences than of life sentences. If the likelihoods were equal, it seems to me that where life imprisonment was improbable enough to make it too distant a possibility to worry much about, a similar low probability of death would have the same effect. After all, we are undeterred by small likelihoods of death every time we walk the streets. And if life imprisonment were sufficiently probable to pose a real deterrent threat, it would pose as much of a deterrent threat as death. And this is just what most of the research we have on the comparative deterrent impact of execution versus life imprisonment suggests.

2. In light of the fact that roughly 500 to 700 suspected felons are killed by the police in the line of duty every year, and the fact that the number of privately owned guns in America is substantially larger than the number of households in America, it must be granted that anyone contemplating committing a crime *already* faces a substantial risk of ending up dead as a result.[38] It's hard to see why anyone *who is not already deterred by this* would be deterred by the addition of the more distant risk of death after apprehension, conviction, and appeal. Indeed, this suggests that people consider risks in a much cruder way than van den Haag's appeal to common sense suggests—which should be evident to anyone who contemplates how

few people use seatbelts (14 percent of drivers, on some estimates), when it is widely known that wearing them can spell the difference between life (outside prison) and death.[39]

3. Van den Haag has maintained that deterrence doesn't work only by means of cost-benefit calculations made by potential criminals. It works also by the lesson about the wrongfulness of murder that is slowly learned in a society that subjects murderers to the ultimate punishment (p. 63). But if I am correct in claiming that the refusal to execute even those who deserve it has a civilizing effect, then the refusal to execute also teaches a lesson about the wrongfulness of murder. My claim here is admittedly speculative, but no more so than van den Haag's to the contrary. And my view has the added virtue of accounting for the failure of research to show an increased deterrent effect from executions *without having to deny the plausibility of van den Haag's commonsense argument that at least some additional potential murderers will be deterred by the prospect of the death penalty.* If there is a deterrent effect from *not executing,* then it is understandable that while executions will deter some murderers, this effect will be balanced out by the weakening of the deterrent effect of not executing, such that no net reduction in murders will result.[40] And this, by the way, also disposes of van den Haag's argument that, in the absence of knowledge one way or the other on the deterrent effect of executions, we should execute murderers rather than risk the lives of innocent people whose murders might have been deterred if we had. If there is a deterrent effect of not executing, it follows that we risk innocent lives either way. And if this is so, it seems that the only reasonable course of action is to refrain from imposing what we know is a horrible fate.[41]

4. Those who still think that van den Haag's commonsense argument for executing murderers is valid will find that the argument proves more than they bargained for. Van den Haag maintains that, in the absence of conclusive evidence on the relative deterrent impact of the death penalty versus life imprisonment, we must follow common sense and assume that if one punishment is more fearful than another, it will deter some potential criminals not deterred by the less fearful punishment. Since people sentenced to death will almost universally try to get their sentences changed to life in prison, it follows that death is more fearful than life imprisonment, and thus that it will deter some additional murderers. Consequently, we should institute the death penalty to save the lives these additional murderers would have taken. But, since people sentenced to be tortured to death would surely try to get their sentences changed to simple execution, the same argument proves that death-by-torture will deter still more potential murderers. Consequently, we should institute death-by-torture to save the lives these additional murderers would have taken. Anyone who accepts van den Haag's argument is then confronted with a dilemma: Until we have conclusive evidence that

capital punishment is a greater deterrent to murder than life imprisonment, he must grant *either* that we should not follow common sense and not impose the death penalty; *or* we should follow common sense and torture murderers to death. In short, either we must abolish the electric chair or reinstitute the rack. Surely, this is the *reductio ad absurdum* of van den Haag's commonsense argument.

CONCLUSION: HISTORY, FORCE, AND JUSTICE

I believe that, taken together, these arguments prove that we should abolish the death penalty though it is a just punishment for murder. Let me close with an argument of a different sort. When you see the lash fall upon the backs of Roman slaves, or the hideous tortures meted out in the period of the absolute monarchs, you see more than mere cruelty at work. Surely you suspect that there is something about the injustice of imperial slavery and royal tyranny that requires the use of extreme force to keep these institutions in place. That is, for reasons undoubtedly related to those that support the second part of Durkheim's first law of penal evolution, we take the amount of force a society uses against its own people as an inverse measure of its justness. And though no more than a rough measure, it is a revealing one nonetheless, because when a society is limited in the degree of force it can use against its subjects, it is likely to have to be a juster society since it will have to gain its subjects' cooperation by offering them fairer terms than it would have to, if it could use more force. From this we cannot simply conclude that reducing the force used by our society will automatically make our society more just—but I think we can conclude that it will have this tendency, since it will require us to find means other than force for encouraging compliance with our institutions, and this is likely to require us to make those institutions as fair to all as possible. Thus I hope that America will pose itself the challenge of winning its citizens' cooperation by justice rather than force, and that when future historians look back on the twentieth century, they will find us with countries like France and England and Sweden that have abolished the death penalty, rather than with those like South Africa and the Soviet Union and Iran that have retained it—with all that this suggests about the countries involved.

NOTES

This paper is an expanded version of my opening statement in a debate with Ernest van den Haag on the death penalty at an Amnesty International conference on capital punishment, held at John Jay College in New York City, on October 17,

1983. I am grateful to the Editors of *Philosophy & Public Affairs* for very thought-provoking comments, to Hugo Bedau and Robert Johnson for many helpful suggestions, and to Ernest van den Haag for his encouragement.

1. Asked, in a 1981 Gallup Poll, "Are you in favor of the death penalty for persons convicted of murder?" 66.25 percent were in favor, 25 percent were opposed, and 8.75 percent had no opinion. Asked the same question in 1966, 47.5 percent were opposed, 41.25 percent were in favor, and 11.25 percent had no opinion (Timothy J. Flanagan, David J. van Alstyne, and Michael R. Gottfredson, eds., *Sourcebook of Criminal Justice Statistics—1981*, U.S. Department of Justice, Bureau of Justice Statistics [Washington, D.C.: U.S. Government Printing Office, 1982], p. 209).

2. Ernest van den Haag and John P. Conrad, *The Death Penalty: A Debate* (New York: Plenum Press, 1983). Unless otherwise indicated, page references in the text and notes are to this book.

3. Some days after the first attempt to execute J. D. Autry by lethal injection was aborted, an editorial in *The Washington Post* (October 14, 1983) asked: "If the taking of a human life is the most unacceptable of crimes, can it ever be an acceptable penalty? Does an act committed by an individual lose its essential character when it is imposed by society?" (p. A26).

4. "Does fining a criminal show want of respect for property, or imprisoning him, for personal freedom? Just as unreasonable is it to think that to take the life of a man who has taken that of another is to show want of regard for human life. We show, on the contrary, most emphatically our regard for it, by the adoption of a rule that he who violates that right in another forfeits it for himself. . . ." (John Stuart Mill, "Parliamentary Debate on Capital Punishment Within Prisons Bill," in *Philosophical Perspectives on Punishment,* ed. Gertrude Ezorsky [Albany: State University of New York Press, 1972], p. 276; Mill made the speech in 1868.)

5. Mill argues that the possibility of executing an innocent person would be an "invincible" objection "where the mode of criminal procedure is dangerous to the innocent," such as it is "in some parts of the Continent of Europe. . . . But we all know that the defects of our [English] procedure are the very opposite. Our rules of evidence are even too favorable to the prisoner" (ibid., pp. 276–77).

6. "As a general rule, a man is undone by waiting for capital punishment well before he dies. Two deaths are inflicted on him, the first being worse than the second, whereas he killed but once" (Albert Camus, "Reflections on the Guillotine," in *Resistance, Rebellion and Death* [New York: Alfred A. Knopf, 1969], p. 205). Based on interviews with the condemned men on Alabama's death row, Robert Johnson presents convincing empirical support for Camus' observation, in *Condemned to Life: Life under Sentence of Death* (New York: Elsevier, 1981).

7. Jeffrie G. Murphy, "Marxism and Retribution," *Philosophy & Public Affairs* 2, no. 3 (Spring 1973): 219.

8. I shall speak throughout of retribution as paying back for "harm caused," but this is shorthand for "harm intentionally attempted or caused"; likewise when I speak of the death penalty as punishment for murder, I have in mind premeditated, first-degree murder. Note also that the harm caused by the offender, for which he is to be paid back, is not necessarily limited to the harm done to his immediate victim. It may include as well the suffering of the victim's relatives or the fear produced in the general populace, and the like. For simplicity's sake, however, I shall continue to speak as if the harm for which retributivism would have us pay the offender back is the harm (intentionally attempted or done) to his immediate victim. Also, retribution is not to be confused with *restitution*. Restitution involves restoring the *status quo ante,* the condition prior to the offense. Since it was in this condition

that the criminal's offense was committed, it is this condition that constitutes the baseline against which retribution is exacted. Thus retribution involves imposing a loss on the offender measured from the *status quo ante*. For example, returning a thief's loot to his victim so that the thief and victim now own what they did before the offense is *restitution*. Taking enough from the thief so that what he is left with is less than what he had before the offense is *retribution*, since this is just what he did to his victim.

9. "The most extreme form of retributivism is the law of retaliation: 'an eye for an eye' " (Stanley I. Benn, "Punishment," *The Encyclopedia of Philosophy* 7, ed. Paul Edwards [New York: Macmillan, 1967], p. 32). Hugo Bedau writes: "retributive justice need not be thought to consist of *lex talionis*. One may reject that principle as too crude and still embrace the retributive principle that the severity of punishments should be graded according to the gravity of the offense" (Hugo Bedau, "Capital Punishment," in *Matters of Life and Death*, ed. Tom Regan [New York: Random House, 1980], p. 177). See also Andrew von Hirsch, "Doing Justice: The Principle of Commensurate Deserts," and Hyman Gross, "Proportional Punishment and Justifiable Sentences," in *Sentencing*, eds. H. Gross and A. von Hirsch (New York: Oxford University Press, 1981), pp. 243–56 and 272–83, respectively.

10. In an article aimed at defending a retributivist theory of punishment, Michael Davis claims that the relevant measure of punishment is not the cost to the offender's victim ("property taken, bones broken, or lives lost"), but the "value of the unfair advantage he [the offender] takes of those who obey the law (even though they are tempted to do otherwise)" (Michael Davis, "How to Make the Punishment Fit the Crime," *Ethics* 93 [July 1983]: 744). Though there is much to be said for this view, standing alone it seems quite questionable. For example, it would seem that the value of the unfair advantage taken of law-obeyers by one who robs a great deal of money is greater than the value of the unfair advantage taken by a murderer, since the latter gets only the advantage of ridding his world of a nuisance while the former will be able to make a new life without the nuisance and have money left over for other things. This leads to the counterintuitive conclusion that such robbers should be punished more severely (and regarded as more wicked) than murderers. One might try to get around this by treating the value of the unfair advantage as a function of the cost imposed by the crime. And Davis does this after a fashion. He takes the value of such advantages to be equivalent to the prices that licenses to commit crimes would bring if sold on the market, and he claims that these prices would be at least as much as what non-licenseholders would (for their own protection) pay licensees not to use their licenses. Now this obviously brings the cost to victims of crime back into the measure of punishment, though only halfheartedly, since this cost must be added to the value to the licensee of being able to use his license. And this still leaves open the distinct possibility that licenses for very lucrative theft opportunities would fetch higher prices on the market than licenses to kill, with the same counterintuitive result mentioned earlier.

11. Stanley Benn writes: "to say 'it is fitting' or 'justice demands' that the guilty should suffer is only to affirm that punishment is right, not to give grounds for thinking so" (Benn, "Punishment," p. 30).

12. Hegel writes that "The sole positive existence which the injury [i.e., the crime] possesses is that it is the particular will of the criminal [i.e., it is the criminal's intention that distinguishes criminal injury from, say, injury due to an accident]. Hence to injure (or penalize) this particular will as a will determinately existent is to annul the crime, which otherwise would have been held valid, and to restore the right" (G. W. F. Hegel, *The Philosophy of Right*, trans. by T. M. Knox [Oxford:

Clarendon Press, 1962; originally published in German in 1821], p. 69, see also p. 331n). I take this to mean that the right is a certain equality of sovereignty between the wills of individuals, crime disrupts that equality by placing one will above others, and punishment restores the equality by annulling the illegitimate ascendance. On these grounds, as I shall suggest below, the desire for revenge (strictly limited to the desire "to even the score") is more respectable than philosophers have generally allowed. And so Hegel writes that, "The annulling of crime in this sphere where right is immediate [i.e., the condition prior to conscious morality] is principally revenge, which is just in its content in so far as it is retributive" (ibid., p. 73).

13. Kant writes that "any undeserved evil that you inflict on someone else among the people is one that you do to yourself. If you vilify him, you vilify yourself; if you steal from him, you steal from yourself; if you kill him, you kill yourself." Since Kant holds that, "If what happens to someone is also willed by him, it cannot be a punishment," he takes pains to distance himself from the view that the offender *wills* his punishment. "The chief error contained in this sophistry," Kant writes, "consists in the confusion of the criminal's [that is, the murderer's] own judgment (which one must necessarily attribute to his reason) that he must forfeit his life with a resolution of the will to take his own life" (Immanuel Kant, *The Metaphysical Elements of Justice, Part I of The Metaphysics of Morals,* trans. by J. Ladd [Indianapolis: Bobbs-Merrill, 1965; originally published in 1797], pp. 101, 105–106). I have tried to capture this notion of attributing a judgment to the offender rather than a resolution of his will with the term 'authorizes'.

14. "Even if a civil society were to dissolve itself by common agreement of all its members . . . , the last murderer remaining in prison must first be executed, so that everyone will duly receive what his actions are worth" (Kant, ibid., p. 102). Interestingly, Conrad calls himself a retributivist, but doesn't accept the strict Kantian version of it. In fact, he claims that Kant "did not bother with justifications for his categorical imperative . . . , [but just] insisted that the Roman *jus talionis* was the reference point at which to begin" (p. 22). Van den Haag, by contrast, states specifically that he is "not a retributivist" (p. 32). In fact he claims that "retributionism" is not really a *theory* of punishment at all, just "a feeling articulated through a metaphor presented as though a theory" (p. 28). This is so, he maintains, because a theory "must tell us what the world, or some part thereof, is like or has been or will be like" (ibid.). "In contrast," he goes on, "deterrence theory is, whether right or wrong, a theory: It asks what the effects are of punishment (does it reduce the crime rate?) and makes testable predictions (punishment reduces the crime rate compared to what it would be without the credible threat of punishment)" (p. 29). Now, it should be obvious that van den Haag has narrowed his conception of "theory" so that it only covers the kind of things one finds in the empirical sciences. So narrowed, there is no such thing as a theory about what justifies some action or policy, no such thing as a Kantian theory of punishment, or, for that matter, a Rawlsian theory of justice—that is to say, no such thing as a *moral* theory. Van den Haag, of course, could use the term 'theory' as he wished, were it not for the fact that he appeals to deterrence theory not merely for predictions about crime rates but also (indeed, in the current context, primarily) as a theory about what justifies punishment—that is, as a *moral* theory. And he must, since the fact that punishment reduces crime does not imply that we should institute punishment unless we *should* do whatever reduces crime. In short, van den Haag is about moral theories the way I am about airplanes: He doesn't quite understand how they work, but he knows how to use them to get where he wants to go.

15. "It may also be pointed out that no one has ever heard of anyone condemned

to death on account of murder who complained that he was getting too much [punishment] and therefore was being treated unjustly; everyone would laugh in his face if he were to make such a statement" (Kant, *Metaphysical Elements of Justice*, p. 104; see also p. 133).

16. Herbert Morris defends retributivism on parallel grounds. See his "Persons and Punishment," *The Monist* 52, no. 4 (October 1968): 475–501 [see chapter 5 in this volume]. Isn't what Morris calls "the right to be treated as a person" essentially the right of a rational being to be treated only as he has authorized, implicitly or explicitly, by his own free choices?

17. Bedau writes: "Where criminals set the limits of just methods of punishment, as they will do if we attempt to give exact and literal implementation to *lex talionis*, society will find itself descending to the cruelties and savagery that criminals employ. But society would be deliberately authorizing such acts, in the cool light of reason, and not (as is often true of vicious criminals) impulsively or in hatred and anger or with an insane or unbalanced mind. Moral restraints, in short, prohibit us from trying to make executions perfectly retributive" (Bedau, "Capital Punishment," p. 176).

18. I am indebted to my colleague Robert Johnson for this suggestion, which he has attempted to develop in "A Life for a Life?" (unpub. ms.). He writes that prisoners condemned to spend their entire lives in prison "would suffer a civil death, the death of freedom. The prison would be their cemetery, a 6′ by 9′ cell their tomb. Their freedom would be interred in the name of justice. They would be consigned to mark the passages of their lives in the prison's peculiar dead time, which serves no purpose and confers no rewards. In effect, they would give their civil lives in return for the natural lives they have taken."

19. "In the case of homicide, the empirical evidence indicates that poverty and poor economic conditions are systematically related to higher levels of homicide" (Richard M. McGahey, "Dr. Ehrlich's Magic Bullet: Economic Theory, Econometrics, and the Death Penalty," *Crime & Delinquency* 26, no. 4 [October 1980]: 502). Some of that evidence can be found in Peter Passell, "The Deterrent Effect of the Death Penalty: A Statistical Test," *Stanford Law Review* (November 1975): 61–80.

20. A similar though not identical point has been made by Jeffrie G. Murphy. He writes: "I believe that retributivism can be formulated in such a way that it is the only morally defensible theory of punishment. I also believe that arguments, which may be regarded as Marxist at least in spirit, can be formulated which show that social conditions as they obtain in most societies make this form of retributivism largely inapplicable within those societies" (Murphy, "Marxism and Retribution," p. 221). Though my claim here is similar to Murphy's, the route by which I arrive at it differs from his in several ways. Most important, a key point of Murphy's argument is that retributivism assumes that the criminal freely chooses his crime while, according to Murphy, criminals act on the basis of psychological traits that the society has conditioned them to have: "Is it just to punish people who act out of those very motives that society encourages and reinforces? If [Willem] Bonger [a Dutch Marxist criminologist] is correct, much criminality is motivated by greed, selfishness, and indifference to one's fellows; but does not the whole society encourage motives of greed and selfishness ('making it,' 'getting ahead'), and does not the competitive nature of the society alienate men from each other and thereby encourage indifference—even, perhaps, what psychiatrists call psychopathy?" (ibid., p. 239) This argument assumes that the criminal is in some sense unable to conform to legal and moral prohibitions against violence, and thus, like the insane, cannot be thought responsible for his actions. This claim is rather extreme, and dubious as a result.

My argument does not claim that criminals, murderers in particular, cannot control their actions. I claim rather that, though criminals can control their actions, when crimes are predictable responses to unjust circumstances, then those who benefit from and do not remedy those conditions bear some responsibility for the crimes and thus the criminals cannot be held *wholly* responsible for them in the sense of being legitimately required to pay their full cost. It should be noted that Murphy's thesis (quoted at the beginning of this note) is stated in a somewhat confused way. Social conditions that mitigate or eliminate the guilt of offenders do not make retributivism *inapplicable*. Retributivism is applied both when those who are guilty because they freely chose their crimes are punished *and* when it is held wrong to punish those who are not guilty because they did not freely choose their crimes. It is precisely by the application of retributivism that the social conditions referred to by Murphy make the punishment of criminals unjustifiable.

21. Van den Haag notes the connection between crime and poverty, and explains it and its implications as follows: "Poverty," he holds, "does not compel crime; it only makes it more tempting" (p. 207). And it is not absolute poverty that does this, only relative deprivation, the fact that some have less than others (p. 115). In support of this, he marshals data showing that, over the years, crime has risen along with the standard of living at the bottom of society. Since, unlike absolute deprivation, relative deprivation will be with us no matter how rich we all become as long as some have more than others, he concludes that this condition which increases the temptation to crime is just an ineradicable fact of social life, best dealt with by giving people strong incentives to resist the temptation. This argument is flawed in several ways. First, the claim that crime is connected with poverty ought not be simplistically interpreted to mean that a low absolute standard of living itself causes crime. Rather, what seems to be linked to crime is the general breakdown of stable communities, institutions and families, such as has occurred in our cities in recent decades as a result of economic and demographic trends largely out of individuals' control. Of this breakdown, poverty is today a sign and a cause, at least in the sense that poverty leaves people with few defenses against it and few avenues of escape from it. This claim is quite compatible with finding that people with lower absolute standards of living, but who dwell in more stable social surroundings with traditional institutions still intact, have lower crime rates than contemporary poor people who have higher absolute standards of living. Second, the implication of this is not simply that it is relative deprivation that tempts to crime, since if that were the case, the middle class would be stealing as much from the rich as the poor do from the middle class. That this is not the case suggests that there is some threshold after which crime is no longer so tempting, and while this threshold changes historically, it is in principle all one could reach. Thus, it is not merely the (supposedly ineradicable) fact of having less than others that tempts to crime. Finally, everything is altered if the temptation to crime is not the result of an ineradicable social fact, but of an injustice that can be remedied or relieved. Obviously, this would require considerable argument, but it seems to me that the current distribution of wealth in America is unjust whether one takes utilitarianism as one's theory of justice (given the relative numbers of rich and poor in America as well as the principle of declining marginal returns, redistribution could make the poor happier without an offsetting loss in happiness among the rich) or Rawls's theory (the worst-off shares in our society could still be increased, so the difference principle is not yet satisfied) or Nozick's theory (since the original acquisition of property in America was marked by the use of force against Indians and blacks, from which both groups still suffer).

22. In arguing that social injustice disqualifies us from applying the death penalty, I am arguing that unjust discrimination in the *recruitment* of murderers undermines the justice of applying the penalty under foreseeable conditions in the United States. This is distinct from the argument that points to the discriminatory way in which it has been *applied* to murderers (generally against blacks, particularly when their victims are white). This latter argument is by no means unimportant, nor do I believe that it has been rendered obsolete by the Supreme Court's 1972 decision in *Furman* v. *Georgia* that struck down then-existing death penalty statutes because they allowed discriminatory application, or the Court's 1976 decision in *Gregg* v. *Georgia,* which approved several new statutes because they supposedly remedied this problem. There is considerable empirical evidence that much the same pattern of discrimination that led to *Furman* continues after *Gregg.* See, for example, William J. Bowers and Glenn L. Pierce, "Arbitrariness and Discrimination in Post-*Furman* Capital Statutes," *Crime & Delinquency* 26, no. 4 (October 1980): 563–635. Moreover, I believe that continued evidence of such discrimination would constitute a separate and powerful argument for abolition. Faced with such evidence, van den Haag's strategy is to grant that discrimination is wrong, but claim that it is not "inherent in the death penalty"; it is a characteristic of "its distribution" (p. 206). Thus discrimination is not an objection to the death penalty itself. This rejoinder is unsatisfactory for several reasons. First of all, even if discrimination is not an objection to the death penalty *per se,* its foreseeable persistence is—as the Court recognized in *Furman*—an objection to instituting the death penalty *as a policy.* Moral assessment of the way in which a penalty will be carried out may be distinct from moral assessment of the penalty itself, but, since the way in which the penalty will be carried out is part of what we will be bringing about if we institute the penalty, it is a necessary consideration in any assessment of the morality of instituting the penalty. In short, van den Haag's strategy saves the death penalty in principle, but fails to save it in practice. Second, it may well be that discrimination is (as a matter of social and psychological fact in America) inherent in the penalty of death itself. The evidence of its persistence after *Furman* lends substance to the suspicion that something about the death penalty— perhaps the very terribleness of it that recommends it to van den Haag—strikes at deep-seated racial prejudices in a way that milder penalties do not. In any event, this is an empirical matter, not resolved by analytic distinctions between what is distributed and how it is distributed. Finally, after he mounts his argument against the discrimination objection, van den Haag usually adds that those who oppose capital punishment "because of discriminatory application are not quite serious . . . , [since] they usually will confess, if pressed, that they would continue their opposition even if there were no discrimination whatsoever in the administration of the death penalty" (p. 225). This is preposterous. It assumes that a person can have only one serious objection to any policy. If he had several, then he would naturally continue to oppose the policy *quite seriously* even though all his objections but one were eliminated. In addition to discrimination in the *recruitment* of murderers, and in the *application* of the death penalty among murderers, there is a third sort that affects the justice of instituting the penalty, namely, discrimination in the *legal definition* of murder. I take this and related issues up in *The Rich Get Rich and the Poor Get Prison: Ideology, Class, and Criminal Justice,* 2d ed. (New York: John Wiley, 1984).

23. Friedrich Nietzsche, *The Birth of Tragedy and The Genealogy of Morals* (New York: Doubleday, 1956), pp. 199–200.

24. Van den Haag writes that our ancestors "were not as repulsed by physical pain as we are. The change has to do not with our greater smartness or moral

superiority but with a new outlook pioneered by the French and American revolutions [namely, the assertion of human equality and with it 'universal identification'], and by such mundane things as the invention of anesthetics, which make pain much less of an everyday experience" (p. 215; cf. van den Haag's *Punishing Criminals* [New York: Basic Books, 1975], pp. 196–206).

25. Emile Durkheim, "Two Laws of Penal Evolution," *Economy and Society* 2 (1973): 285 and 294; italics in the original. This essay was originally published in French in *Année Sociologique* 4 (1899–1900). Conrad, incidentally, quotes Durkheim's two laws (p. 39), but does not develop their implications for his side in the debate.

26. Durkheim writes that "of the two laws which we have established, the first contributes to an explanation of the second" (Durkheim, "Two Laws of Penal Evolution," p. 299).

27. The "two causes of the evolution of punishment—the nature of the social type and of the governmental organ—must be carefully distinguished" (ibid., p. 288). Durkheim cites the ancient Hebrews as an example of a society of the less developed type that had milder punishments than societies of the same social type due to the relative absence of absolutist government among the Hebrews (ibid., p. 290).

28. Durkheim's own explanation of the progressive moderation of punishments is somewhat unclear. He rejects the notion that it is due to the growth in sympathy for one's fellows since this, he maintains, would make us more sympathetic with victims and thus harsher in punishments. He argues instead that the trend is due to the shift from understanding crimes as offenses against God (and thus warranting the most terrible of punishments) to understanding them as offenses against men (thus warranting milder punishments). He then seems to come round nearly full circle by maintaining that this shift works to moderate punishments by weakening the religious sentiments that overwhelmed sympathy for the condemned: "The true reason is that the compassion of which the condemned man is the object is no longer overwhelmed by the contrary sentiments which would not let it make itself felt" (ibid., p. 303).

29. Van den Haag seems to waffle on the question of the unique awfulness of execution. For instance, he takes it not to be revolting in the way that earcropping is, because "We all must die. But we must not have our ears cropped" (p. 190), and here he cites John Stuart Mill's parliamentary defense of the death penalty in which Mill maintains that execution only *hastens* death. Mill's point was to defend the claim that, "There is not . . . any human infliction which makes an impression on the imagination so entirely out of proportion to its real severity as the punishment of death" (Mill, "Parliamentary Debate," p. 273). And van den Haag seems to agree since he maintains that, since "we cannot imagine our own nonexistence . . . , [t]he fear of the death penalty is in part the fear of the unknown. It . . . rests on a confusion" (pp. 258–59). On the other hand, he writes that, "Execution sharpens our separation anxiety because death becomes clearly foreseen. . . . Further, and perhaps most important, when one is executed he does not just die, he is put to death, forcibly expelled from life. He is told that he is too depraved, unworthy of living with other humans" (p. 258). I think, incidentally, that it is an overstatement to say that we cannot imagine our own nonexistence. If we can imagine any counterfactual experience, for example, how we might feel if we didn't know something that we do in fact know, then it doesn't seem impossible to imagine what it would "feel like" not to live. I think I can arrive at a pretty good approximation of this by trying to imagine how things "felt" to me in the eighteenth century. And, in fact, the sense of the awful difference between being alive and not that enters my experience

when I do this, makes the fear of death—not as a state, but as the absence of life—seem hardly to rest on a confusion.

30. I am not here endorsing this view of voluntarily entered slavery or prostitution. I mean only to suggest that it is *the belief* that these relations involve the extreme subjugation of one person to the power of another that is at the basis of their offensiveness. What I am saying is quite compatible with finding that this belief is false with respect to voluntarily entered slavery or prostitution.

31. This is no doubt partly due to modern skepticism about an afterlife. Earlier peoples regarded a foreseen death as a blessing allowing time to make one's peace with God. Writing of the early Middle Ages, Phillippe Aries says, "In this world that was so familiar with death, sudden death was a vile and ugly death; it was frightening; it seemed a strange and monstrous thing that nobody dared talk about" (Phillippe Aries, *The Hour of Our Death* [New York: Vintage, 1982], p. 11).

32. George Orwell, *1984* (New York: American Library, 1983; originally published in 1949), p. 197.

33. I say "might" here to avoid the sticky question of just how effective a deterrent the death penalty would have to be to justify overcoming our scruples about executing. It is here that the other considerations often urged against capital punishment—discrimination, irrevocability, the possibility of mistake, and so on—would play a role. Omitting such qualifications, however, my position might crudely be stated as follows: *Just desert limits what a civilized society may do to deter crime, and deterrence limits what a civilized society may do to give criminals their just deserts.*

34. Isaac Ehrlich, "The Deterrent Effect of Capital Punishment: A Question of Life or Death," *American Economic Review* 65 (June 1975): 397–417. For reactions to Ehrlich's work, see Alfred Blumstein, Jacqueline Cohen, and Daniel Nagin, eds., *Deterrence and Incapacitation: Estimating the Effects of Criminal Sanctions on Crime Rates* (Washington, D.C.: National Academy of Sciences, 1978), esp. pp. 59–63 and 336–60; Brian E. Forst, "The Deterrent Effect on Capital Punishment: A Cross-State Analysis," *Minnesota Law Review* 61 (May 1977): 743–67; Deryck Beyleveld, "Ehrlich's Analysis of Deterrence," *British Journal of Criminology* 22 (April 1982): 101–23; and Isaac Ehrlich, "On Positive Methodology, Ethics and Polemics in Deterrence Research," *British Journal of Criminology* 22 (April 1982): 124–39. Much of the criticism of Ehrlich's work focuses on the fact that he found a deterrence impact of executions in the period from 1933–1969, which includes the period of 1963–1969, a time when hardly any executions were carried out and crime rates rose for reasons that are arguably independent of the existence or nonexistence of capital punishment. When the 1963–1969 period is excluded, no significant deterrence effect shows. Prior to Ehrlich's work, research on the comparative deterrent impact of the death penalty versus life imprisonment indicated no increase in the incidence of homicide in states that abolished the death penalty and no greater incidence of homicide in states without the death penalty compared to similar states with the death penalty. See Thorsten Sellin, *The Death Penalty* (Philadelphia: American Law Institute, 1959).

35. Van den Haag writes: "Other studies published since Ehrlich's contend that his results are due to the techniques and periods he selected, and that different techniques and periods yield different results. Despite a great deal of research on all sides, one cannot say that the statistical evidence is conclusive. Nobody has claimed to have *disproved* that the death penalty may deter more than life imprisonment. But one cannot claim, either, that it has been proved statistically in a conclusive manner that the death penalty does deter more than alternative penalties. This lack of proof does not amount to disproof" (p. 65).

36. An alternative formulation of this "commonsense argument" is put forth and defended by Michael Davis in "Death, Deterrence, and the Method of Common Sense," *Social Theory and Practice* 7, no. 2 (Summer 1981): 145–77. Davis's argument is like van den Haag's except that, where van den Haag claims that people *do* fear the death penalty more than lesser penalties and *are* deterred by what they fear most, Davis claims that it is *rational* to fear the death penalty more than lesser penalties and thus *rational* to be more deterred by it. Thus, he concludes that the death penalty is the most effective deterrent *for rational people*. He admits that this argument is "about rational agents, not actual people" (ibid., p. 157). To bring it back to the actual criminal justice system that deals with actual people, Davis claims that the criminal law makes no sense unless we suppose the potential criminal to be (more or less) "rational" (ibid., p. 153). In short, the death penalty is the most effective deterrent because it would be rational to be most effectively deterred by it, and we are committed by belief in the criminal law to supposing that people will do what is rational. The problem with this strategy is that a deterrence justification of a punishment is valid only if it proves that the punishment actually deters actual people from committing crimes. If it doesn't prove that, it misses its mark, no matter what we are committed to supposing. Unless Davis's argument is a way of proving that the actual people governed by the criminal law will be more effectively deterred by the death penalty than by lesser penalties, it is irrelevant to the task at hand. And if it is a way of proving that actual people will be better deterred, then it is indistinguishable from van den Haag's version of the argument and vulnerable to the criticisms of it which follow.

37. David A. Conway writes: "given the choice, I would strongly prefer one thousand years in hell to eternity there. Nonetheless, if one thousand years in hell were the penalty for some action, it would be quite sufficient to deter me from performing that action. The additional years would do nothing to discourage me further. Similarly, the prospect of the death penalty, while worse, may not have any greater deterrent effect than does that of life imprisonment" (David A. Conway, "Capital Punishment and Deterrence: Some Considerations in Dialogue Form," *Philosophy & Public Affairs* 3, no. 4 [Summer 1974]: 433).

38. On the number of people killed by the police, see Lawrence W. Sherman and Robert H. Langworthy, "Measuring Homicide by Police Officers," *Journal of Criminal Law and Criminology* 70, no. 4 (Winter 1979): 546–60; on the number of privately owned guns, see Franklin Zimring, *Firearms and Violence in American Life* (Washington, D.C.: U.S. Government Printing Office, 1968), pp. 6–7.

39. *AAA World* (Potomac ed.) 4, no. 3 (May–June 1984): 18c and 18i.

40. A related claim has been made by those who defend the so-called brutalization hypothesis by presenting evidence to show that murders *increase* following an execution. See, for example, William J. Bowers and Glenn L. Pierce, "Deterrence or Brutalization: What Is the Effect of Executions?" *Crime & Delinquency* 26, no. 4 (October 1980): 453–84. They conclude that each execution gives rise to two additional homicides in the month following, and that these are real additions, not just a change in timing of the homicides (ibid., p. 481). My claim, it should be noted, is not identical to this, since, as I indicate in the text, what I call "the deterrence effect of not executing" is not something whose impact is to be seen immediately following executions but over the long haul, and, further, my claim is compatible with finding no net increase in murders due to executions. Nonetheless, should the brutalization hypothesis be borne out by further studies, it would certainly lend support to the notion that there is a deterrent effect of not executing.

41. Van den Haag writes: "If we were quite ignorant about the marginal deterrent

effects of execution, we would have to choose—like it or not—between the certainty of the convicted murderer's death by execution and the likelihood of the survival of future victims of other murderers on the one hand, and on the other his certain survival and the likelihood of the death of new victims. I'd rather execute a man convicted of having murdered others than put the lives of innocents at risk. I find it hard to understand the opposite choice" (p. 69). Conway was able to counter this argument earlier by pointing out that the research on the marginal deterrent effects of execution was not *inconclusive* in the sense of *tending to point both ways,* but rather in the sense of *giving us no reason to believe that capital punishment saves more lives than life imprisonment.* He could then answer van den Haag by saying that the choice is not between risking the lives of murderers and risking the lives of innocents, but between killing a murderer with no reason to believe lives will be saved, and sparing a murderer with no reason to believe lives will be lost (Conway, "Capital Punishment and Deterrence," pp. 442–43). This, of course, makes the choice to spare the murderer more understandable than van den Haag allows. Events, however, have overtaken Conway's argument. The advent of Ehrlich's research, contested though it may be, leaves us in fact with research that tends to point both ways.

16

Refuting Reiman and Nathanson

Ernest van den Haag

I shall consider Jeffrey Reiman's view of the punishment offenders deserve before turning to his moral scruples, alleged to justify lesser punishments, and to the discriminatory distribution of the death penalty which Stephen Nathanson stresses.

Reiman believes the death penalty is deserved by some murderers, but should never be imposed. Moral scruples should preclude it. If the punishment deserved according to the *lex talionis* is morally repugnant, we may impose less, provided the suffering imposed *in lieu of* what is deserved is proportional to the suffering inflicted on the crime victim. However, suffering exceeding that of his victim can never be deserved by the offender; to impose it would be "unjust for the same reasons that make punishment of the innocent unjust."[1]

MEASUREMENT

How do we know whether the punitive suffering to be imposed on the offender is less or "equal to that which he imposed on the victim" so as not to exceed what he deserves?[2] Cardinal and interpersonal measurement of suffering would be required to find out. Although ordinal measurement is possible in some cases, the cardinal and interpersonal measurement required by Reiman's scheme is not.[3] How many days must the kidnapper be confined, to suffer as much, but no more, than his victim? If he kept his victim three days, are three days of confinement correct? Or three hundred? Or one

From *Philosophy & Public Affairs* 14, no. 2 (Spring 1985). Copyright © 1985 by Princeton University Press. Reprinted with permission of Princeton University Press.

thousand? If he half-starved his victim, should we do as much to him, or, how do we commute starvation into additional time?

Punishment for kidnapping can be, within limits, of the same kind as the crime, although all we can actually do to conform to Reiman's prescription even here is to confine for a longer time the kidnapper who kept his victim for a longer time. We have no way of comparing the victim's suffering with the victimizer's, and to limit the latter accordingly. Execution, too, bears some similarity to the murderer's crime. But confinement? How do we make it commensurate with murder? What about the punishment for assault, burglary, or rape? How do we compare the pain suffered by the victims with the pain to be imposed on the offender by confinement, to make sure that the latter not exceed the former? There is no way of applying Reiman's criterion of desert. Fortunately, we don't need to.

ACTUAL DESERT

Even if, somehow, we knew that three days' confinement inflicts as much pain as his victim suffered on the kidnapper who kept his victim three days, we would feel that the kidnapper deserves much more punishment. That feeling would be appropriate. The offender imposed undeserved suffering on his victim. Why should society not impose undeserved (in Reiman's terminology) suffering on the offender? It would be undeserved only if one accepts Reiman's flawed view of retribution, for, in addition to whatever he deserves for what his victim suffered, the offender also deserves punishment for breaking the law, for imposing undeserved, unlawful suffering on someone. Retributionism of any kind cannot authorize less, despite Reiman's view that suffering imposed on the criminal is unjust when it exceeds the suffering of his victim.

Although occasionally he indicates awareness of the social harm caused by crime and even of the social function of punishment, Reiman treats crimes as though involving but a relationship between victim and offender implemented by judicial authorities.[4] From this faulty premise he infers that retribution should not exceed the harm done to the victim, an idea derived from the *lex talionis*. But that primitive rule was meant to limit the revenge private parties could exact for what was regarded as private harm. The function of the rule was to guard against social disruption by unlimited and indefinitely extended vengeance.

Crimes are no longer regarded merely as private harms. Retribution for the suffering of the individual victims, however much deserved, is not punishment any more than restitution is. Punishment must vindicate the disrupted public order, the violated law, must punish for the social harm done. If my neighbor is burglarized or robbed, he is harmed. But we all must take costly precautions, and we all feel and are threatened: crime harms society as it harms victims. Hence, punishment must, whenever possible, impose pain believed to exceed the pain suffered by the individual victim of crime. No less is deserved. Punishment must be determined by the total gravity of the crime, the social as well as the individual harm, and by the need to deter from the harmful crime. There are ordinal limits to deserved punishments, but cardinal upper limits are set only by harm, habit and sentiment—not by victim suffering.

Let me now turn to the moral scruples which should lead us to reduce punishment to less than what is deserved in some cases. I share some of Reiman's scruples: although he deserves it, I do not want to see the torturer tortured. Other scruples strike me as unjustified.

POVERTY AND CULPABILITY

Reiman believes "that the vast majority of murders in America are a predictable response to the frustrations and disabilities of impoverished social circumstances" which could be, but are not remedied because "others in America benefit," wherefore we have "no right to exact the full cost . . . from our murderers until we have done everything possible to rectify the conditions that produce their crimes."[5] Murder here seems to become the punishment for the sins of the wealthy. According to Reiman, "the vast majority" of current murderers are not fully culpable, since part of the blame for their crimes must be placed on those who fail to "rectify the conditions that produce their crimes."

I grant that certain social conditions predictably produce crime more readily than others. Does it follow that those who commit crimes in criminogenic conditions are less responsible, or blameworthy, than they would be if they did not live in these conditions? Certainly not. Predictability does not reduce responsibility. Reiman remains responsible for his predictable argument. Culpability is reduced only when the criminal's ability to control his actions, or to realize that they are wrong, is abnormally impaired. If not, the social conditions in which the criminal lives have no bearing on his irresponsibility for his acts. Conditions, such as poverty, just or unjust, may increase the temptation to commit crimes. But poverty is neither a necessary nor a sufficient condition for crime, and thus certainly not a coercive one. If there is no compulsion, temptation is no excuse. The law is meant to restrain, and to hold responsible, those tempted to break it. It need not restrain those not tempted, and it cannot restrain those who are unable to control their actions.

Reiman's claim, that even "though criminals can control their actions, when crimes are predictable responses to unjust circumstances, then those who benefit from and do not remedy those conditions bear some responsibility for the crimes and thus the criminals cannot be held *wholly* responsible for them . . ." seems quite unjustified. Those responsible for unjust conditions must be blamed for them,[6] but not for crimes that are "predictable responses to unjust circumstances," if the respondents could have avoided these crimes, as most people living in unjust conditions do.

If crimes are political, that is, address not otherwise remediable "unjust circumstances," they may be held to be morally, if not legally, excusable, on some occasions.[7] But the criminal's moral, let alone legal, responsibility for a crime which he committed for personal gain and could have avoided, is not diminished merely because he lives in unjust circumstances, and his crime was a predictable response to them. Suppose the predictable response to unjust wealth were drunken driving, or rape. Would his wealth excuse the driver or the rapist? Why should poverty, if wealth would not?[8]

Crime is produced by many circumstances, "just" and "unjust." The most just society may have no less crime than the least just (unless "just" is defined circularly as the absence of crime). Tracing crime to causal circumstances is useful and may help us to control it. Suggesting that they *eo ipso* are excuses confuses causality with nonresponsibility. *Tout comprendre ce n'est pas tout pardonner,* Mme. de Staël's followers to the contrary notwithstanding. Excuses require specific circumstances that diminish the actor's control over his actions.

Since "unjust circumstances" do not reduce the responsibility of criminals for their acts, I shall refrain from discussing whether Reiman's circumstances really are unjust, or merely unequal, and whether they do exist because someone benefits from them and could be eliminated if the alleged beneficiaries wished to eliminate them. I am not sure that unjust circumstances always can be remedied, without causing worse injustices. Nor do I share Reiman's confidence that we know what social justice is, or how to produce it.

CIVILIZATION

Reiman thinks that the death penalty is not civilized, because it involves the total subjugation of one person to others, as does slavery, or prostitution.[9]

Whereas slavery usually is not voluntary, the murderer runs the risk of execution voluntarily; he could avoid it by not murdering. I find nothing uncivilized in imposing the risk of subjugation and death on those who decide to murder.

Nota bene: Persons who act with diminished capacity, during moments of passion, are usually convicted of manslaughter rather than murder. Even if convicted of murder, they are not sentenced to death; only if the court believes that the murderer did have a choice, and intended to murder, can he receive the death sentence.

Reiman refers to research finding a brutalization effect, such that executions lead to more homicides. The data are unpersuasive. Some researchers find an increase, some a decrease, of homicides immediately after an execution.[10] Either effect seems ephemeral, involving bunching, rather than changes in the annual homicide rate.

To argue more generally, as Reiman also does, that capital punishment is inconsistent with the advancement of civilization, is to rely on arbitrary definitions of "advancement" and "civilization" for a circular argument. If civilization actually had "advanced" in the direction Reiman, quoting Durkheim, thinks it has, why is that a reason for not preferring "advancement" in some other, perhaps opposite, direction? I cannot find the *moral* (normative) argument in Reiman's description.

DETERRENCE

The death penalty should be retained if abolition would endanger us, Reiman believes. But he does not believe that abolition would. He may be right. However, some of his arguments seem doubtful.

He thinks that whatever marginal deterrent effect capital punishment has, if it has any, is not needed, since life imprisonment provides all the deterrence needed. How can it be ascertained that punishment X deters "everyone who can be deterred" so that punishment X-plus would not deter additional persons? I can see no way to determine this, short of experiments we are unlikely to undertake. Reiman may fear life imprisonment as much, or more, than death. Couldn't someone else fear death more and be insufficiently deterred by life imprisonment?

I cannot prove conclusively that the death penalty deters more than life imprisonment, or that the added deterrence is needed. Reiman cannot prove conclusively that the added deterrence is not needed, or produced. I value the life of innocents more than the life of murderers. Indeed, I value the life of murderers negatively. Wherefore I prefer over- to under-protection. I grant this is a preference.

SELF-DEFENSE

Reiman also believes that murderers who are not deterred by the risk they run because their victims may defend themselves with guns will not be deterred by the risk of execution. This seems unrealistic. Murderers rarely run much risk from self-defense since they usually ambush unsuspecting victims.

TORTURE

On my reasoning, Reiman contends, torture should be used, since it may deter more than execution; or else, even if more deterrent than alternatives, the death penalty should be abolished as torture was: "either we must abolish the electric chair or reinstitute the rack," is his colorful phrase. But there is a difference. I do not oppose torture as undeserved or nondeterrent (although I doubt that the threat of the rack, or of anything adds deterrence to the threat of execution), but simply as repulsive. Death is not; nor is the death penalty. Perhaps repulsiveness is not enough to exclude the rack. If Reiman should convince me that the threat of the rack adds a great deal of deterrence to the threat of execution he might persuade me to overcome my revulsion and to favor the rack as well. It certainly can be deserved.

MORAL THEORY

In *The Death Penalty: A Debate*[11] I noted that only when punishments are based not on retribution alone, but also on deterrence, they rest on a theory, that is, on a correlation of recurrent facts to a prediction: punishment X will, *ceteris paribus,* reduce the rate of crime Y by 10 percent, and X-plus will bring a reduction of 20 percent. Reiman censures me for using "theory" when I should have written "empirical theory." He is right. Further, deterrence does not morally justify any punishment, unless one has first accepted the moral desirability of reducing crime, and the tolerability of the costs. I should have pointed that out. Finally, I did not mean to deny that there are moral theories to justify retribution. They strike me as more dependent on feeling than empirical theories are. More to the point, unlike deterrence theory, justice theories are not meant to predict the effect of various punishments, and are not capable of determining, except ordinally, what these punishments should be, although they can help to justify the distribution of punishments.[12]

MODES OF EXECUTION

As Reiman stresses, the spectacle of execution is not pretty. Nor is surgery. Wherefore both should be attended only by the necessary personnel.[13] I do not find Reiman's aesthetic or moral scruples sufficient to preclude execution or surgery. However, I share his view that lethal injections are particularly unpleasant, not so much because of the subjugation which disturbs him, but because of the veterinary air. (We put animals "to sleep" when sick or inconvenient.) In contrast, shooting strikes me as dignified; it is painless, too, and probably the best way of doing what is necessary.

LIFE IMPRISONMENT

Reiman proposes life imprisonment without parole instead of execution. Although less feared, and therefore likely to be less deterrent, actual lifelong imprisonment strikes me as more cruel than execution even if perceived as less harsh. Its comparative cruelty was stressed already by Cesare Bonesana, Marchese di Beccaria, and by many other since.

Life imprisonment also becomes undeserved over time. A person who committed a murder when twenty years old and is executed within five years—far too long and cruel a delay in my opinion—is, when executed, still the person who committed the crime for which he is punished. His identity changes little in five years. However, a person who committed a murder when he was twenty years old and is kept in prison when sixty years old, is no longer the same person who committed the crime for which he is still being punished. The sexagenarian is unlikely to have much in common with the twenty-year-old for whose act he is being punished; his legal identity no longer reflects reality. Personality and actual identity are not that continuous. In effect, we punish an innocent sexagenarian who does not deserve punishment, instead of a guilty twenty-year-old who did. This spectacle should offend our moral sensibilities more than the deserved execution of the twenty-year-old. Those who deserve the death penalty should be executed while they deserve it, not kept in prison when they no longer deserve any punishment.

DISCRIMINATION

Disagreeing with the Supreme Court, Stephen Nathanson believes that the death penalty still is distributed in an excessively capricious and discriminatory manner. He thinks capital punishment is "unjust" because poor blacks are more likely to be sentenced to death than wealthy whites. Further, blacks who murdered whites are more likely to be executed than those who murdered blacks.[14] This last discrimination has been thrown into relief recently by authors who seem to be under the impression that they have revealed a new form of discrimination against black murderers. They have not. The practice invidiously discriminates against black victims of murder, who are not as fully, or as often, vindicated as white victims are. However, discrimination against a class of victims, although invidious enough, does not amount to discrimination against their victimizers. The discrimination against black victims, the lesser punishment given their murderers, actually favors black murderers, since most black victims are killed by black murderers. Stephen Nathanson and Jeffrey Reiman appear to think that they have captured additional discrimination against black defendants. They are wrong.

Neither the argument from discrimination against black victims, nor the argument from discrimination against black murderers, has any bearing on the guilt of black murderers, or on the punishment they deserve.

Invidious discrimination is never defensible. Yet I do not see wherein it, in Reiman's words, "would constitute a separate and powerful argument for abolition," or does make the death penalty "unjust" for those discriminatorily selected to suffer it, as Stephen Nathanson believes.[15] If we grant that some (even all) murderers of blacks, or, some (even all) white and rich murderers, escape the death penalty, how does that reduce the guilt of murderers of whites, or of black and poor murderers, so that they should be spared execution, too? Guilt is personal. No murderer becomes less guilty, or less deserving of punishment, because another murderer was punished leniently, or escaped punishment altogether. We should try our best to bring every murderer to justice. But if one got away with murder wherein is that a reason to let anyone else get away? A group of murderers does not become less deserving of punishment because another equally guilty group is not punished, or punished less. We can punish only a very small proportion of all criminals. Unavoidably they are selected accidentally. We should reduce this accidentality as much as possible but we cannot eliminate it.[16]

EQUAL INJUSTICE AND UNEQUAL JUSTICE

Reiman and Nathanson appear to prefer equal injustice—letting all get away with murder if some do—to unequal justice: punishing some guilty offenders according to desert, even if others get away. Equal justice is best, but unattainable. Unequal justice is our lot in this world. It is the only justice we can ever have, for not all murderers can be apprehended or convicted, or sentenced equally in different courts. We should constantly try to bring every offender to justice. But meanwhile unequal justice is the only justice we have, and certainly better than equal injustice—giving no murderer the punishment his crime deserves.

MORE DISCRIMINATION

Nathanson insists that some arbitrary selections among those equally guilty are not "just." He thinks that selecting only bearded speeders for ticketing, allowing the cleanshaven to escape, is unjust. Yet the punishment of the bearded speeders is not unjust. The escape of the cleanshaven ones is. I never maintained that a discriminatory distribution is just—only that it is irrelevant to the guilt and deserved punishment of those actually guilty.

Nathanson further suggests that it is not just to spare some student plagiarizers punishment for (I suppose) irrelevant reasons, while punishing others. Again the distribution is discriminatory, i.e., unjust. But the punishment of the plagiarizers selected is not. (The nonpunishment of the others is.) Nathanson thinks that giving a prize only to one of three deserving children (his own) is unjust. Not to the deserving child. Only to the others, just as it was unjust not to punish the others who deserved it, but not unjust to punish the deserving plagiarizers who were irrelevantly selected.[17]

Nathanson taxes me with inconsistency because in a footnote I wrote that irrelevant discriminations are "not acceptable to our sense of justice." They are not. But I did not say that those who deserved the punishment received, or the reward, were unjustly treated, that is, did not deserve it and should not have received it. Rather those equally situated also should have received it, and the distribution was offensive because they did not. Whenever possible this inequality should be corrected, but certainly not by not distributing the punishment, or the reward at issue, or by not giving it to the deserving. Rather by giving it as well to those who because of discrimination did not get it. (I might have done better to write in my footnote that discriminatory distributions offend our sense of *equal* justice. But neither the Constitution nor I favor replacing justice with equality.)

Nathanson quotes the late Justice Douglas suggesting that a law which deliberately prescribes execution only for the guilty poor, or which has that effect, would be unconstitutional. Perhaps. But the vice would be in exempting the guilty rich; the guilty poor would remain guilty, and deserving of prescribed punishment even if the guilty rich escape legally or otherwise.[18]

Further on Nathanson points out that the inevitable capriciousness in the distribution of punishments (only a very small percentage of offenders are ever punished and the selection unavoidably is morally arbitrary), while no reason to abolish punishment in general, may still be an argument for abolishing capital punishment because of its unique severity, and because we could survive without. We can survive without many things, which is not reason for doing without, if one thinks, as I do, that we survive *better* with. As for the unique severity of the death penalty it is, of course, the reason for imposing it for uniquely heinous crimes. The guilt of those who committed them is not diminished, if they are selected by a lottery from among all those guilty of the crime.

Following Charles Black, Nathanson notes that those executed are not necessarily the worst murderers, since there is no way of selecting these. He is right. It seems quite sufficient, however, that those executed, though not the worst, are bad enough to deserve execution. That others who deserved it even more got away, does not make those executed insufficiently deserving.

Nathanson goes on to insist that "not every person who kills another is guilty of the same crime." True. Wherefore the law makes many distinctions, leaving only a small group of those guilty of homicide eligible for the death penalty. Further, capital punishment is not mandated. The court must decide in each case whether or not to impose it. To impose capital punishment, courts must find that the aggravating circumstances attending the murder outweigh the mitigating ones, both of which must be listed in the law. Nathanson is right in pointing out that the criteria listed in the law are not easy to apply. If they were, we would not need the judgment of the court. That judgment is not easy to make. It may seem too severe, or not severe enough, in some cases, as would mandated penalties. So what else is new?

NOTES

1. See Jeffrey H. Reiman, "Justice, Civilization, and the Death Penalty: Answering van den Haag," *Philosophy & Public Affairs* 14, no. 2: 128. Unless otherwise noted, all my quotations are taken from Reiman's article.

2. This question arises only when the literal *lex talionis* is abandoned—as Reiman proposes to do, for good reason—in favor of the proportional retribution he suggests. How, by the way, would we punish a skyjacker? Summing up the suffering of all the skyjacked passengers? What about the damage to air traffic?

3. The order of punishments is notoriously hard to coordinate with the order of crimes; even when punishments are homogeneous, crimes are not.

4. Perhaps Reiman's excessive reliance on the Hegelian justification of retribution (to vindicate the equality of victim and offender) or on the Kantian version (to vindicate the rationality of both) is to blame.

5. Reiman does not say here that murder deserves less than the death penalty, but only that "the vast majority of murderers" deserve less because impoverished. However, wealthy murderers can be fully culpable, so that we may "exact the full cost" from them.

6. Who are they? They are not necessarily the beneficiaries, as Reiman appears to believe. I benefit from rent control, which I think unjust to my landlord, but I'm not responsible for it. I may benefit from low prices for services or goods, without being responsible for them, or for predictable criminal responses to them. Criminals benefit from the unjust exclusionary rules of our courts. Are they to blame for these rules?

7. See my *Political Violence & Civil Disobedience, passim* (New York: Harper & Row, 1972), for a more detailed argument.

8. Suppose unjust wealth tends to corrupt, and unjust poverty does not. Would the wealthy be less to blame for their crimes?

9. Prostitution does not involve total subjugation and is voluntary. In an ambiguous footnote Reiman asserts that it is the perception of prostitution as subjugation that makes it offensive. But this perception, derived from pulp novels more than from reality, is not what makes the voluntary act offensive. Rather, it is the sale of sex as a fungible service, divorced from affection and depersonalized that is offensive. Anyway, when something is offensive because misperceived it is not the thing that is offensive.

10. David P. Phillips, "The Deterrent Effect of Capital Punishment: New Evidence on an Old Controversy," *The American Journal of Sociology* (July 1980).

For further discussion see loc. cit., July 1982. See also Lester, *Executions as a Deterrent to Homicides,* 44 *Psychological Rep.* 562 (1979).

11. Ernest van den Haag and John P. Conrad (New York: Plenum Press, 1983).

12. See my *Punishing Criminals* (New York: Basic Books, 1975) which is superseded to some extent by the views expressed in my "Criminal Law as a Threat System," 73 *Journal of Criminal Law and Criminology* 2 (1982).

13. Both spectacles when graphically shown may also give rise to undesirable imitations or inspirations.

14. Despite some doubts, I am here granting the truth of both hypotheses.

15. Stephen Nathanson, "Does It Matter if the Death Penalty Is Arbitrarily Administered?" *Philosophy & Public Affairs* 14, no. 2 (this issue). Unless otherwise noted, all further quotations are taken from Nathanson's article.

16. Discrimination or capriciousness is (when thought to be avoidable and excessive) sometimes allowed by the courts as a defense. Apparently this legal device is meant to reduce discrimination and capriciousness. But those spared because selected discriminatorily for punishment do not become any less deserving of it as both Reiman and Nathanson think, although not punishing them is used as a means to foster the desired equality in the distributions of punishments.

17. There will be some difficulty in explaining to the children who did not get the reward, why they did not, but no difficulty in explaining why one deserving child got it—unless the children share Nathanson's difficulty in distinguishing between justice and equality.

18. See note 16.

17

Safely Executed

Christie Davies

In November 1974, bombs exploded in two pubs in Birmingham, England, killing twenty-one and injuring 162. Six Irishmen were arrested, convicted for murder, and sentenced to life imprisonment. This March [1991], after the longest criminal appeal in British history, their convictions were overturned.

One side effect of this successful appeal has been to make it impossible for capital punishment to be reintroduced in Britain. It may also affect the American debate on retaining the death penalty. Among the Western democracies, America is now the odd one out, for no one else executes.

Regarding the Birmingham Six, the opponents of capital punishment are smugly saying that had the death penalty not been abolished in 1964, innocent men would have been hanged. Given that our systems of criminal justice are of necessity fallible, this seems to be an irrefutable argument against capital punishment. Mistaken convictions do occur, and pardons for the dead are of little consolation.

However, although difficult, it is by no means impossible to design a test that will meet the triple requirements of infallibility, retribution, and deterrence that are necessary for a just and objective system of capital punishment. In order to do so, it is first necessary to reverse the curious blurring of the notions of retribution and deterrence that has occurred.

Some econometricians claim that each execution saves several lives as other would-be murderers are deterred. But anyone who is not a statistician—judges, say—will want to feel that the murderer *deserves* to be executed rather than that he is merely introducing a useful deterrent effect on the gallows. When there is a direct link between the fate of a particular helpless victim whose life has been snuffed out and the convicted villain on the dock, the judiciary have been all in favor of execution. They found it much more difficult to justify sentencing someone to death in the interests of a group of unknown "statistical persons." Capital punishment has to be used on retribution *as well as* deterrence. It must be seen as a just penalty for a horrid crime as well as being a demonstrably effective means of protecting potential victims.

While thinking about this problem, my mind was mightily concentrated on the coincidence that I gave lifts in the course of one week to two hitchhikers who had just been released from the penitentiary. While driving through Britain's equivalent of Silicon Valley, I gave a lift to a small, sad, shabby, middle-aged artisan who was traveling in search of work. He had, he explained, just come out of jail, and this prejudiced employers against him despite his being a skilled worker with a trade.

"What were you in for?" I asked.

"Murder," came the reply.

When I later told my family about this, they were horrified at the risk they thought I had taken, but in fact the meek little man was very unlikely ever to be violent again, unless he were to remarry and once more find his spouse in bed with a neighbor.

In retrospect I am much more fearful of the Scotsman to whom in the following week I gave a lift down the highway that runs westward from London to the furnaces and foundries of Wales. He had never committed murder, but he had a long history of violent offenses—including assaults on prison guards—which stopped just short of killing his victims. He told me all this without a trace of remorse, while taking swigs from a hip flask, which confirmed all my Welsh ancestral prejudices in favor of total abstinence. I remembered an observation made by a criminologist colleague that repeatedly violent nonmurderers are far more of a threat to the public than the one-time murderer who has suddenly exploded under stress.

JUSTICE SERVED

It would not be unjust to execute someone with a long string of separate convictions for serious violent offenses stopping just short of murder—such as armed robbery, forcible rape, or inflicting grievous bodily harm—but it would be unwise, for it would encourage him to finish off his victims to silence potential witnesses. However, there can be no such objection to executing such a person if he does finally commit murder. Also, the chance of a *totally* innocent person being wrongly convicted of violent offenses on several separate occasions would be very close to zero. Executing such a person for murder would serve the purpose of deterring others, and it would also satisfy the requirement of just retribution—in this case, not for a single homicidal crime but for a lifetime's thuggery. A law to the effect that murderers with a long string of previous convictions for acts of heinous violence (and only those with such convictions) should be executed ought to satisfy both the inchoate British sense of fairness and the strict rules laid down by the U.S. Supreme Court.

Such executions would, though, only be effective if citizens are willing to support capital punishment as enthusiastically in the case of particular individual criminals as they are in the abstract when pestered by an opinion pollster. When faced with a politicized uproar calling for the reprieve rather than the execution of a popular local villain, they would have to be willing to become a vociferous majority reveling in the assertion of just retribution and thus getting the message of deterrence home to the members of the criminal classes.

18

Capital Punishment and Contemporary Values: People's Misgivings and the Court's Misperceptions*

William Bowers

Twenty years after the Supreme Court struck down existing death penalty statutes (*Furman* v. *Georgia* 1972) and a day after Justice Thurgood Marshall's death, the senior Justice of the U.S. Supreme Court, Harry Blackmun, charged the Court with coming "perilously close to murder" in its latest death penalty ruling. He made this charge in an unusual oral dissent from a decision which held that a federal appeals court could not hear newly developed evidence of a death row inmate's impossible innocence (*Herrera* v. *Collins* 1992). The Court, nine months earlier, had barred a lower federal court from hearing new evidence challenging execution by asphyxiation as cruel punishment (*Gome* v. *U.S. District Court* 1992) and had then taken the unprecedented step of ordering no further stays of execution (*Vasquez* v. *Harris* 1992). . . . How did we reach this point when twenty years earlier the Court had declared that the death penalty as applied was too arbitrary to be constitutionally acceptable, and when virtually all other modern industrialized nations of the free world either had already, or soon would, do away with capital punishment?

Law & Society Review 27, no. 1 (1993). Reprinted by permission of the Law and Society Association.

*I wish to thank Margaret Vandiver, Ken Haas, and Joe Hoffmann for helpful comments on short notice, and Patricia Dugan, Andrea Waldo, Heather MacAskill, and Peter Wong for helping me get the data and references together.

The Court's answer is that we got where we now are—191 executions, 2,676 people awaiting execution, and perhaps a million hours of state, federal, and Supreme Court time devoted to capital cases since *Furman*[1]—because it changed its mind about the arbitrariness of capital punishment. . . . In 1976, the Court decided that "on their face," the new "guided discretion" capital statutes enacted after 1972 would curb the arbitrariness *Furman* declared unconstitutional (*Gregg* v. *Georgia* 1976, and companion cases, including *Jurek* v. *Texas* 1976 and *Profitt* v. *Florida* 1976). States that had such statutes could go ahead with capital punishment. . . .

Yet, this legalistic account leaves out, I think, an essential ingredient for understanding why the Court acted as it did; namely, the Court's misplaced apprehension about public opinion. That is to say, the Court's 1976 affirmation and 1987 reaffirmation of capital punishment (1) may reflect the Court's belief that the public wants capital punishment and to do away with it would be disastrous for the Court's credibility with the public; when, in fact, (2) the public's expressed support for capital punishment is not a genuine but a spurious function of people's desire for harsh but meaningful punishment for convicted murderers. I will review the Court's own opinions for evidence bearing on the first proposition, and then turn to recent citizen survey data and ongoing interviews with capital jurors for evidence concerning the second proposition.

I. THE COURT'S APPREHENSION ABOUT PUBLIC OPINION

The Court has paid close attention to public opinion polls on the death penalty. In a 1968 decision that said people could not be kept off capital juries simply because they personally opposed the death penalty (*Witherspoon* v. *Illinois* 1968), Justice Stewart, writing for the Court, declared that the United States was a "nation less than half of whose people believe in the death penalty" (p. 520), citing a 1966 Gallup poll showing 42 percent in favor, 47 percent opposed, and 11 percent undecided. He went on to say that a jury consisting entirely of death penalty supporters would "speak only for a distinct and dwindling minority" (ibid.), contrasting the 1966 figures with an earlier 1960 poll showing 51 percent in favor, 36 percent opposed, and 13 percent undecided.

By 1972 when the Court declared the death penalty unconstitutionally arbitrary in *Furman*,[2] death penalty support was on the rise in the polls. Chief Justice Burger noted that a 1969 poll showed a 51 percent majority in favor of the death penalty and 40 percent opposed, and he contrasted these results with those of the 1966 Gallup poll showing 42 percent in favor and 47 percent opposed (dissenting, p. 386). . . . Justice Marshall responded with serious questions about the adequacy of the polls for judging whether capital punishment comports with contemporary values. He observed that the American people were poorly informed about the ways the death penalty was used and that their expressed support for capital punishment should be given little weight because only a public "fully informed as to the purposes of the penalty and its liabilities would find the penalty shocking, unjust, and unacceptable" (concurring, p. 361).

By 1976, when the *Gregg* Court changed its mind about arbitrariness, death penalty support had reached about 60 percent in the polls. A 1972 Gallup poll showed 57 percent in favor; a 1973 Harris survey showed 59 percent in favor. Justice Stewart, writing for Stewart, Powell, and Stevens in *Gregg*, reiterated that the Eighth Amendment " 'must draw its meaning from the evolving standards of decency that mark the progress of a maturing society' [citing] (*Trop* v. *Dulles* [356 U.S. (1958)] at 101)." "The assessment of contemporary values," he wrote (p. 173), "is not to be decided subjectively, but by 'objective indicia,' " and he pointed to the enactment of new capital statutes in thirty-five states and the returning of death sentences by juries under these new statutes as objective indications of public support following *Furman*. He then cited the 1972 Gallup and 1973 Harris polls in support of his conclusion that "a large proportion of American society continues to regard [the death penalty] as an appropriate and necessary criminal sanction" (p. 179). . . . Justice Stewart's earlier reliance on the polls in *Witherspoon* returned perhaps to haunt him in *Gregg*.

In *Gregg*, then, the Court effectively converted the constitutional question of the death penalty's comportment with the values of a maturing society into a political question of what state legislatures have done about capital punishment. Instead of following Justice Marshall's urging to adopt a standard that looked to informed opinion about the death penalty, . . . the Court rested its judgment above all on the popularity of the death penalty with the public, as reflected in the actions of legislators and the behavior of jurors.

Why was the Court so interested in the polls and so ready to defer to state legislatures? Concerning the polls, the Eighth Amendment's protection against punishments that violate "the evolving standards of decency that mark the progress of a maturing society" would seem to give the Justices the latitude to look beyond majority attitudes to an "informed public," as Justice Marshall did, or to "other enlightened nations," as Justice Brennan did. Yet, the specter of rising majority support for capital punishment in the polls was surely too hard for most Justices to reconcile with claims that the death penalty violates "evolving standards of decency" and undoubtedly had a chilling effect on their readiness to outlaw the death penalty for good, or even to stick with their earlier judgment that its application was too arbitrary.[3] Historically, the Court has been reluctant to use the Eighth Amendment so long as it believed that most people approved of a punishment (Hoffmann 1993).

Concerning the Court's deference to state legislatures, perhaps the stormy prior decade of conflict with states over school desegregation and civil rights cases made the Court reluctant to do more than ban the death penalty's mandatory use. . . . The Court may not have wanted to risk what it thought would be another unpopular, emotionally charged decision, especially in those states where its reputation and credibility were already tarnished (Bass 1990). Ironically, it was Justice Marshall as Chief Counsel for the NAACP Legal Defense Fund in 1954 who brought the landmark school desegregation cases (*Brown* v. *Board of Education* 1954) that contributed perhaps most of all to the Court's troubles during this period.

By 1987, when the Court rejected McCleskey's challenge that the death penalty was racially biased and hence too arbitrary, public support had risen above 70 percent. These polling results have been interpreted as solid public support for capital punishment by the pollsters, the news media, and the politicians. Indeed, they prompted pollsters to declare "deep-seated pro-death penalty attitudes" and "continuing strong support for [the] death penalty" (Field Institute 1990), politicians to make capital punishment a campaign issue (Oreskes 1990), . . . and researchers to focus attention on the polling results (Bohm 1991; Fox et al. 1990–91). And haven't we all—opponents, supporters and the public at large—now come to believe that Americans solidly support the death penalty?

II. A SPURIOUSNESS THEORY OF EXPRESSED DEATH PENALTY SUPPORT

Consider the possibility that we all, including the Court, have misinterpreted the polls. Perhaps the expressed support they reflect is not a deep-seated or strongly held commitment to capital punishment but actually a reflection of the public's desire for a genuinely harsh but meaningful punishment for convicted murderers. . . . This spuriousness theory is built on three specific hypotheses. The first, and most important, of these is that (1) people will abandon the death penalty when presented with a genuinely harsh and meaningful alternative. This central claim is substantiated by two subordinate hypotheses, which I also seek to confirm: (2) people see fundamental shortcomings in the death penalty as a punishment, and (3) they accept the death penalty because they believe the currently available alternatives are insufficiently harsh or meaningful.

In support of this theory, I will offer evidence for each of these hypotheses from two sources: (1) surveys of citizens in New York and Nebraska that Margaret Vandiver and I conducted in 1991[4] and (2) interviews with capital jurors in California, Florida, and South Carolina, the first three states in which such interviews have been virtually completed in a 13-state study now underway.[5]

Hypothesis 1: People will abandon the death penalty
when presented with a harsh but meaningful alternative.

In a series of surveys beginning with one conducted by Amnesty International USA in Florida in 1985 and followed up by surveys in other states, the following question, or one very much like it, was asked: "Suppose convicted first-degree murderers in this state could be sentenced to life in prison without parole and also be required to work in prison for money that would go to the families of their victims. Would you prefer this as an alternative to the death penalty?"

This question was asked in surveys in Florida, Georgia, New York, and California 1985–89 and replicated in our 1991 New York and Nebraska surveys. Our New York survey included both a New York City sample[6] and a representative statewide sample. Panel B of Table 1 shows the responses to this question in the four earlier surveys and in our three samples (the New York State and City samples are shown separately). Panel A of the table shows the responses to the standards "favor/oppose" death penalty polling question.

In all instances where this alternative of life without parole combined with a restitution requirement (LWOP+R) was posed, expressed death penalty support plummeted. Among the earlier surveys, it dropped 62 percentage points in Florida; 32 points in Georgia; 40 points in New York; and 54 points in California. Among our own samples, it dropped 52, 49, and 56 points, respectively, in New York State, in New York City, and in Nebraska.

What is more, this obviously harsh but meaningful punishment, which puts the offender to work to pay restitution for the loss and suffering his crime has caused, is preferred to the death penalty by a majority in every state where it was posed as an alternative.[7] Even among respondents who said they "strongly" favored the death penalty on the standard favor/oppose question, majorities of 56 percent, 66 percent, and 57 percent abandoned it in favor of the LWOP+R alternative, respectively, in our New York State, New York City, and Nebraska samples.[8] Public preference for this alternative is unmistakable.

Does the experience of serving on a capital jury reinforce people's commitment to the death penalty, or sour them on capital punishment? And does it matter whether or not the jury on which they served condemned the defendant to death? We asked the capital jurors the same question we used in the New York and Nebraska surveys. Table 2 shows their responses.

Again, in all instances majorities prefer LWOP+R over the death penalty. This is so for jurors who imposed the death sentence and those who did not in all three states. The experience of serving on a capital jury obviously did not make jurors into advocates for the death penalty. Like their counterparts who have not been capital jurors, they prefer the LWOP+R alternative.[9]

Table 1
Responses to Death Penalty Polling Questions in States Where Respondents
Were Asked about Alternatives to Capital Punishment (Percent)

A. Favoring or Opposing Capital Punishment

	Favor	Oppose	Not Sure[a]	Poll Date
Florida	84.0	13.0	3.0	5/86
Georgia	75.0	25.0	—	6/86
New York	72	—	—	5/89
California	79.5	19.0	—	12/89
New York State	70.6	21.8	8.0	3/91
New York City	68.1	21.9	10.0	3/91
Nebraska	80.4	13.4	6.1	4/91

**B. Preferring the Death Penalty or Sentence of Life without Parole
plus Restitution (LWOP+R) as Alternative to Death Penalty**

	Prefer Alternative	Prefer Death Penalty	Undecided/ No Opinion	Poll Date
Florida	70	24	6	5/86
Georgia	51	43	5	12/86
New York	62	32	6	5/89
California	67	26	7	12/89
New York State	73	19	8	3/91
New York City	73	19	8	3/91
Nebraska	64	26	10	4/91

Source: *Florida:* Cambridge Survey Research 1986; *Georgia:* Thomas & Hutcheson 1986; *California:* Haney & Murtado 1989; *New York* (1989): Cambridge Survey Research 1989; *New York & Nebraska* (1991): Bowers & Vandiver 1991a, 1991b.
[a]Includes "don't know," "depends," "not sure," "no opinion," and "undecided."

Note that if the polls had asked this question at the time of *Gregg*—when considerably fewer would have had to abandon the death penalty to produce an overwhelming preference for LWOP+R—politicians might have been persuaded to convert these preferences into law or have been replaced by those who would. In terms of legislative enactments and jury decisions, the death penalty would then have failed the Court's test of contemporary values.

*Hypothesis 2: People see fundamental shortcomings
in the death penalty as a punishment.*

Our citizen surveys included a battery of statements about people's punishment attitudes and priorities. Seven of these in our New York and nine

Table 2

California, Florida, and South Carolina Capital Jurors' Responses
to Questions about Alternatives to Capital Punishment

	California		Florida		South Carolina	
	Death	Prison	Death	Prison	Death	Prison
Yes	50.8	53.1	50.8	56.9	61.4	56.8
No	35.4	39.1	32.8	27.5	21.4	27.3
Not sure	13.8	7.8	14.8	13.7	17.1	13.6
No answer	0.0	0.0	0.0	1.9	0.0	2.3
No.	65	64	61	51	70	44

in our Nebraska surveys referred specifically to the death penalty. The statement with which most people agreed in each of our three samples read, "The death penalty is too arbitrary because some people are executed and others are sent to prison for the very same crimes."

This is, of course, a classic definition of unfairness, and it is precisely the kind of unfairness that caused the *Furman* Court to declare the death penalty unconstitutional under existing statutes in 1972.

Four out of five people in each of our three citizen samples agreed that the death penalty was "too arbitrary," and virtually half in each sample agreed "strongly" with this statement, as shown in Table 3. Even more people agreed with this statement than with one that read, "If we used the death penalty more often there would be fewer murders across the country," or indeed, said they favored the death penalty in response to the standard polling question (see Table 1, panel A).

Does actually having to decide whether a convicted capital defendant should live or die relieve people's misgivings about the arbitrariness of capital punishment? After all, people who make such a life-or-death decision may develop a commitment to believing that what they are doing is not arbitrary, especially perhaps those who impose a death sentence. The answers appear in Table 4.

Serving on a capital jury makes no apparent difference. Like the public at large, 80 percent of the capital jurors said the death penalty is too arbitrary, and nearly half agreed strongly with this judgment. There is no consistent difference across states between jurors who did and did not choose death, although the death jurors in California are a bit more reluctant than others to endorse this judgment "strongly." There is no telling what the level of agreement might have been among these people before serving as capital jurors or in these states as compared with people in New York and Nebraska. But it is unmistakably clear that capital jurors, like other citizens, see the death penalty as too arbitrary in overwhelming numbers.

Table 3

1991 New York and Nebraska Respondents' Agreement with Statement:
"The death penalty is too arbitrary because some people are executed
and others go to prison for the very same crimes"

	New York State	New York City	Nebraska
Strongly agree	46.0	50.0	46.4
Moderately agree	29.2	22.8	29.2
Probably agree	7.4	5.4	8.1
Probably disagree	2.2	2.8	1.4
Moderately disagree	5.6	7.2	5.3
Strongly disagree	5.8	8.6	2.4
Don't know/refused/NA	3.8	4.3	7.1

Table 4

California, Florida, and South Carolina Capital Jurors' Agreement with Statement:
"The death penalty is too arbitrary because some people are executed
and others go to prison for the very same crimes"

	California		Florida		South Carolina	
	Death	Prison	Death	Prison	Death	Prison
Agree strongly	35.4	46.9	45.9	47.1	54.3	54.5
Agree moderately	30.8	21.9	32.8	19.6	27.1	25.0
Agree slightly	7.7	9.4	8.2	11.8	5.7	4.5
Disagree slightly	7.7	7.8	3.3	1.9	1.4	0.0
Disagree moderately	7.7	4.7	8.2	7.8	4.3	4.5
Disagree strongly	1.5	1.6	0.0	3.9	1.4	2.3
Don't know/not sure	7.7	6.3	1.6	1.9	5.7	9.1
No answer	1.5	0.0	0.0	1.9	0.0	0.0
No.	65	64	61	51	70	44

If the polls had included this question and had obtained results in 1976 and perhaps earlier, could the *Gregg* Court in good conscience have said the death penalty was not too arbitrary or did not violate contemporary values? Arbitrariness is, after all, a value judgment about the fundamental unfairness of the application of the punishment in question. It was the value judgment the Court itself used under Eighth Amendment authority to invalidate existing capital statutes in *Furman*. Politicians might have ignored such value judgments in favor of expressions of support for capital punishment in which fear of crime, desire for harsh punishment, and dissatisfaction with available alternatives could override such value judgments. But doesn't the Eighth Amendment require the Supreme Court to consider con-

Table 5
1991 New York and Nebraska Respondents' Estimate of Number of Years
Convicted Murderers Usually Serve before Parole or Release

	New York State	New York City	Nebraska
Less than 10 years	25.6	31.0	20.4
10–15 years	29.6	29.0	27.9
16 or more years	24.0	17.8	38.7
Don't know/NA	20.8	22.2	13.0

temporary values as reflected in such judgments instead of broad endorsements in which value judgments may play only a minor role?

Hypothesis 3: People accept the death penalty because they believe the currently available alternatives are insufficiently harsh or meaningful.

If people feel the death penalty is too arbitrary (and they will abandon it for LWOP+R), why do so many of them say they favor it in respone to the favor/oppose question? Hypothesis 3 suggests that the death penalty is accepted because it is viewed as better than the presently available alternative in their states. We asked: "How many years do you think a convicted first degree murderer in [this state] will usually spend in prison before being paroled or released back into society?"

Roughly half the people surveyed said that the usual punishment for murderers not sentenced to death will be fifteen years or less in prison. Slightly more than half the people in the New York samples though this, and slightly less than half in Nebraska (Table 5). If we exclude those who did not venture an estimate, a clear majority in all three samples said fifteen years or less. One in four said less than ten years in the two New York samples, and one in five gave this response in Nebraska.[10]

In New York the mandatory minimum for murder is not less than fifteen years, and in Nebraska it is life without parole (LWOP) for death-eligible murder. In both states, at least half the citizens' estimates are well below the mandatory minimum sentences on the statute books and the terms actually served by convicted murderers not sentenced to death.[11] No doubt, the public's exaggerated sense that convicted murderers will be back on the streets so soon is the product of selective media reporting of crime by previously incarcerated inmates and the absence of statistics that distinguish persons convicted of the kinds of murder that might be punishable by death from other lesser forms of criminal homicide.

The point here is not that people underestimate the current punishment for convicted murderers but that the term of years they imagine imprisoned murderers will serve is short enough to make the incapacitative aspect of capital punisment attractive to them, however arbitrary they believe it is. Of course, the LWOP+R alternative they prefer to the death penalty also eliminates the possibility of recidivism. Notably, there is evidence that a majority of the public would also be willing to accept parole after a fixed term of at least twenty-five years in preference to the death penalty on the condition that it was coupled with a restitution requirement and that the defendant had fully met the restitution requirement (Bowers et al. 1995).

Does serving as a capital juror enlighten people about what the punishment will be if the death penalty is not imposed? Not surprisingly, a 1991 South Carolina survey indicated that three out of four people said that if they were jurors in a capital case, it would be "extremely" or "very" important for them to know what the punishment would be if they did not vote for death.[12] Moreover, recent research indicates that one in four capital juries in Georgia interrupted their deliberations to ask the trial judge for further information or instructions, and that nine out of ten times the question they asked was what the punishment would be if they did not impose a deatth sentence (Lane 1993). In Georgia and most other states, the law prevents the judge from answering this question.

So first of all, we might expect jurors not to be much more enlightened than the public at large and, hence, subject to the same misperceptions about the leniency of current options. Second, if people are more likely to favor the death penalty when they think the alternative option is too lenient, our theory suggests that as jurors they might be more willing to impose a death sentence. The answers to both of these suppositions are evident in Table 6.

To begin with, the data show that jurors, like the public at large, imagine that murderers not sentenced to death will be paroled or released relatively soon—not quite as soon as the public thinks but sooner than the laws of their states actually permit. Overall, roughly a third of the jurors as compared to about half of the public thought that murderers not sentenced to death would be back on the streets in fifteen years or less. Jurors' longer estimates may be due, in part, to the fact that the mandatory minimum sentences in Florida and South Carolina are longer than in New York (which accounts for two of the three citizen samples). Thus, South Carolina requires that convicted murderers not sentenced to death serve a mandatory minimum of thirty years in prison, and Florida keeps convicted murderers not sentenced to death in prison twenty-five years before they become eligible for parole. California, like Nebraska, automatically imposes life without parole when the death sentence is not handed down.[13]

Using the mandatory minimum as the basis for comparison, we can say that most jurors in each of these three states imagine that convicted murderers not sentenced to death will serve less than the mandatory mini-

Table 6
California, Florida, and South Carolina Capital Jurors' Estimate of
Number of Years Convicted Murderers Usually Serve before Parole or Release

	California		Florida		South Carolina	
	Death	Prison	Death	Prison	Death	Prison
<10 years	13.8	15.6	14.8	15.7	18.6	4.5
10 years	9.2	6.3	6.6	3.9	11.4	6.8
11–14 years	6.2	4.7	4.9	1.9	12.9	2.3
15 years	4.6	4.7	13.1	1.9	4.3	6.8
16–19 years	3.1	1.6	4.9	3.9	10.0	4.5
20 years	9.2	4.7	8.2	13.7	8.6	15.9
21–24 years	0.0	1.6	6.6	1.9	5.7	9.1
25 years	0.0	0.0	29.5	33.3	5.7	11.4
26–29 years	0.0	0.0	3.3	5.8	0.0	2.3
30 years	1.5	0.0	1.6	0.0	7.1	22.7
31+ years	0.0	3.2	0.0	0.0	1.4	4.5
LWOP	36.9	31.3	3.3	3.9	1.4	2.3
Don't know/NA	15.3	21.9	3.3	11.8	12.9	6.8
No.	65	64	61	51	70	44

mum sentence. Thus, both citizen and juror grossly underestimate the time that will usually be served by murderers not sentenced to death.

Moreover, there is a consistent difference between jurors who did and did not impose death as punishment. In each of these three states, believing that convicted first-degree murderers not sentenced to death would get out sooner is associated with voting for death. Notably, the relationship between belief in early release and voting for death is more pronounced as fewer jurors in the state appear to know what the mandatory minimum sentence is. Thus the difference is least evident in California where a third of the jurors appear to know that life without parole is the sentence that will be imposed in lieu of death, and most pronounced in South Carolina where fewer than 15 percent appear to know the mandatory minimum.

The results are consistent with the hypothesis that *jurors who underestimate the currently available alternative are more apt to impose the death penalty.* It is possible, of course, that jurors who did not impose a death sentence were more motivated to learn what the sentence would actually be after not recommending death. But if so, they should appear more often in the mandatory minimum categories and less often among the "don't knows/ NAs." In fact, this happens only for South Carolina and is by no means strong enough there to account for the greater tendency of jurors who underestimate the current option to impose a death sentence in that state.

This pattern in the data raises the specter of arbitrariness in the sentencing behavior of capital jurors owing quite specifically to laws prohibiting them from being told what the sentence would be if they do not impose the death penalty. It may be argued in theory that a jury's decision should be based strictly on whether the defendant's blameworthiness merits execution, and that having judges describe or explain what the sentence would otherwise be introduces the possibility of bias. But whatever the arguments, the empirical evidence indicates that not informing the jury about the sentence that would otherwise be imposed is biasing the jury's sentencing decision and that the bias is in favor of death as punishment since most jurors underestimate the sentence that would otherwise be served.

From the standpoint of the spuriousness theory, the data in Tables 5 and 6 are doubly confirming. The fact that citizens and jurors underestimate the severity of the punishment alternatives to death for convicted first-degree murderers is consistent with them favoring the death penalty in the polls and, consequently, with legislators enacting capital statutes. Further, the fact that jurors who see the available alternative to death as relatively lenient are more apt to impose a death sentence means that death sentences are much more common than they would be if jurors did not underestimate the severity of current alternatives. The theory thus explains how the Court's allegedly "objective" indicia of contemporary values in terms of legislative enactments and jury decisions are corrupted first by the public's ignorance of the current options and second by the absence of severe but meaningful alternative forms of punishment. Hence, the Court's indicia do not reflect genuine death penalty support.

III. CONCLUSION

The Supreme Court had all it needed to make good on doing away with the death penalty in 1976. The rest of the world was moving away from capital punishment, the Court itself had taken one bold step toward ending executions in *Furman,* there was ample historical evidence of its arbitrary and discriminatory use, there was no credible evidence of its allged deterrent advantage, and the Court itself in 1971 had said that capital sentencing decisions cannot be guided (*McGautha* v. *California* 1971). Instead, the court broke with the worldwide trend, ignored the legacy of racism in the application of the death penalty, declared that the death penalty must be a superior deterrent (contrary to its own evaluation in *Gregg* that the evidence was "inconclusive"), and went on to affirm guided discretion capital statutes "on their face" without waiting to see whether "in practice" they actually curbed the arbitrariness that rendered earlier statutes, if not the thousands of executions they authorized, unconstitutional.

The factors underlying the Court's decision to permit capital punishment in 1976 are uncertain. The Court paid close attention to the polls showing a persistent rise in the percentage who said they favored capital punishment for a decade prior to its 1976 decision. The Court may have been leery about the consequences of doing away with the death penalty after most states returned to it following *Furman* and after a protracted period of conflict with the states over school desegregation and civil rights rulings. The Court's choice of legislative enactments as its foremost indicator of the death penalty's comportment with contemporary values was clearly a sign of deference to state law and perhaps an indication that the Court wanted to avoid another decision it thought would be unpopular with the states.

Now, twenty years after *Furman,* the current Court is adamant in its commitment to the operative laws and their application by juries as the indicia of contemporary values.[14] Justice Scalia has disparaged empirical research including polls challenging the execution of juveniles as "ethicoscience" (*Stanford* v. *Kentucky* 1989:323), and the Court has dismissed 66–73 percent opposition in the polls of several states to the execution of the mentally retarded (*Penry* v. *Lynaugh* 1989:334–35).[15] For now, the Court appears to be as unimpressed with polls showing opposition to the death penalty for certain defendants as it was impressed in *Furman* and *Gregg* with those showing support on the favor/oppose death penalty polling question.

But this could change if the Court became persuaded that it is mistaken about the public's view of capital punishment. The tide could turn because Supreme Court Justices don't like to be wrong and because the Eighth Amendment requires the Court to act on its most enlightened interpretation of contemporary values. The evidence sketched out here, if replicated and confirmed in other studies, could have the critical effect of changing the perspectives of legislators, judges, the media, and the public on how people think about capital punishment. The obvious political implication of a clear public preference for an alternative to the death penalty is that it will prompt lawmakers to convert the public's punishment preference into laws or they will be replaced by those who will. The apparently exorbitant costs of maintaining a system of capital punishment (Death Penalty Information Center 1992), as well as the public's interest in restitution requirements as a component of punishment and in seeing prisoners work during their incarceration (Bowers et al. 1995), will add to the political attractiveness of an alternative that puts prisoners to work for money that would go to their victims' families.

The recognition that we have been wrong about how the public thinks about the death penalty will take time to sink in, but if and when it becomes the new wisdom on this matter, it will surely affect the Supreme Court, perhaps not directly or immediately in a shift of the Court's interpretation of contemporary values, but perhaps indirectly by fostering a renewed receptivity to death penalty challenges. This is a situation in which a "face-saving" decision could compensate for many past mistakes. Maybe the study of how jurors make their sentencing decisions will provide the kind of evidence the court will find compelling.[16] For instance, if jurors make it clear in their own words (as suggested in Table 6 above) that they are more apt to impose death when they are unsure about what the alternative would be, the Court's presuppositions about how such decisions are made cannot stand. And, likewise, other presuppositions about how capital jurors make their sentencing decisions may also fall.

My purpose has been more to raise than to resolve questions with a few choice findings from research now underway. Concerning the public generally, there is more to be said about people's punishment preferences and particularly about the appeal of an alternative to the death penalty that incorporates the principle of restitution to murder victims' families (Bowers et al. 1995). This is just the first glimpse of capital jurors' thinking and at what the implciation may be for capital punishment in the United States.

NOTES

1. The execution and death row figures are current as of January 15, 1993; NAACP Legal Defense & Educational Fund 1993.

2. In addition to the arbitrariness of its application, the Eighth Amendment challenge to the death penalty in *Furman* required the Court to consider the contemporary meaning of the amendment's "cruel and unusual punishment" clause. Its meaning is not static: it "may acquire meaning as public opinion becomes enlightened by a humane justice" (*Weems* v. *United States* 1910:378). Thus, a previously acceptable punishment such as the death penalty could become unconstitutional, owing to "evolving standards of decency" (*Trop* v. *Dulles* 1958:101).

3. As an Eighth Amendment violation, the death penalty's arbitrariness was a judgment of the Court that extended the notion of "cruel and unusal punishment" beyond the absolute excessiveness of a punishment or its disproportionality relative to a particular crime, to include the fairness or utility of its administration.

4. The initial finds of these two surveys were reported in Bowers and Vandiver 1991a, 1991b. A more detailed analysis of these data [is] published . . . in Bowers et al. (1995).

5. The co-investigators for these states are Scott Sundby, Gordon Waldo, and Ted Eisenberg, respectively. The target sample in each state is 120 interviews: four each in thirty capital cases since 1988, fifteen cases in which the jury's sentence was death and fifteen in which it was not. The target sample of sixty jurors in death cases has been met in all three states, although a few interviews remain to be completed with people who served on juries that did not impose a death sentence.

6. The New York City sample was drawn to represent state senatorial districts 16, 19, and 21 in the Queens and Brooklyn burroughs of New York City, so it is not representative of the city as a whole. We include this grouping of respondents because it constitutes an urban sample distinctively different from the statewide samples used in other studies.

7. There is some indication in the available studies (mostly unpublished) that

people would be willing to accept parole for convicted first-degree murderers after a fixed period of at least twenty-five years if by then the offender had also met the restitution requirements in full. Bowers et al. (1995).

8. These data are presented in Bowers et al. (1995).

9. Obviously, the citizen samples in Table 1 and the juror samples in Table 2 are not directly comparable since they come from different states. Even for California and Florida where earlier citizen survey results might be compared with our juror interview responses, direct comparisons are confounded because the process of jury selection for capital cases disproportionately eliminates death penalty opponents. Also for California the citizen sample is statewide, but the juror sample was drawn from northern California.

10. The greater number of "no answers" and "don't knows" in the New York samples is due to the fact that the question was open-ended; respondents had to volunteer an answer rather than simply choose a five-year interval response category as in the Nebraska survey. One other difference that keeps the two surveys from being strictly comparable is a problem of overlapping response categories in the Nebraska survey. Thus, for example, Nebraskans could choose categories such as "ten to fifteen years" or "fifteen to twenty years." Strictly speaking, the percentages in the 10–15-year category is a more conservative estimate for Nebraska than for New York since we have no way of identifying Nebraskans in the 15–20-year category whose estimate would have been fifteen years if asked to make a point rather than an interval estimate.

11. The mandatory minimum sentence before parole eligibility in New York State is no less than fifteen or more than twenty-five years at the judge's discretion for categories of murder that might be capital offenses if the state had the death penalty. Thus only murderers whose convictions or sentences were reversed or reduced on appeal or commuted by the governor would get out of prison in less than fifteen years. The New York State Division of Parole indicates that the average time served was 202.1 months (sixteen years and ten months) for all prisoners initially convicted of murder and released on parole in 1991. This is a conservative estimate since it includes prisoners whose convictions or sentences were reversed or reduced on appeal and excludes prisoners who served lengthy sentences and died in prison without ever being granted parole (information from personal communication with New York State Division of Parole, February 1993).

12. The 1991 statewide South Carolina survey of 500 residents eighteen years of age and older was conducted by the Survey Research Laboratory of the University of South Carolina's Institute for Public Affairs and submitted in the form of an affidavit for the petitioner in *Sate* v. *Simmons* (1993). The question read, "If you were a juror . . . how important would it be for you to know how much time the peson would serve . . . ?" Some 45.3 percent replied "extremely important; 31.5 percent "very important"; 9.3 percent "somewhat important"; 2.4 percent "not too important"; 4.6 percent "not at all important"; and 6.3 percent "don't know."

13. In Florida for a prisoner to be released in less than twenty-five years would require that the governor recommend clemency and at least half of the state's six-person elected cabinet must accept the recommendation. In South Carolina and California, gubernatorial clemency is the only source of relief from, respectively, the mandatory thirty years in prison and life without parole alternatives to the death penalty. The exercise of such clemency is virtually unheard of in recent years in these states.

14. Twenty years ago Chief Justice Burger conceded in *Furman* (dissenting, pp. 385, 386) that public opinion polls could indicate that legislatures had lost touch

with community values. For evidence of a vast discrepancy between the death penalty attitudes and preferences of voters and their legislators, see Bowers & Vandiver 1991a; Bowers et al. . . .

15. The Court in *Penry* v. *Lynaugh* (1989:288–89, O'Connor, J., for the Court) explained:

> Penry does not offer any evidence of the general behavior of juries with respect to sentencing mentally retarded defendants, nor of decisions of prosecutors. He points instead to several public opinion surveys that indicate strong public opposition to execution of the retarded. For example, a poll taken in Texas found that 86 percent of those polled supported the death penalty, but 73 percent opposed its application to the mentally retarded. . . . A Florida poll found 71 percent of those surveyed were opposed to the execution of mentally retarded capital defendants, while only 12 percent were in favor. . . . A Georgia poll found 66 percent of those polled opposed to the death penalty for the retarded, 17 percent in favor, with 16 percent responding that it depends how retarded the person is. . . . The public sentiment expressed in these and other polls and resolutions may ultimately find expression in legislation, which is an objective indicator of contemporary values upon which we can rely. But at present, there is insufficient evidence of a national consensus against executing mentally retarded people convicted of capital offenses for us to conclude that it is categorically prohibited by the Eighth Amendment.

16. The Court has signaled in *Lockhart* v. *McCree* (1986) that to understand how capital jurors exercise their discretion, it is not enough to examine the behavior and thinking of persons who "were not actual jurors sworn under oath to apply the law to the facts of an actual case involving the fate of an actual capital defendant. We have serious doubts about the value of these studies in predicting the behavior of actual jurors."

Perhaps, then, the Court will be interested in evidence about real jurors in actual cases (as, indeed, its complaining in *Penry* v. *Lynaugh* about not having evidence on the reactions of capital jurors to mentally retarded capital defendants suggests (see passage quoted in note 15).

REFERENCES

Baldus, David C., George Woodworth, and Charles A. Pulaski, Jr. (1990). *Equal Justice and the Death Penalty: A Legal and Empirical Analysis.* Boston: Northeastern University Press.

Bass, Jack (1990). *Unlikely Heroes.* Tuscaloosa: University of Alabama Press.

Black, Charles L., Jr. (1981). *Capital Punishment: The Inevitability of Caprice and Mistake.* 2d ed. New York: W. W. Norton.

Bohm, Robert M. (1991). "American Death Penalty Opinion. 1936–1986: A Critical Examination of the Gallup Polls," in R. M. Bohm, ed., *The Death Penalty in America: Current Research.* Cincinnati: Anderson Publishing Co.

Bowers, William J., and Margaret Vandiver (1991a). *New Yorkers Want an Alternative to the Death Penalty: Executive Summary of a New York State Survey.* Boston: Criminal Justice Research Center, Northeastern University (April).

——— (1991b). *Nebraskans Want an Alternative to the Death Penalty: Executive Summary of Nebraska State Survey.* Boston: Criminal Justice Research Center, Northeastern University (May).

Bowers, William J., Margaret Vandiver, and Patricia H. Dugan (1995). "People

Want an Alternative to the Death Penalty: A New Look at Public Opinion." Criminal Justice Research Center, Northeastern University.

Cambridge Survey Research (1986). *An Analysis of Political Attitudes towards the Death Penalty in the State of Florida: Executive Summary.* Washington, D.C.: Cambridge Survey Research.

——— (1989). *New York Public Opinion Poll—The Death Penalty: An Executive Summary.* Washington, D.C.: Cambridge Survey Research.

Death Penalty Information Center (1992). *Millions Misspent: What Politicians Don't Say about the High Costs of the Death Penalty.* Washington, D.C.: The Center.

Field Institute (1990). *Press Release: Continuing Strong Support for Death Penalty.* San Francisco: Field Institute (March 27).

Fox, James Alan, Michael L. Radelet, and Julie L. Bonsteel (1990–91). "Death Penalty Opinion in the Post-*Furman* Years," *New York University Review of Law & Social Change* 18.

Good, Andrew (1993). "Book Review," 17 *Champion.*

Gross, Samuel R., and Robert Mauro (1989). *Death and Discrimination: Racial Disparities in Capital Sentencing.* Boston: Northeastern University Press.

Haney, Craig, and Aida Hurtado (1989). *Californians' Attitudes about the Death Penalty: Results of a Statewide Survey.* Santa Cruz: University of Califorina, Santa Cruz.

Hoffmann, Joseph L. (1993). "The 'Cruel and Unusual Punishment' Clause: A Limit on the Power to Punish, or Constitutional Rhetoric?" in D. J. Bodenhamer and J. W. Ely, Jr., eds., *The Bill of Rights in Modern America: After 200 Years.* Bloomington: Indiana University Press.

Jurow, George L. (1971). "New Data on the Effect of a 'Death Qualified' Jury on the Guilt Determination Process," 84 *Harvard Law Review* 567.

Lane, J. Mark (1993). "Is There Life without Parole? A Capital Defendant's Right to a Meaningful Alternative Sentence," 26 *Loyola of Los Angeles Law Review* 325.

NAACP Legal and Educational Defense Fund (1993). *Death Row U.S.A. Reporter.* New York: NAACP Legal and Educational Defense Fund.

Oreskes, Michael (1990). "The Political Stampede on Execution." *New York Times,* April 4, sec. A, p. 16.

Reinhardt, Stephen (1992). "The Supreme Court, the Death Penalty, and the *Harris* Case," 102 *Yale Law Journal* 205.

Sarat, Austin, and Neil Vidmar (1976). "Public Opinion, the Death Penalty, and the Eighth Amendement: Testing the Marshall Hypothesis," 1976 *Wisconsin Law Review* 171.

Stinchcombe, Arthur L., Rebecca Adams, Carol A. Heimer, Kim Lane Scheppele, Tom W. Smith, and D. Garth Taylor (1980). *Crime and Punishment—Changing Attitudes in America.* San Francisco: Jossey-Bass.

Thomas, Robert H., and John Hutchinson, Jr. (1986). *Georgia Residents' Attitudes toward the Death Penalty, the Disposition of Juvenile Offenders, and Related Issues.* Atlanta: Center for Public & Urban Research, Georgia State University.

Vidmar, Neil, and Phoebe Ellsworth (1974). "Public Opinion and the Death Penalty," 26 *Stanford Law Review* 1245.

Weisberg, Robert (1983). "Deregulating Death," 1983 *The U.S. Supreme Court Review* 305.

Zimring, Franklin E., and Gordon Hawkins (1986). *Capital Punishment and the American Agenda.* Cambridge: Cambridge University Press.

CASES CITED

Booth v. *Maryland,* 482 U.S. 496 (1987).

Brown v. *Board of Education,* 347 U.S. 483 (1954).

Fowler v. *North Carolina,* 285 N.C. 90, *cert. granted,* 419 U.S. 963 (1974), *order for reargument revoked,* 424 U.S. 903 (1976).

Furman v. *Georgia,* 408 U.S. 238 (1972).

Gomez v. *U.S. District Court,* 112 S. Ct. 1652, 119 L. Ed.2d 561 (1992).

Gregg v. *Georgia,* 428 U.S. 153 (1976).

Herrera v. *Collins,* 112 S.Ct., 2936, 119 L..Ed.2d. 561 (1993).

Jurek v. *Texas,* 428 U.S. 262 (1976).

Lockhart v. *McCree,* 476 U.S. 162 (1976).

McCleskey v. *Kemp,* 481 U.S. 279 (1987).

McGautha v. *California,* 402 U.S. 183 (1971).

Payne v. *Tennessee,* 111 S.Ct. 2597, 115 L.Ed.2d 720 (1991).

Penry v. *Lynaugh,* 492 U.S. 302 (1989).

Proffitt v. *Florida,* 428 U.S. 242 (1976).

Stanford v. *Kentucky,* 492 U.S. 361 (1989).

State v. *Simmons,* S.C. S.Ct., #23784, February 1, 1993 (unpub.).

Trop v. *Dulles,* 356 U.S. 86 (1958).

Vasquez v. *Harris,* 112 S.Ct. 1713, 118 L.Ed.2d 419 (1992).

Weems v. *United States,* 217 U.S. 349 (1910).

Witherspoon v. *Illinois,* 391 U.S. 510 (1968).

Woodson v. *North Carolina,* 428 U.S. 280 (1976).

19

Callins v. *Collins*

Justice Blackmun's Dissenting Opinion

Callins v. *Collins,* Director, Texas Department of Criminal Justice, Institutional Division. The petition for a writ of certiorari is denied.

Justice Blackmun, dissenting.

On February 23, 1994, at approximately 1:00 A.M., Bruce Edwin Callins will be executed by the State of Texas. Intravenous tubes attached to his arms will carry the instrument of death, a toxic fluid designed specifically for the purpose of killing human beings. The witnesses, standing a few feet away, will behold Callins, no longer a defendant, an appellant, or a petitioner, but a man, strapped to a gurney, and seconds away from extinction.

Within days, or perhaps hours, the memory of Callins will begin to fade. The wheels of justice will churn again, and somewhere, another jury or another judge will have the unenviable task of determining whether some human being is to live or die. We hope, of course, that the defendant whose life is at risk will be represented by competent counsel—someone who is inspired by the awareness that a less-than-vigorous defense truly could have fatal consequences for the defendant. We hope that the attorney will investigate all aspects of the case, follow all evidentiary and procedural rules, and appear before a judge who is still committed to the protection of defendants' rights—even now, as the prospect of meaningful judicial oversight has diminished. In the same vein, we hope that the prosecution, in urging the penalty of death, will have exercised its discretion wisely, free from bias, prejudice, or political motive, and will be humbled, rather than emboldened, by the awesome authority conferred by the State.

The United States Law Week, February 22, 1994, 62 U.S.L.W. 3546.

But even if we can feel confident that these actors will fulfill their roles to the best of their human ability, our collective conscience will remain uneasy. Twenty years have passed since this Court declared that the death penalty must be imposed fairly, and with reasonable consistency, or not at all, see *Furman* v. *Georgia* . . . (1972), and, despite the effort of the States and courts to devise legal formulas and procedural rules to meet this daunting challenge, the death penalty remains fraught with arbitrariness, discrimination, caprice, and mistake. This is not to say that the problems with the death penalty today are identical to those that were present twenty years ago. Rather, the problems that were pursued down one hole with procedural rules and verbal formulas have come to the surface somewhere else, just as virulent and pernicious as they were in their original form. Experience has taught us that the constitutional goal of eliminating arbitrariness and discrimination from the administration of death . . . can never be achieved without compromising an equally essential component of fundamental fairness—individualized sentencing. See *Lockett* v. *Ohio* . . . (1978).

It is tempting, when faced with conflicting constitutional commands, to sacrifice one for the other or to assume that an acceptable balance between them already has been struck. In the context of the death penalty, however, such jurisprudential maneuvers are wholly inappropriate. The death penalty must be imposed "fairly, and with reasonable consistency, or not at all." *Eddings* v. *Oklahoma* . . . (1982).

To be fair, a capital sentencing scheme must treat each person convicted of a capital offense with that "degree of respect due the uniqueness of the individual." *Lockett* v. *Ohio*. . . . That means affording the sentencer the power and discretion to grant mercy in a particular case, and providing avenues for the consideration of any and all relevant mitigating evidence that would justify a sentence less than death. Reasonable consistency, on the other hand, requires that the death penalty be inflicted evenhandedly, in accordance with reason and objective standards, rather than by whim, caprice, or prejudice. Finally, because human error is inevitable, and because our criminal justice system is less than perfect, searching appellate review of death sentences and their underlying convictions is a prerequisite to a constitutional death penalty scheme.

On their face, these goals of individual fairness, reasonable consistency, and absence of error appear to be attainable: Courts are in the very business of erecting procedural devices from which fair, equitable, and reliable outcomes are presumed to flow. Yet, in the death penalty area, this Court, in my view, has engaged in a futile effort to balance these constitutional demands, and now is retreating not only from the *Furman* promise of consistency and rationality, but from the requirement of individualized sentencing as well. Having virtually conceded that both fairness and rationality cannot be achieved in the administration of the death penalty, see

McCleskey v. *Kemp* . . . (1987), the Court has chosen to deregulate the entire enterprise, replacing, it would seem, substantive constitutional requirement with mere aesthetics, and abdicating its statutorily and constitutionally imposed duty to provide meaningful judicial oversight to the administration of death by the States.

From this day forward, I no longer shall tinker with the machinery of death. For more than twenty years I have endeavored—indeed, I have struggled—along with a majority of this Court, to develop procedural and substantive rules that would lend more than the mere appearance of fairness to the death penalty endeavor.[1] Rather than continue to coddle the Court's delusion that the desired level of fairness has been achieved and the need for regulation eviscerated, I feel morally and intellectually obligated simply to concede that the death penalty experiment has failed. It is virtually self-evident to me now that no combination of procedural rules or substantive regulations ever can save the death penalty from its inherent constitutional deficiencies. The basic question—does the system accurately and consistently determine which defendants "deserve" to die?—cannot be answered in the affirmative. It is not simply that this Court has allowed vague aggravating circumstances to be employed, see, e.g., *Arave* v. *Creech* . . . (1993), relevant mitigating evidence to be disregarded, see, e.g., *Johnson* v. *Texas* . . . (1993), and vital judicial review to be blocked, see, e.g., *Coleman* v. *Thompson* . . . (1991). The problem is that the inevitability of factual, legal, and moral error gives us a system that we know must wrongly kill some defendants, a system that fails to deliver the fair, consistent, and reliable sentences of death required by the Constitution.[2]

In 1971, in an opinion which has proved partly prophetic, the second Justice Harlan, writing for the Court, observed:

> Those who have come to grips with the hard task of actually attempting to draft means of channeling capital sentencing discretion have confirmed the lesson taught by the history recounted above. To identify before the fact those characteristics of criminal homicides and their perpetrators which call for the death penalty, and to express these characteristics in language which can be fairly understood and applied by the sentencing authority, appear to be tasks which are beyond present human ability. . . . For a court to attempt to catalog the appropriate factors in this elusive area could inhibit rather than expand the scope of consideration, for no list of circumstances would ever be really complete. *McGautha* v. *California* . . . (1971)

In *McGautha,* the petitioner argued that a statute which left the penalty of death entirely in the jury's discretion, without any standards to govern its imposition, violated the Fourteenth Amendment. Although the Court did not deny that serious risks were associated with a sentencer's unbounded discretion, the Court found no remedy in the Constitution for the inevitable failings of human judgment.

A year later, the Court reversed its course completely in *Furman* v. *Georgia* . . . (1972). . . . The concurring Justices argued that the glaring inequities in the administration of death, the standardless discretion wielded by judges and juries, and the pervasive racial and economic discrimination, rendered the death penalty, at least as administered, "cruel and unusual" within the meaning of the Eighth Amendment. Justice White explained that, out of the hundreds of people convicted of murder every year, only a handful were sent to their deaths, and that there was "no meaningful basis for distinguishing the few cases in which [the death penalty] is imposed from the many cases in which it is not." . . . If any discernible basis could be identified for the selection of those few who were chosen to die, it was "the constitutionally impermissible basis of race." Ib., at 310 (Stewart, J., concurring).

I dissented in *Furman*. Despite my intellectual, moral, and personal objections to the death penalty, I refrained from joining the majority because I found objectionable the Court's abrupt change of position in the single year that had passed since *McGautha*. While I agreed that the Eighth Amendment's prohibition against cruel and unusual punishments "may acquire meaning as public opinion becomes enlightened by a humane justice," . . . I objected to the "suddenness of the Court's perception of progress in the human attitude since decisions of only a short while ago." . . . Four years after *Furman* was decided, I concurred in the judgment in *Gregg* v. *Georgia,* . . . (1976), and its companion cases which upheld death sentences rendered under statutes passed after *Furman* was decided. . . .

There is little doubt now that *Furman*'s essential holding was correct. Although most of the public seems to desire, and the Constitution appears to permit, the penalty of death, it surely is beyond dispute that if the death penalty cannot be administered consistently and rationally, it may not be administered at all. *Eddings* v. *Oklahoma*. . . . I never have quarreled with this principle; in my mind, the real meaning of *Furman*'s diverse concurring opinions did not emerge until some years after *Furman* was decided. See *Gregg* v. *Georgia*. . . . ("*Furman* mandates that where discretion is afforded a sentencing body on a matter so grave as the determination of whether a human life should be taken or spared, that discretion must be suitably directed and limited so as to minimize the risk of wholly arbitrary and capricious action"). Since *Gregg,* I faithfully have adhered to the *Furman* holding and have come to believe that it is indispensable to the Court's Eighth Amendment jurisprudence.

Delivering on the *Furman* promise, however, has proved to be another matter. *Furman* aspired to eliminate the vestiges of racism and the effects of poverty in capital sentencing; it deplored the "wanton" and "random" infliction of death by a government with constitutionally limited power. *Furman* demanded that the sentencer's discretion be directed and limited by procedural rules and objective standards in order to minimize the risk of arbitrary and capricious sentences of death.

In the years following *Furman,* serious efforts were made to comply with its mandate. State legislatures and appellate courts struggled to provide judges and juries with sensible and objective guidelines for determining who should live and who should die. Some States attempted to define who is "deserving" of the death penalty through the use of carefully chosen adjectives, reserving the death penalty for those who commit crimes that are "especially heinous, atrocious, or cruel," . . . or "wantonly vile, horrible or inhuman." . . . Other States enacted mandatory death penalty statutes, reading *Furman* as an invitation to eliminate sentencer discretion altogether. . . . Still other States specified aggravating and mitigating factors that were to be considered by the sentencer and weighed against one another in a calculated and rational manner. . . .

Unfortunately, all this experimentation and ingenuity yielded little of what *Furman* demanded. It soon became apparent that discretion could not be eliminated from capital sentencing without threatening the fundamental fairness due a defendant when life is at stake. Just as contemporary society was no longer tolerant of the random or discriminatory infliction of the penalty of death . . . , evolving standards of decency required due consideration of the uniqueness of each individual defendant when imposing society's ultimate penalty. . . .

This development in the American conscience would have presented no constitutional dilemma if fairness to the individual could be achieved without sacrificing the consistency and rationality promised in *Furman.* But over the past two decades, efforts to balance these competing constitutional commands have been to no avail. Experience has shown that the consistency and rationality promised in *Furman* are inversely related to the fairness owed the individual when considering a sentence of death. A step toward consistency is a step away from fairness.

There is a heightened need for fairness in the administration of death. This unique level of fairness is born of the appreciation that death truly is different from all other punishments a society inflicts upon its citizens. "Death, in its finality, differs more from life imprisonment than a 100-year prison term differs from one of only a year or two." Woodson [1958]. . . . Because of the qualitative difference of the death penalty, "there is a corresponding difference in the need for reliability in the determination that death is the appropriate punishment in a specific case." Ibid. In *Woodson,* a decision striking down mandatory death penalty statutes as unconstitutional, a plurality of the Court explained: "A process that accords no significance to relevant facets of the character and record of the individual offender or the circumstances of the particular offense excludes from consideration in fixing the ultimate punishment of death the possibility of compassionate or mitigating factors stemming from the diverse frailties of humankind." . . .

While the risk of mistake in the determination of the appropriate penalty may be tolerated in other areas of the criminal law, "in capital cases the fundamental respect for humanity underlying the Eighth Amendment . . . requires consideration of the character and record of the individual offender and the circumstances of the particular offense as a constitutionally indispensable part of the process of inflicting the penalty of death." Ibid. Thus, although individualized sentencing in capital cases was not considered essential at the time the Constitution was adopted, *Woodson* recognized that American standards of decency could no longer tolerate a capital sentencing process that failed to afford a defendant individualized consideration in the determination whether he or she should live or die. . . .

The Court elaborated on the principle of individualized sentencing in *Lockett* v. *Ohio* . . . (1978). In that case, a plurality acknowledged that strict restraints on sentencer discretion are necessary to achieve the consistency and rationality promised in *Furman,* but held that, in the end, the sentencer must retain unbridled discretion to afford mercy. Any process or procedure that prevents the sentencer from considering "as a mitigating factor, any aspect of a defendant's character or record and any circumstances of the offense that the defendant proffers as a basis for a sentence less than death," creates the constitutionally intolerable risk that "the death penalty will be imposed in spite of factors which may call for a less severe penalty." . . . See also *Sumner* v. *Shuman* . . . (1987) (invalidating a mandatory death penalty statute reserving the death penalty for life-term inmates convicted of murder). The Court's duty under the Constitution therefore is to "develop a system of capital punishment at once consistent and principled but also humane and sensible to the uniqueness of the individual." *Eddings* v. *Oklahoma.*

I believe the *Woodson-Lockett* line of cases to be fundamentally sound and rooted in American standards of decency that have evolved over time. The notion of prohibiting a sentencer from exercising its discretion "to dispense mercy on the basis of factors too intangible to write into a statute," *Gregg* . . . is offensive to our sense of fundamental fairness and respect for the uniqueness of the individual. In *California* v. *Brown* . . . (1987), I said in dissent:

> The sentencer's ability to respond with mercy towards a defendant has always struck me as a particularly valuable aspect of the capital sentencing procedure. . . . [W]e adhere so strongly to our belief that a sentencer should have the opportunity to spare a capital defendant's life on account of compassion for the individual because, recognizing that the capital sentencing

decision must be made in the context of "contemporary values." *Gregg*
v. *Georgia* . . . we see in the sentencer's expression of mercy a distinc-
tive feature of our society that we deeply value. . . .

Yet, as several Members of the Court have recognized, there is real
"tension" between the need for fairness to the individual and the consistency
promised in *Furman*. . . . On the one hand, discretion in capital sentencing
must be "controlled by clear and objective standards so as to produce non-
discriminatory [and reasoned] application." *Gregg*. . . . On the other hand,
the Constitution also requires that the sentencer be able to consider "any
relevant mitigating evidence regarding the defendant's character or background, and the circumstances of the particular offense." *California* v. *Brown*.
. . . (1987). The power to consider mitigating evidence that would warrant
a sentence less than death is meaningless unless the sentencer has the discretion
and authority to dispense mercy based on that evidence. Thus, the Constitution, by requiring a heightened degree of fairness to the individual, and
also a greater degree of equality and rationality in the administration of
death, demands sentencer discretion that is at once generously expanded
and severely restricted.

This dilemma was laid bare in *Penry* v. *Lynaugh* . . . (1989). The
defendant in *Penry* challenged the Texas death penalty statute, arguing that
it failed to allow the sentencing jury to give full mitigating effect to his
evidence of mental retardation and history of child abuse. The Texas statute
required the jury, during the penalty phase, to answer three "special issues";
if the jury unanimously answered "yes" to each issue, the trial court was
obligated to sentence the defendant to death. . . . Only one of the three
issues—whether the defendant posed a "continuing threat to society"—was
related to the evidence Penry offered in mitigation. But Penry's evidence
of mental retardation and child abuse was a two-edged sword as it related
to that special issue: "it diminish[ed] his blameworthiness for his crime even
as it indicate[d] that there [was] a probability that he [would] be dangerous
in the future." . . . The Court therefore reversed Penry's death sentence,
explaining that a reasonable juror could have believed that the statute
prohibited a sentence less than death based upon his mitigating evidence.

After *Penry*, the paradox underlying the Court's post-*Furman* jurisprudence was undeniable. Texas had complied with Furman by severely
limiting the sentencer's discretion, but those very limitations rendered Penry's
death sentence unconstitutional.

The theory underlying *Penry* and *Lockett* is that an appropriate balance
can be struck between the *Furman* promise of consistency and the *Lockett*
requirement of individualized sentencing if the death penalty is conceptual-
ized as consisting of two distinct stages. In the first stage of capital sentencing,
the demands of *Furman* are met by "narrowing" the class of death-eligible

offenders according to objective, fact-bound characteristics of the defendant or the circumstances of the offense. Once the pool of death-eligible defendants has been reduced, the sentencer retains the discretion to consider whatever relevant mitigating evidence the defendant chooses to offer. See *Graham* v. *Collins* . . . (arguing that providing full discretion to the sentencer is not inconsistent with *Furman* and may actually help to protect against arbitrary and capricious sentencing).

Over time, I have come to conclude that even this approach is unacceptable: It simply reduces, rather than eliminates, the number of people subject to arbitrary sentencing.[3] It is the decision to sentence a defendant to death—not merely the decision to make a defendant eligible for death—that may not be arbitrary. While one might hope that providing the sentencer with as much relevant mitigating evidence as possible will lead to more rational and consistent sentences, experience has taught otherwise. It seems that the decision whether a human being should live or die is so inherently subjective—rife with all of life's understandings, experiences, prejudices, and passions—that it inevitably defies the rationality and consistency required by the Constitution.

The arbitrariness inherent in the sentencer's discretion to afford mercy is exacerbated by the problem of race. Even under the most sophisticated death penalty statutes, race continues to play a major role in determining who shall live and who shall die. Perhaps it should not be surprising that the biases and prejudices that infect society generally would influence the determination of who is sentenced to death, even within the narrower pool of death-eligible defendants selected according to objective standards. No matter how narrowly the pool of death-eligible defendants is drawn according to objective standards, *Furman*'s promise still will go unfulfilled so long as the sentencer is free to exercise unbridled discretion within the smaller group and thereby to discriminate. " 'The power to be lenient [also] is the power to discriminate.' " *McCleskey* v. *Kemp* . . . (1973).

A renowned example of racism infecting a capital-sentencing scheme is documented in *McCleskey* v. *Kemp* . . . (1987). Warren McCleskey, an African-American, argued that the Georgia capital-sentencing scheme was administered in a racially discriminatory manner, in violation of the Eighth and Fourteenth Amendments. In support of his claim, he proffered a highly reliable statistical study (the Baldus study) which indicated that, "after taking into account some 230 nonracial factors that might legitimately influence a sentencer, the jury more likely than not would have spared McCleskey's life had his victim been black." . . . The Baldus study further demonstrated that blacks who kill whites are sentenced to death "at nearly twenty-two times the rate of blacks who kill blacks, and more than seven times the rate of whites who kill blacks." . . .

Despite this staggering evidence of racial prejudice infecting Georgia's capital-sentencing scheme, the majority turned its back on McCleskey's claims, apparently troubled by the fact that Georgia had instituted more procedural and substantive safeguards than most other states since *Furman,* but was still unable to stamp out the virus of racism. Faced with the apparent failure of traditional legal devices to cure the evils identified in *Furman,* the majority wondered aloud whether the consistency and rationality demanded by the dissent could ever be achieved without sacrificing the discretion which is essential to fair treatment of individual defendants:

> [I]t is difficult to imagine guidelines that would produce the predictability sought by the dissent without sacrificing the discretion essential to a humane and fair system of criminal justice. . . . The dissent repeatedly emphasizes the need for "a uniquely high degree of rationality in imposing the death penalty." . . . Again, no suggestion is made as to how greater "rationality" could be achieved under any type of statute that authorizes capital punishment. . . . Given these safeguards already inherent in the imposition and review of capital sentences, the dissent's call for greater rationality is no less than a claim that a capital punishment system cannot be administered in accord with the Constitution. . . .

I joined most of Justice Brennan's significant dissent which expounded McCleskey's Eighth Amendment claim, and I wrote separately . . . to explain that McCleskey also had a solid equal protection argument under the Fourteenth Amendment. I still adhere to the views set forth in both dissents, and, as far as I know, there has been no serious effort to impeach the Baldus study. Nor, for that matter, have proponents of capital punishment provided any reason to believe that the findings of that study are unique to Georgia.

The fact that we may not be capable of devising procedural or substantive rules to prevent the more subtle and often unconscious forms of racism from creeping into the system does not justify the wholesale abandonment of the *Furman* promise. To the contrary, where a morally irrelevant—indeed, a repugnant—consideration plays a major role in the determination of who shall live and who shall die, it suggests that the continued enforcement of the death penalty in light of its clear and admitted defects is deserving of a "sober second thought." Justice Brennan explained:

> Those whom we would banish from society or from the human community itself often speak in too faint a voice to be heard above society's demand for punishment. It is the particular role of courts to hear these voices, for the Constitution declares that the majoritarian chorus may not alone dictate the conditions of social life. The Court thus fulfills, rather than disrupts, the scheme of separation of powers by closely scrutinizing the imposition of the death penalty, for no decision of a society is more deserving of the "sober second thought." Stone, "The Common Law in the United States," 50 *Harvard Law Review* 4, 25 (1936). . . .

In the years since *McCleskey,* I have come to wonder whether there was truth in the majority's suggestion that discrimination and arbitrariness could not be purged from the administration of capital punishment without sacrificing the equally essential component of fairness—individualized sentencing. Viewed in this way, the consistency promised in *Furman* and the fairness to the individual demanded in *Lockett* are not only inversely related, but irreconcilable in the context of capital punishment. Any statute or procedure that could effectively eliminate arbitrariness from the administration of death would also restrict the sentencer's discretion to such an extent that the sentencer would be unable to give full consideration to the unique characteristics of each defendant and the circumstances of the offense. By the same token, any statute or procedure that would provide the sentencer with sufficient discretion to consider fully and act upon the unique circumstances of each defendant would "thro[w] open the back door to arbitrary and irrational sentencing." . . . All efforts to strike an appropriate balance between these conflicting constitutional commands are futile because there is a heightened need for both in the administration of death.

But even if the constitutional requirements of consistency and fairness are theoretically reconcilable in the context of capital punishment, it is clear that this Court is not prepared to meet the challenge. In apparent frustration over its inability to strike an appropriate balance between the *Furman* promise of consistency and the *Lockett* requirement of individualized sentencing, the Court has retreated from the field, allowing relevant mitigating evidence to be discarded, vague aggravating circumstances to be employed, and providing no indication that the problem of race in the administration of death will ever be addressed. In fact some members of the Court openly have acknowledged a willingness simply to pick one of the competing constitutional commands and sacrifice the other. See *Graham* . . . (calling for the reversal of *Penry*); *Walton* v. *Arizona* . . . (1990) (Scalia, J., concurring in part and concurring in the judgment) (announcing that he will no longer enforce the requirement of individualized sentencing, and reasoning that either *Furman* or *Lockett* is wrong and a choice must be made between the two). These developments are troubling, as they ensure that death will continue to be meted out in this country arbitrarily and discriminatorily, and without that "degree of respect due the uniqueness of the individual." *Lockett.* . . . In my view, the proper course when faced with irreconcilable constitutional commands is not to ignore one or the other, nor to pretend that the dilemma does not exist, but to admit the futility of the effort to harmonize them. This means accepting the fact that the death penalty cannot be administered in accord with our Constitution.

My belief that this Court would not enforce the death penalty (even if it could) in accordance with the Constitution is buttressed by the Court's "obvious eagerness to do away with any restriction on the States' power to execute whomever and however they please." *Herrera*. . . . I have explained at length on numerous occasions that my willingness to enforce the capital punishment statutes enacted by the States and the Federal Government, "notwithstanding my own deep moral reservations . . . has always rested on an understanding that certain procedural safeguards, chief among them the federal judiciary's power to reach and correct claims of constitutional error on federal habeas review, would ensure that death sentences are fairly imposed." *Sawyer* v. *Whitley* . . . (1992). . . . See also *Herrera* v. *Collins* [1991]. In recent years, I have grown increasingly skeptical that "the death penalty really can be imposed fairly and in accordance with the requirements of the Eighth Amendment," given the now limited ability of the federal courts to remedy consitutional errors. . . .

Federal courts are required by statute to entertain petitions from state prisoners who allege that they are held "in violation of the Constitution or the treaties of the United States." 28 U.S.C. Section 2254 (a). Serious review of these claims helps to ensure that government does not secure the penalty of death by depriving a defendant of his or her constitutional rights. At the time I voted with the majority to uphold the constitutionality of the death penalty in *Gregg* v. *Georgia* . . . (1976), federal courts possessed much broader authority than they do today to address claims of constitutional error on habeas review. In 1976, there were few procedural barriers to the federal judiciary's review of a State's decision to impose death in a particular case. Since then, however, the Court has "erected unprecedented and unwarranted barriers" to the federal judiciary's review of the constitutional claims of capital defendants. . . .

The Court's refusal last term to afford Leonel Torres Herrera an evidentiary hearing, despite his colorable showing of actual innocence, demonstrates just how far afield the Court has strayed from its statutorily and constitutionally imposed obligations. . . . In *Herrera,* only a bare majority of this Court could bring itself to state forthrightly that the execution of an actually innocent person violates the Eighth Amendment. This concession was made only in the course of erecting nearly insurmountable barriers to a defendant's ability to get a hearing on a claim of actual innocence. . . . Certainly there will be individuals who are actually innocent who will be unable to make a better showing than what was made by Herrera without the benefit of an evidentiary hearing.[4] The Court is unmoved by this dilemma, however; it prefers "finality" in death sentences to reliable determinations of a capital defendant's guilt. Because I no longer can state with any confidence that this Court is able to reconcile the Eighth Amendment's competing constitutional commands, or that the federal judiciary will provide meaningful oversight to the state courts as they exercise their authority to inflict the penalty of death, I believe that the death penalty, as currently administered, is unconstitutional.

Perhaps one day this Court will develop procedural rules or verbal formulas that actually will provide consistency, fairness, and reliability in a capital-sentencing scheme. I am not optimistic that such a day will come. I am more optimistic, though, that this Court eventually will conclude that the effort to eliminate arbitrariness while preserving fairness "in the infliction of [death] is so plainly doomed to failure that it—and the death penalty—must be abandoned altogether." . . . I may not live to see that day, but I have faith that eventually it will arrive. The path the Court has chosen lessens us all. I dissent.

NOTES

1. As a member of the United States Court of Appeals, I voted to enforce the death penalty, even as I stated publicly that I doubted its moral, social, and constitutional legitimacy. . . .

2. Because I conclude that no sentence of death may be constitutionally imposed under our death penalty scheme, I do not address Callins' individual claims of error. I note, though, that the Court has stripped "state prisoners of virtually any meaningful federal review of the constitutionality of their incarceration." *Butler* v. *McKellar* . . . (1990) (Brennan, J., dissenting). Even if Callins had a legitimate claim of constitutional error, this Court would be deaf to it on federal habeas unless "the state court's rejection of the constitutional challenge was so clearly invalid under then-prevailing legal standards that the decision could not be defended by any reasonable jurist." . . . That a capital defendant facing imminent execution is required to meet such a standard before the Court will remedy constitutional violations is indefensible.

3. The narrowing of death-eligible defendants into a smaller subgroup coupled with the unbridled discretion to pick among them arguably emphasizes rather than ameliorates the inherent arbitrariness of the death penalty. . . .

4. Even the most sophisticated death penalty schemes are unable to prevent human error from condemning the innocent. Innocent persons have been executed, see Bedau and Radelet, *Miscarriages of Justice in Potentially Capital Cases,* 40 *Stanford Law Review* 21, 36, 173–79 (1987), perhaps recently, see *Herrera* v. *Collins,* supra, and will continue to be executed under our death penalty scheme.

20

Callins v. *Collins*

Justice Scalia's Concurring Opinion

Callins v. *Collins,* Director, Texas Department of Criminal Justice, Institutional Division. The petition for a writ of cetiorari is denied.

Justice Scalia, concurring.

Justice Blackmun dissents from the denial of certiorari in this case with statement explaining why the death penalty "as currently administered," . . . is contrary to the Constitution of the United States. That explanation often refers to "intellectual, moral and personal" perceptions, but never to the text and tradition of the Constitution. It is the latter rather than the former that ought to control. The Fifth Amendment provides that "[n]o person shall be held to answer for a capital . . . crime, unless on a presentment or indictment of a Grand Jury, . . . nor be deprived of life . . . without due process of law." This clearly permits the death penalty to be imposed, and establishes beyond doubt that the death penalty is not one of the "cruel and unusual punishments" prohibited by the Eighth Amendment.

As Justice Blackmun describes, however, over the years since 1972 this Court has attached to the imposition of the death penalty two quite incompatible sets of commands: the sentencer's discretion to impose death must be closely confined, see *Furman* v. *Georgia* . . . (1972) . . . but the sentencer's discretion not to impose death (to extend mercy) must be unlimited, see *Eddings* v. *Oklahoma* . . . (1982); *Lockett* v. *Ohio* . . . (1978). These commands were invented without benefit of any textual or historical support; they are the product of just such "intellectual, moral, and personal" perceptions as Justice Blackmun expresses today, some of which (viz., those

The United States Law Week, February 22, 1994, 62 U.S.L.W. 3546.

that have been "perceived" simultaneously by five members of the Court) have been made part of what is called "the Court's Eighth Amendment jurisprudence."

Though Justice Blackmun joins those of us who have acknowledged the incompatibility of the Court's *Furman* and *Lockett-Eddings* lines of jurisprudence . . . he unfortunately draws the wrong conclusion from the acknowledgment. He says:

> [T]he proper course when faced with irreconcilable constitutional commands is not to ignore one or the other, nor to pretend that the dilemma does not exist, but to admit the futility of the effort to harmonize them. This means accepting the fact that the death penalty cannot be administered in accord with our Constitution.

Surely a different conclusion commends itself—to wit, that at least one of these judicially announced irreconcilable commands which cause the Constitution to prohibit what its text explicitly permits must be wrong.

Convictions in opposition to the death penalty are often passionate and deeply held. That would be no excuse for reading them into a Constitution that does not contain them, even if they represented the convictions of a majority of Americans. Much less is there any excuse for using that course to thrust a minority's views upon the people. Justice Blackmun begins his statement by describing with poignancy the death of a convicted murderer by lethal injection. He chooses, as the case in which to make that statement, one of the less brutal of the murders that regularly come before us—the murder of a man ripped by a bullet suddenly and unexpectedly, with no opportunity to prepare himself and his affairs, and left to bleed to death on the floor of a tavern. The death-by-injection which Justice Blackmun describes looks pretty desirable next to that. It looks even better next to some of the other cases currently before us which Justice Blackmun did not select as the vehicle for his accouncement that the death penalty is always unconsitutional—for example, the case of the 11-year-old girl raped by four men and then killed by stuffing her panties down her throat. See *McCollum* v. *North Carolina,* No. 93-7200, cert. now pending before the Court. How enable a quiet death by lethal injection compared with that! If the people conclude that such more brutal deaths may be deterred by capital punishment; indeed, if they merely conclude that justice requries such brutal deaths to be avenged by capital punishment; the creation of false, untextual and unhistorical contradictions within "the Court's Eighth Amendment jurisprudence" should not prevent them.

Selected Bibliography

Bedau, Hugo Adam. *Death Is Different: Studies in the Morality, Law, and Politics of Capital Punishment.* Boston: Northeastern University Press, 1987.

———, ed. *The Death Penalty in America.* 3rd. ed. New York: Oxford University Press, 1982.

Berns, Walter. *For Capital Punishment: Crime and the Morality of the Death Penalty.* New York: Basic Books, Inc., 1979.

Bohm, Robert M., ed. *The Death Penalty in America: Current Research.* Cincinnati, Ohio: Anderson Pub. Co., 1991.

Bowers, William J. *Legal Homicide: Death as Punishment in America 1864–1982.* Boston: Northeastern University Press, 1984.

Conrad, John, and Ernest van den Haag. *The Death Penalty: A Debate.* New York: Plenum, 1983.

Garland, David. *Punishment and Modern Society: A Study in Social Theory.* Chicago: University of Chicago Press, 1990.

Hart, H. L. A. *Punishment and Responsibility.* New York: Oxford University Press, 1968.

Hook, Donald D., and Lothan Kahn. *Death in the Balance: The Debate over Capital Punishment.* Lexington, Mass.: Lexington Books, 1989.

Nakell, Barry, and Kennth A. Hardy. *The Arbitrariness of the Death Penalty.* Philadelphia: Temple University Press, 1987.

Nathanson, Stephen. *An Eye for an Eye: The Morality of Punishing Death.* Totowa, N.J.: Rowman & Littlefield, Publishers, 1987.

Radelet, Michael L.; Hugo Adam Bedau; and Constance E. Putnam. *In Spite of Innocence: Erroneous Convictions in Capital Cases.* Boston: Northeastern University Press, 1992.

Van den Haag, Ernest. *Punishing Criminals: Concerning a Very Old and Painful Question.* Lanham, Md.: University Press of America, 1991.

Yant, Martin. *Presumed Guilty: When Innocent People Are Wrongly Convicted.* Amherst, N.Y.: Prometheus Books, 1991.

Zimring, Franklin E., and Gordon Hawkins. *Capital Punishment and the American Agenda.* Cambridge: Cambridge University Press, 1986.

List of Contributors

Hugo Adam Bedau is Professor of Philosophy, Tufts University.

Walter Berns is John M. Olin University Professor, Georgetown University.

Harry Blackmun is a member of the United States Supreme Court.

William Bowers is Principal Research Scientist in the College of Criminal Justice, Northwestern University.

Richard Dagger is Associate Professor of Political Science at Arizona State University.

Christie Davies is Professor of Sociology at the University of Reading, England.

J. D. Mabbott, who died in 1988, was a member of the faculty of St. John's College, Oxford University.

J. Gordon Melton is Director of the Institute for the Study of American Religion, Santa Barbara, California.

Karl Menninger, who died in 1990, was Clinical Professor of Psychiatry, University of Kansas, and co-founder of the Menninger Foundation for Psychiatric Education and Research.

Herbert Morris is Professor of Philosophy, University of California, Los Angeles.

Stephen Nathanson is Professor of Philosophy, Northeastern University.

Constance E. Putnam collaborated with Hugo Adam Bedau and Michael L. Radelet in the project resulting in the 1992 book *In Spite of Innocence: Erroneous Convictions in Capital Cases.*

Michael L. Radelet is Professor of Sociology, University of Florida.

257

John Rawls is James Bryant Conant University Professor, Harvard University.

Jeffrey H. Reiman is Professor of Philosophy and Justice at The American University in Washington, D.C.

Antonin Scalia is a member of the United States Supreme Court.

Lloyd Steffen is Professor of Philosophy and Religion, Northland College, Ashland, Wisconsin.

Ernest van den Haag is the John M. Olin Professor of Jurisprudence and Public Policy, Fordham University.

Richard Wasserstrom is Professor of Philosophy, University of California, Santa Cruz.